44261

Anton Dvořák

Da Capo Press Music Reprint Series

GENERAL EDITOR

FREDERICK FREEDMAN

VASSAR COLLEGE

ANTON DVOŘÁK

By

PAUL STEFAN

Translated by

Y. W. VANCE

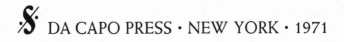 DA CAPO PRESS · NEW YORK · 1971

A Da Capo Press Reprint Edition

This Da Capo Press edition of
Anton Dvořák
is an unabridged republication of the
first edition published in New York in 1941.

Library of Congress Catalog Card Number 79-146147

SBN 306-70105-7

Published by Da Capo Press
A Division of Plenum Publishing Corporation
227 West 17th Street, New York, N.Y. 10011

Anton Dvořák

Anton Dvořák

ANTON DVOŘÁK

By

PAUL STEFAN

Translated by

Y. W. VANCE

THE GREYSTONE PRESS

NEW YORK

Printed in the United States of America
THE WILLIAM BYRD PRESS, INC.
RICHMOND, VIRGINIA

Foreword and Acknowledgment

In 1929 I had the honor of speaking on the Vienna radio in commemoration of the twenty-fifth anniversary of Anton Dvořák's death. On that occasion, I called attention to the fact that there was no serviceable bibliographical material covering the life and works of the great master of modern Czech music, for at that time the authoritative work by Otokar Šourek was still unfinished. The first volume had appeared in 1916; the fourth and last was scheduled for 1933. In the United States, however, there is no genuinely authoritative work; this is strange because Dvořák made his home in America for three years, and the whole field of his activities in this country was of the greatest possible significance for the evolution of American music.

In 1886, when Dvořák was only 45 and the most important part of his life-work was yet to be accomplished, one of his friends, Professor Zubatý, wrote a short biographical sketch which did not purport to do more than draw attention to the man and his work. When, thirty years after Dvořák's death, no thorough study of his work had yet appeared, I decided to undertake the task. Virtually all the available material had been dealt with in Šourek's four volumes. With the consent of this excellent musicologist, I therefore made use of his findings and even incorporated in

5

my book much of his analysis and critical examination of Dvořák's works. It was both a pleasure and an honor for me to name Šourek as co-author of the German edition of my Dvořák book.

In its preparation I had, in 1934, the valuable assistance of Jiří Dohalský, son of a member of the Czechoslovakian legation in Vienna, who helped me in linguistic matters; of the Secretary of Foreign Affairs of the Czech Republic, Professor Krofta, himself a great music lover; of Professor Krofta's secretary, Jaroslav Jindra; and of Legation Secretary Šrom. Of great assistance in preparing this book were also that enthusiastic propagator of Czech music abroad, Doctor Jan Löwenbach, and my old friend, the composer, Paul A. Pisk, Professor of Music at Redlands, California. My hearty thanks are due to all of these for their friendly and ever-ready collaboration.

Since the German edition of my book first appeared, the world has been overwhelmed by a cataclysm, and all men of good will are trying, each in his own small way, to lay the foundations for a new order after the earthquake shall have passed. In these times of stress and strain, regardless of national boundaries and the disposition of armies, all those who love and appreciate Czech music will unite to celebrate the hundredth anniversary of Dvořák's birthday, September 8th, 1941.

This volume has been revised, rearranged and adapted to meet the needs of the American reading public, and in its new guise it bears the name of only one author, who is none the less fully aware of how much he owes to his former co-author. Circumstances and conditions of today make it impossible to communicate with anyone now living under a "protectorate." Nevertheless, I live in the hope and faith that, at a day not too far distant, I shall be able to present to him a copy of this latest life of Anton Dvořák.

It is a pleasure to take this opportunity of expressing my thanks to Mr. Joseph J. Kovařík, the friend and helper of Anton Dvořák. For forty-one years a member of the New York Philharmonic Orchestra, as violinist and later violist, Mr. Kovařík has played under virtually all the famous conductors who have visited this country. Accompanying the Philharmonic on its European tour with Toscanini, he revisited his native Bohemia in 1930.

Kovařík's notes and data provided the foundation for the monumental work in Czechish by Otakar Šourek. With the assistance of Mr. Kovařík, at his summer home in Ridgefield, Connecticut, I have checked and revised once more all my own sources of information. The Kovařík collection of Dvořák programs and press clippings was presented some years ago to the Dvořák Museum in Prague.

In recognition of their helpful co-operation in preparing this American edition, I wish to express my thanks to my old friend, the translator, Yandray Wilson Vance; and to the composer, Dr. Elliott Griffis, who most kindly consented to read the proofs.

PAUL STEFAN

Plymouth, New Hampshire
August, 1941

Contents

Illustrations

Introduction

In Praise of the Bohemian Music-Maker

Such a master as Dvořák did not drop out of the blue upon the world. At a superficial glance, it seems as if with Smetana and Dvořák the flower of Czech music had sprung suddenly into being. In reality, this was only the blossoming of a renascent spirit. Centuries of enforced silence weighed down upon the Czechs of the pre-romantic age. There was no actual Czechish life and hence, apparently, no Czechish music. But there was the Bohemian "Musikant" (music-maker). It is true, he was to be found not merely in Bohemia but everywhere.

He has to be seen at work, and perhaps, we must even have something of his being in ourselves, if we are to understand and interpret the Bohemian Musikant. Then words will no longer be necessary. Picture him to yourself, this fiddler, clarinettist, trombone-player, or what have you, sitting at a table, probably in some rustic inn-garden, with his glass of beer before him, having enjoyed a hearty meal of coarse but savory Bohemian food. Suddenly the spirit moves him, he is transformed into an artist. There follows inevitably the full flood of melody, unfailing rhythm, infectious temperament. Nobody and nothing can withstand this thraldom.

In Bohemian folk-tales, the Musikant fetches back the

13

prey of hell from its gorge, wresting the devil's plunder out of his very claws. In the fable of "Schwanda the Doodle-sack-piper", the imps are compelled to dance to his will. Man, animal, inanimate nature, all must obey the Bohemian Musikant: they cannot help themselves. In every piece of Czechish music, along with the folk-song and dance elements, the Musikant is to be heard. Everywhere, and in serious music, too, there is a role for him to play.

One is reminded of Nedbal, with his powerful bowing sustaining the viola's leading voice in the opening of Smetana's Quartet, "Aus meinem Leben" ("Scenes from my Life"). Listening to him, you could see the forest, the fields, the village with its people, the geese on the pond, the peasant children, the organist, the school-teacher, the priest, the authorities, the gentry—all that early world of a lovable, unspoiled people.

There are all varieties of the Bohemian Musikant, from the public-house fiddler in the village of Biedermeier times to the much-sought-after strings and horns of one of the élite American orchestras of today. A brief resumé of their historical backgrounds will shed some light on the too-little explored field of creative forces at work in the Bohemia of former days.

Bohemian-Czech music is known to us from the writings of contemporaries about the end of the Tenth Century. The old songs of a later day in honor of St. Adalbert and St. Wenceslas have been preserved. Music flourished at the courts of the Bohemian kings, had much to say in the battles of the Hussites, and in the struggles attending the Reformation and Counter-Reformation. (When we say Bohemian, we are also thinking of Moravia and Silesia, all parts of that Czechish-and-German land formerly integrated in the Austro-Hungarian Empire.) The ominous song of the Hussites pulsates throughout one of Dvořák's most inspiring works.

Prague, the City of an Hundred Towers, was not lacking in lustre among the world capitals of those times. National demarcations were not so clearly defined. In harmony with the spirit of universality surviving from the Middle Ages, various languages and cultures intermingled to form a higher cultural unity. It was, indeed, at the Chancellery of the Luxemburg rulers of Bohemia that the German language of letters came into being. In the person of that strange figure, Kaiser Rudolf, dramatically depicted in Grillparzer's "Fraternal Strife in the House of Habsburg", the blessings of peace were united in Prague in one last efflorescence before the Thirty Years War.

Then came the Battle of the White Mountain, the victory of the Habsburgs and the Counter-Reformation, the overthrow of Bohemian independence. But music soon flourished once again. When Gluck, born not far from the Bohemian border, arrived in Prague, he became the pupil of the famous Bohuslav Černohorský, a Franciscan Father, who had been Tartini's master in Padua. Gluck admired the high standards evidenced by the cultivation of music in Prague. Compelled to earn enough on which to live and study, Gluck used to play his violin in the villages about Prague.

Bach esteemed his Bohemian contemporary, Johann Dismas Zelenka, who lived and composed in Dresden. In 1722, on his travels through Bohemia, Charles Burney met the great organist, Seeger, with whom, as Seeger did not speak German, he conversed in Italian. Bohemians are proud of Burney's description of the Čáslau village school whose organist had four pianos on which the pupils diligently practiced.

The nobility—the families of Auersperg, Bouquoi, Clam-Gallas, Czernin, Hartig, Kinský, Lobkowitz, Pachta, and Schwarzenberg—regularly maintained their own house orchestras on their country estates as well as in Prague. Toward the close of the Eighteenth Century, Prague still had three theater orchestras and nineteen church choirs, to contemporary historians a deplorable decline. Practically every retainer in the homes of the nobility was required to play an instrument in the house orchestra. While conducting such an orchestra retained by Count Morzin on his Lukawetz estate, Haydn composed his First Symphony in 1759.

Many Bohemian musicians went abroad, among them both composers and interpretative artists; often, composer and virtuoso in one. The violinist Heinrich von Biber, wrote his "program violin sonatas" far from home. Johann Stamitz with both his sons went to live in Mannheim, where they were responsible for establishing the fame of the strings in the Mannheim Court Orchestra. Stamitz originated "the Mannheim style" of symphonic composition which came to have so much importance for Vienna's composers in the classic tradition and thus for the entire evolution of music.

Four Benda brothers also migrated to Germany. Franz, the eldest, at first a street-musician, later became the concert-master of Frederick the Great; George, the youngest, was the originator of the German music-"melodrama". Josef Mysliveček went to Italy where he changed his name to Venatorini and, as an opera composer, became known as "il divino Boemo". Mozart found a great deal of stimulus in Venatorini's musical ideas.

On the coronation of Karl VI, in 1723, the opera, "Costanza e Fortezza" by Fux was performed in Prague. From that time forth the people of Prague were seized with a passion for opera. Count Nostiz built a theater on the Fruit Market. Consecrated by the world première of "Don Giovanni", this building known as the "Ständetheater" (Guild Theater) is still in use. "Don Giovanni" was the logical successor to the frenetic acclaim that had attended the première of "The Marriage of Figaro" in the Bohemian capital. The Italian Director, Bondini, commissioned a new opera by Mozart, who completed "Don Giovanni" in Prague, celebrating an unprecedented triumph there with his masterpiece. (Vienna did not care so much for it!) The Prague incident was one of those pieces of good fortune unhappily rare in Mozart's life. His reported saying rings true: "My friends in Prague understand me."—(as much as to say, "only my Prague friends"!)

Indeed, Mozart's music came to have such an importance for Prague that for half a century no one dared surpass him! Only imitators of Mozart were tolerated; Beethoven was considered a detestable innovator. The most outspoken Mozart fanatics were Dionys Weber, Director of the Prague Conservatory, founded in 1811, and the "music-dictator", Tomaschek. The first biography of Mozart was published, immediately after his death, in Prague.

The dawn of a new age began with the coming of Carl Maria von Weber as conductor of the Prague Theater Orchestra; it lightened still more with the romantics, to whom Beethoven was religion; with Schumann, whose magazine had the most subscribers in Prague; and with the tempestuous receptions accorded to Liszt and Berlioz. In 1865 they held a Wagner Festival in Prague; Wagner, too, loved and esteemed the musical gifts of Bohemia.

Tomaschek and Worzischek became the forerunners of the romantic piano composers (Schubert, Schumann, etc.). Bohemia produced not only Sechter, the theorist, who was to have taught Schubert and did teach Bruckner, but the piano virtuoso, Dusík (Dussek) and the tenor, Tichatschek, whom Wagner extravagantly revered. The music historian Ambros made his foundational studies in Bohemia, as did also at a later date Guido Adler of Vienna.

About the beginning of the Sixties, Gustav Mahler was growing up on the Bohemian-Moravian border, imbibing the Bohemian folk-song, the dances and marches of the countryside. Right down to the present time, the continuity is unbroken: the Bohemian Musikant in all his types and roles has not died out. Until its most recent enslavement, Prague was one of the most stimulating musical cities of the world, chiefly because of the friendly competition of two great musical peoples, each of which concentrated its forces about its own flourishing and exemplary opera organization. The German Theater, under the direction of Angelo Neumann (a figure out of one of E. T. A. Hoffmann's tales) was for many years the operatic preparatory school of Europe. As long ago as 1892, at the Vienna Music and Theater Exposition, the Czechish National Theater triumphed with its works of marked individuality and their spontaneous, lusty interpretation. And Smetana's "The Bartered Bride", pearl of Czechish operatic art, on that occasion began its triumphal career throughout the world.

Instead, however, of talking about German and Czechish music, we have thus far with entire justification spoken only of Bohemian music. Both the peoples of Bohemia lived together in peace. There was as yet no expression of national idiosyncracies. Just as people conversed in both languages, so music in those days was the common property of both peoples. German was the language of society. But Zelenka had already set to music several Czechish texts, and Tomaschek did the same "so as not to forget his mother tongue".

On the other hand, it was the Czech, Tuma, in Vienna, who was cited as the exemplar of "an honest German man"; and it was J. A. Steffan from the Czechish town of Kopidlno who smoothed the path of Schubert in his studies of the German Lied. Both Smetana and Dvořák composed to German texts, and Dvořák even wrote an entire German opera.

The Czechs only awakened to self-determination with the

opening up of the world of romantic ideas on whose threshold Herder and Goethe both proclaimed the rightful place of the Slav peoples in the world's literature. Goethe came to know Bohemia at first hand and distinctly sensed the hidden forces at work that were root and soil of the spiritual landscape of a future nation. The enthusiasm evinced by German poets, such as Ebert, Meissner and Moritz Hartmann, for the history of their Bohemian compatriots, was in the genuine romantic tradition.

Germans, too, believed in the authenticity and antiquity of the so-called "Königinhof" Manuscript discovered in 1818. It offered intimations of the past greatness of Czech poetry and it certainly contained genuine poetry. Both Tomaschek and, later, Dvořák, wrote musical settings to some of the Königinhof verses. Nevertheless, it was none other than the undaunted intellectual fighter and "realist", Masaryk, afterwards President of the Republic, who proved the Königinhof Manuscript a forgery.

In a similar manner to that in which Arnim and Brentano compiled "Des Knaben Wunderhorn" (The Boy's Magic Horn) out of the imperishable treasure of German folk-poetry, so in Bohemia Jaromir Erben compiled the anthology "Kytice" (Nosegay), a collection imbued with the true spirit of the people. Thereafter it became the fashion for German composers to draw upon the "Nosegay" for poems to set to music. Hanslick, growing up in the midst of Prague's musical life, followed suit.

In 1826, the first Czechish play with music was composed by the theater-conductor, Škroup, entitled "Dráteník"

(Wire-binder). Involuntarily one is reminded of Lehar's operetta "Rastelbinder" (The Tinker). Lehar himself, certainly owes a great deal to the magic of Slav music.

Indeed, no Austrian composer was able to rid himself altogether of the Slav influence. The former metropolis of Vienna derived from German, Latin, Slav, Hungarian and Oriental elements the very atmosphere in which a universal Austrian music, its audience, and generations of music-lovers could thrive.

A century ago, Škroup in a short folk-play had a masterly inspiration when he wrote the song, "Kde domov můj" (Where is my Native Land?), giving undreamt-of, forceful expression to national aspirations. It became the hymn of the Czech nation and, finally, of the new Czecho-Slovakian state.

Nevertheless, a long time was to elapse before a Czech opera with seeds of vitality in it could be written and produced. Smetana, born in 1824, in the early days of national romanticism, at last produced such a work for his people. Entitled "The Brandenburger in Bohemia", it is not so well known as his other operas.

In the early Sixties, the Czechs and the outside world were granted the privilege of hearing that delightful masterpiece, "The Bartered Bride". Along with the great works composed by Czech masters, the Czechish people were given a theater in which those masterpieces could be produced. But music in Bohemia still had its struggles. Smetana himself voiced the most vehement criticism of Czech musical life. In so doing, he was defending himself before the hyper-nationalists who called him a Wagnerian, a despiser of Czech poesy, and a German imitator.

Today, Czech opera has a long and honorable history. Outside of Smetana, our gratitude is chiefly due to Dvořák. And sooner or later some of his works for the theater will find their way to other stages outside Bohemia.

Anton Dvořák

CHAPTER I

THE YOUNG DVOŘÁK

Country Village and Organ School

UNLIKE those of other countries, Bohemian musicians did not congregate for generation after generation about specific centers of the arts. In Bohemia, in those days, Prague was the only art center. The musicians, however, mostly of peasant stock, came from all parts of the country. Dvořák, like Smetana, was of the peasantry.

He was born on the Birthday of the Virgin, September 8th, 1841, in the tiny village of Nelahozeves, otherwise known by the German name of Mühlhausen. The surrounding country is entirely Czechish. Nelahozeves itself lies on the banks of the Moldau, that stream celebrated in Bohemian song and story, in the pleasant, fruitful valley north of Prague.

In the midst of farmlands, meadows and orchards, Nelahozeves-Mühlhausen is a typical Bohemian village, with tidy houses on gentle slopes and a few by the waterside. In the quiet streets there are straggling geese and children at play. Now and then a dog barks. Otherwise, the quietude of Mother Earth, the peace of fertility, seems to envelop everything.

The palace of the Lobkowitz family dominates the surroundings. The red-roofed inn that once belonged to Dvořák's father still stands on the village square. Son of a publican and butcher, and one of fourteen children, Dvořák's father, Franz, lived to be eighty, dying only ten years before his famous son. A man of splendid stamina, Franz Dvořák married Anna Zdeněk, a servant at the Lobkowitz palace. Simple, healthy, industrious folk, Franz and Anna did their best to rear eight children, five sons and three daughters, to be as simple and Godfearing as themselves. Anton was the eldest.

(All his life, Dvořák was at pains to be sure the Czech form of his name, "Antonín", was printed on the title-pages of his works alongside the more cosmopolitan "Anton".)

Like all Bohemians when it came to music-making, Dvořák's father could hold his own with the best of them; he played both violin and zither and was a member of the village band that functioned on all festive and religious occasions. We can hardly deduce from this that Anton inherited his musical gifts from his father; among his fellow countrymen, that much musicality was native as the air they breathed.

At eight years of age, Anton entered the village school, which knew no mysteries of "grades". The schoolmaster and village organist in one, Josef Spitz, could, it goes without saying, "play all instruments". Anton learned to play the violin, much to the enjoyment of those who frequented his father's inn. His parents were naturally very proud, but no one thought that he would ever become a musician; they intended, of course, that he should learn a trade.

At fourteen, he was sent to the not far distant town of Zlonitz (Zlonice) to stay with his maternal uncle and learn to speak German, essential to the business of innkeeping. Zlonitz, rather more citified, was noted for its love of music. The schoolmaster and choir-conductor in one, Josef Toman, and the German teacher, Anton Liehmann, were both excellent musicians.

Liehmann conducted his own orchestra and gave music lessons among the families of the palace officials and town burghers. The church choir even maintained paid singers. Liehmann composed all kinds of pieces for his orchestra. A whole chestful of these, betraying the influence both of the classics and of Bohemian folk-music has been preserved.

Liehmann at once noticed the exceptional talent of young Anton, whom he taught to play the viola, piano and organ, further supplementing this instruction with lessons in harmony. His method was simple and direct: whoever did not know his lesson received as many blows with the pointer as the notes he misread. In later years, however, Dvořák never forgot to be grateful to his former master.

Dvořák's father did not prosper in Nelahozeves; he moved his family and business to Zlonitz where he opened another inn. Liehmann and Uncle Zdeněk tried to convince him that his talented son must receive further musical instruction; but Franz Dvořák was not yet doing so well at his new place of business that he could think of such plans. He insisted that Anton should first learn to speak German properly, and the boy was sent to Böhmisch-Kamnitz, away from admiring friends and well-wishers.

In Böhmisch-Kamnitz, as it turned out, he found another Liehmann in the person of Herr Hancke. Soon Dvořák was able to conduct the village choir without this new teacher's supervision.

A year passed and he returned to Zlonitz to help his father in the inn and butcher-shop. He went on working with Liehmann, composing marches and dances for his orchestra. At last Uncle Zdeněk promised the necessary financial support for regular music lessons. They decided to send Anton to the Organ School in Prague.

Neither Prague nor his work at the School could affect his unspoiled, countrified disposition. Sprung from the soil, Dvořák remained his whole life true to his peasant origins. Even while staying in Prague, Dvořák used to make frequent visits to his early musical friend and mentor, Liehmann. And after Liehmann died, in 1879, Dvořák conducted a concert in Zlonitz, in September, 1880, in order to raise funds for the gravestone. A more enduring memorial to Liehmann he created in the character of the village school-teacher, Benda, in his opera, "Jacobin". (This historically significant name was intentionally chosen; the important role of the Bendas was mentioned in the preceding chapter.)

In the fall of 1857, an accomplished young musician at the age of 16, Anton Dvořák arrived in Prague and found passable quarters next to the German Technical High School, in the house (now Dominikanergasse 238) of his cousin, married to a tailor by the name of Pleva. It was not very comfortable.

The Organ School Dvořák attended had been founded in 1830 by the Society of the Friends of Church Music in Bohemia. For sixty years, until in 1890 it became merged with the Prague Conservatory of Music, the Organ School was of outstanding importance to whole generations of Czech composers. (Dvořák himself was later to become Professor and then Director of this enlarged Conservatory.) Besides the numerous teachers on its staff, who provided the music in the churches of Prague, the Organ School turned out many composers and practicing musicians, whereas the Conservatory restricted itself almost exclusively to cultivating the interpretative artist.

During Dvořák's first year, the venerable Pitsch was Director of the Organ School; when Pitsch died in 1858, Josef Krejčí, a Czech with a passion for nagging his compatriots, became Director. In his eyes, anybody who wanted to accomplish anything must be able to speak German. Inasmuch as this was Dvořák's weak point, he could not very well demonstrate what he knew. The musician's techniques were taught with religious severity, but equal attention was given to an exact knowledge of the works by the great masters. The faculty comprised the best musicians in Prague.

Dvořák, however, made his acquaintance with music at first hand from other sources as well. He played viola in the orchestra of the St. Cecilia Society, thus becoming initiated into the world of Schumann and Wagner, to both of whom he owed much of his later musical evolution. One of his fellow students was Karel Bendl, later a well-known composer and the son of a well-to-do inn-keeper. In his house there was a piano and a library of scores, and it was here that Dvořák laid the foundations of his wide knowledge of musical literature.

All would have been well if his material circumstances had only been a little better. But Uncle Zdeněk soon had to cease paying for his studies and Dvořák was thrown on his own, forced to give lessons and look for aid to his other relatives in Prague. Fortunately, his Uncle Dušek was able to give him lodging.

Dvořák finished his two years at the Organ School in 1859, his certificate stating, in German, that he showed rather more talent for the practice of music; his grasp of theory was held to be somewhat weaker. Most likely this was because he could not express himself so well in German. What was meant by "practice" is not perfectly clear. It should be noted that Dvořák used to write intentionally in false relations and consecutive fifths, both forbidden by his teachers, and this naturally earned their disapproval. In spite of this severity (characteristic of the times) in judging his theoretical abilities, Dvořák stood second at the head of a graduating class of twelve. The first was a certain Siegmund Glanz, known to posterity only as a name, who had received the mark, "very good", on all his work.

First Chamber Music and Symphonic Works

DVOŘÁK AT EIGHTEEN was now a full-fledged musician ready to take his part in life, and almost immediately he earns our attention as a creative musician. It is true of his beginnings as of his later works that the traditions not only of his people but of the classic age of music awakened to new life in him. As prolific as Haydn and Mozart, he made music in the same joyous spirit with which they approached it; in the realm of the symphony and of chamber-music writing, his spiritual guide was Beethoven. He never spoke of Beethoven except with awe.

"Why don't you all kneel?" he would cry out in his explosive manner to the class whenever his students at the Conservatory were playing a Beethoven Sonata.

In his jubilant love of life (with a faint trace of melancholy), in the sheer facility of his creating, in his rapturous melodizing, however, he felt himself akin to Schubert. He derived a great deal from the German romantics, especially Schumann, and something from Wagner whose fascination he felt. In his latter years, despite all admonitions to abjure him, Dvořák finally made full confession of his love for Wagner. But the most vital elements in his composition have their source in his own native land and in the wealth of his own inner being.

Just as Smetana had already given his people a national opera, so Dvořák now gave them the symphonies and chamber music they lacked. His earliest works still plainly reveal their artistic dependence on the great masters; but those works carried him farther than any of his compatriots had hitherto ventured.

Leaving out of account two polkas, the first of which was composed in 1854, Dvořák's actual Opus 1 is the *String Quintet in A minor with two Violas*. The manuscript, dated

June 6th, 1861 (not the date of its completion), is signed "Antonín Leopold Dvořák." (Leopold must have been his confirmation name since it is not in his baptismal certificate.) The work is in three movements with no scherzo; its character is correspondingly melancholy, eloquent of early struggles. It remained for many years unknown and was only finally performed from the manuscript in 1921 by the pupils of the Prague Conservatory at the Emmaus Monastery in commemoration of the eightieth anniversary of Dvořák's birth.

The themes are remarkably similar to a Mozart in minor key; the song-theme of the First Movement might have come from Mozart's pen. But towards the end of this movement, a mystic light, reminiscent of Beethoven, is shed on the meditative musical mood. In the Slow Movement and especially in the Finale, there is rather less of the singing euphony of Dvořák than there is of Beethovenesque defiance. In the Finale there is to be remarked for the first time a peculiarity of Dvořák's: a dotted figure played simultaneously with triplets. One of the themes reveals its inner kinship with a motive in the Second Movement. As in Dvořák's earlier efforts, the whole formal structure is surprisingly mature, the instrumentation is clear, emphatic and of his characteristic beautiful sonority. This is a full-throated music of the late classic period. The only thing lacking is that national note without which we can scarcely imagine Dvořák.

One year later, in March 1862, Dvořák wrote the words "Thank God!" at the conclusion of his *String Quartet in A major*, and these words appear on all his later manuscripts. By great good fortune, this work was preserved by a merchant of Prague who saved it from being destroyed, as Dvořák destroyed most of his other compositions of the Sixties. Dvořák was delighted when, in 1887, his friend restored this early Quartet to him. He gave him in exchange some of the manuscript sketches for his "Stabat mater"; and in 1888 he consented to have the Quartet performed.

The Quartet in A major, in four movements, contains a Scherzo still in thrall to Beethoven but none the less pointing to Dvořák's later use of Bohemian folk-dance motives. The national note is also struck in the melody of the Slow Movement. The whole is markedly in contrast to the Quintet; the invention is freer and more spontaneous, Dvořák's characteristic use of irregular periods is more distinct, the modulation is richer. There is a contentment with the things of this life and a greater maturity.

He still had to spend most of his time giving lessons and playing in orchestras. He had joined the very popular Komzák Orchestra and was of course, expected to play with it in the larger inns and restaurants. He still had no access to a piano except at Bendl's and he had to share a room with other lodgers at his Uncle Dušek's.

For the Komzák Orchestra, Dvořák composed a *"Polka With Galop"* included in a "Dance Album". Later on, when Dvořák was a famous composer, it was held much against him that these harmless effusions were reprinted in a special edition, designated Opus 53—as if he had given way to weakness in his old age! They were simply "pot-boilers" of his youth. Opus 53 later became the catalogue number of his Violin Concerto. (In later chapters, we shall have more to say about oddities in the numbering of Dvořák's compositions.)

It was pure chance, too, that led to the preservation of these dances. For Dvořák took pains to destroy all his compositions of the years 1863 to 1865 and 1866 to 1869. Some, it may have been, he disliked himself; others, perhaps, he felt had met with merited disapproval. Another work that escaped destruction was the *Symphony in C Minor*, composed in February and March, 1865, and entitled "The Bells of Zlonitz". It remained undiscovered until 1923.

Had Dvořák ever happened to find it, he would unquestionably have made up for certain deficiencies in the instrumentation. The same thematic material, in parts reminiscent of the Quintet and Quartet, reappears in the "Silhouettes" for Piano of 1879. The best movement of the Symphony in C minor is the Scherzo, and the whole work speaks clearly of the hardships of youth, the undaunted will to live and the playful spirit of an original inventor. Never published, this Symphony was not performed until a few years ago.

As violist, along with the entire Komzák Orchestra, Dvořák became a member of the new Czechish National Theater Orchestra. For the time being, however, the Orchestra still had to play three times a week in the inns of Prague. It was only later that its members came to have no duties outside of the theater. For Dvořák, his playing in the theater meant only more work, with no increase in pay, a paltry eighteen gulden a month.

He soon perceived that in order to go on composing he would have to have a piano at his own disposal; he therefore accepted the invitation of a fellow-member of the Orchestra, Moritz Anger, to stay with him on the Heumarkt, now Havlíček Square. There it was not exactly quiet, either, since five young musicians shared the place together. But they all had some consideration for each other and Dvořák found it possible to work.

From 1865 on, this was to be the scene of his labors: here he composed the Symphony in C minor, the Symphony in B, a 'Cello Concerto and a Song Cycle. This cycle, "*The Cypresses*" bears witness to the joys and sufferings of his heart. It was while giving piano lessons at the home of the goldsmith, Čermák, that Dvořák made the acquaintance of Čermák's daughters, Josefa (later an accomplished actress who married Count Kaunitz) and Anna, a gifted contralto, who was one day to become his wife. Before he found out that it was Anna he loved, he fell in love with Josefa, the elder sister, but met with no response. Consequently, these songs express alternating moods of joy and pain.

Because of these tender memories, The Cypresses, with words by Gustav Pfleger-Moravský, was among his favorite compositions. Whereas he discarded most of his youthful output, Dvořák always treasured this. Eight of the songs appear in a revised version as the group of "*Love Songs*", Op. 83, published in 1888. The tenth in this cycle he employed as an aria in the opera, "King and Charcoal-burner". And when Dvořák discarded his first version of that work, he used the same aria again in his opera, "Wanda". In the "Silhouettes" for Piano, besides themes from the C Minor Symphony, there is a theme from The Cypresses. In 1882, he published four of the same cycle revealing a masterly improvement in their revision, and in 1887, he rearranged twelve of the original cycle, this time for string quartet. Dvořák re-christened them "Evening Songs". They remained unpublished until 1921, when ten of them were brought out.

Although Dvořák had Schubert distinctly in mind, the Cypress lieder do not much resemble their prototype. True, they contain a wealth of melody and colorful harmony, but Dvořák's declamation was poor and he was far more concerned with the melodic line than with the text. The piano accompaniment is just passable and none too playable. These reproaches, however, are only valid with respect to the original, youthful version. Whatever material from the songs he later employed was transmuted by the supreme artistry of the master.

The 'Cello Concerto in A Major (June, 1865)—not to be confused with his later "famous" B Minor 'Cello Concerto —was written for and dedicated to his good friend, Peer, (who later became virtuoso in attendance at the Court of Prince Hohenzollern-Hechingen). This manuscript was rediscovered in 1925, edited and published by Günther Raphael, who also arranged the original piano accompaniment for small orchestra. Dvořák's typically romantic, neo-

Wagnerian yet beautifully warm-hearted, work thereby suffered some drastic changes and elisions.

The B major Symphony follows immediately upon the first Symphony in C minor just as, previously, one chamber-music work succeeded another. This habit of composing "in pairs" is characteristic of Dvořák's creative method; he cannot manage to express himself fully in a single work, so great is the flood of ideas. Even his operas appear in pairs.

The B major Symphony was written from August to October, 1865. He intended to destroy it but his friend Anger, so runs the anecdote, was instrumental in helping to save it. Dvořák wanted to have the score bound, but he did not have the money to pay the bookbinder. Anger lent him the money but demanded it back again when he heard that Dvořák, having changed his mind, now intended to burn the score. Dvořák was unable to pay and so the work remained unharmed. He later touched up the score, designating it as Opus 4, 1888, with the intention of having Simrock publish it. Unpublished until the present day, it has been several times performed.

The Symphony in B major is flooded throughout by a far-reaching, wide-embracing, almost cosmic joyousness. The first indications of a Wagnerian diffuseness make this work much less concentrated in detail. Likewise the mightily billowing instrumentation pays its respects to Wagner. Dvořák's somewhat capricious voice-leading in the bass and his wealth of counterpoint lend interest to this work, which also contains remarkable premonitions of the thematic material in his later works. One of these motives, in the First

Movement, reappears in "King and Charcoal-burner", in the First Slav Rhapsody and in "Jacobin". It is also akin to a folk-song echoed in Smetana's "The Kiss". The beau-

tiful Slow Movement is rich in emotional quality, the Scherzo is brilliantly witty. Dvořák's characteristic toying with the first subject before it assumes its final form, a sort of "masking" of his primal thematic idea, is in keeping with the broad dimensions of this work. These are all signs of a naive yet conscious and masterful handling of forms.

As time went on, Dvořák found it too unquiet at Anger's. He decided, since he was now earning twenty gulden a month in the orchestra, to spend two of them on a piano, rented from a tailor, and once more, in 1873, he took up his abode at Uncle Dušek's. Among the compositions he had destroyed were two overtures, a mass, a clarinet quintet and some incidental music written for the Czechish National

Theater. (One of these pieces according to the orchestral conductor, Čech, was rather a symphony than stage-music.)

Czechish Opera with German Text

THIS was about the time of the beginnings of Czechish opera. Smetana had already written his masterpieces, "The Bartered Bride" and "Dalibor". Each Czechish composer considered it his duty to do everything in his power to serve the theater of his people. As a member of the orchestra, Dvořák came to know from rehearsals every detail of those works about to be performed. Inevitably, he could not resist the temptation to try his hand at opera.

Smetana had already been reproached for following in Wagner's footsteps. What was there about this Wagner? Dvořák, hearing Liszt play Wagner's compositions, felt himself spellbound by the magic of their genius and their great creative power. He went to hear Wagner's music-dramas at the German Theater; he played in the orchestra when Smetana conducted Liszt's "St. Elizabeth". The urge became irresistible; like Wagner, Dvořák, too, must be heard upon the stage.

Being unknown, however, he could find nobody to write a libretto. Nothing daunted, he chanced upon Theodor Körner's *"Alfred the Great"* in an old German almanac, seized upon it, and, betwixt spring and autumn of 1870, composed an "Heroic Opera in Three Acts", using the German text. (The name of the author, withheld in the almanac, was only later ascertained by Otakar Fischer and Jan Löwenbach.)

The story is as follows: The Danes are celebrating their victory over the Britons. Among the prisoners of war is Alvine, the betrothed of Alfred of Britain; she rejects the marriage overtures of Harald, the Dane. Disguised as a harpist, Alfred comes to the tower in which Alvine is captive, throws off his disguise, and in the midst of the wild melée that ensues, escapes with Alvine. In the following battle, the Britons are victorious over the Danes. But Alfred promises the Danes an unhindered departure so long as they cease to besiege England. Harald prefers death. The poem culminates in an apotheosis of British freedom.

The tremendous force of these events and the determination with which Dvořák sets out to translate them into musical terms—all this works out to the disadvantage of the music. The whole affair does not really concern Dvořák, he is merely determined to make it conform to his ends. Wherever the opportunity presents itself, as in the prayer for victory or in the outbursts in the name of freedom (reminiscent of the yearning of the Czechish people and something like Verdi's innuendos in his operas), Dvořák takes fire.

For the rest, "Alfred" contains some constructions admirable in themselves, especially for a beginner, clearly indicating their Wagnerian archetypes. Nevertheless, as in his songs, Dvořák, the composer of absolute music, triumphs over the composer of music to a given text. For this reason neither here nor in his later works does he bind himself to the scheme of leitmotifs, although he uses them. At no time does he renounce his own broad, flowing melodies, but turns them over to the orchestra and handles the voices purely as recitative.

The work is interesting in more than one respect. Notwithstanding, only the Overture was ever heard. Preserved among the posthumous works as a "Tragic Overture", it was published in 1912 by Simrock, unaware that it was intended for an opera, under the title *"Dramatic Overture"*. In the same manner as Wagner, the Overture introduces the four main themes of this memorable attempt at an opera. It was performed under Nedbal in 1905.

Despite everything, as time went on, the "Wagner crisis" gained an ever stronger ascendancy over the absolute musician in Dvořák. The Second and Third String Quartets of 1870, by chance preserved, give evidence of this. Dvořák had destroyed the scores, but a few copies containing mistakes and corrections were somehow left intact. Significant is the manner in which Dvořák's music overflows and bursts the confines of formal structure. In the *E minor Quartet No. 3,* moreover, there is the remarkable attempt to contrive a new form, a single movement in five parts: A, B, A, B, A. In the final movement of *Quartet No. 2,* Dvořák for the first time writes a rondo. In this work, as if in need of protection from too much Wagner, he quotes the Czechish national song, "Hej Slované".

Wagner's dramatic style is preponderant in the whole structure of this chamber music: melodically and harmonically it seems to point to the stage. The one quartet corresponds in spirit and in treatment to the early Wagner; the other, to the Wagner of "Tristan" whose harmonies are even intensified. The voices often move entirely in melodic lines.

The B-part of the Second Quartet, as it takes form in the Andante religioso, reappears in the *"Nocturne" in B major for Strings*, Op. 40 (Bote & Bock) with the additional part for double-bass. The first half of this Nocturne consists of that section from the Quartet; the rest of it, though composed in the same vein, is new. What a pity that both Quartets have remained in manuscript! Could they be published, we should have accessible a rare example of the struggles of an absolute musician with a form conditioned by influences outside the province of absolute music. (The 'cello part of a 'cello sonata, for which the piano is missing, gives further testimony of this.)

Dvořák soon overcame the most acute stage of the crisis. There remained in him the longing to compose an opera, together with the realization that he would have to conform to new and totally different laws governing this form. It offered him the possibilities of developing the leitmotif after his own fashion, of letting the orchestra predominate over the stage, of audacity in harmonic writing. Above all, he was stirred to his depths by the being and music of Wagner.

At the end of a triumphant career of devotion to absolute music, Dvořák was once again seized by this longing for the opera and its new world of forms. Too little attention has been paid to this fact, bearing witness to the unqualified honesty and adaptability of an artist, unblinded by success, for whom material security could never dull the appeal of the spirit, the command of destiny.

Comic Opera

In June, 1871, a musical periodical published the news that Anton Dvořák, a member of the National Theater Orchestra, had completed a comic opera and submitted it to the management. The text of this three-act opera, *"King and Charcoal-burner"* ("Král a uhlíř"), was by a writer and notary, Bernhard Guldener. Despite his many years of tireless creative activity, this was the first time that Dvořák's name had appeared in print. Hitherto, he had lived a life of virtual obscurity, poverty, and hard work.

The Philharmonic Orchestra, comprising the orchestras of both Theaters, the Czechish and the German, conducted by Smetana, performed the *Overture to King and Charcoal-burner*, and it met with success. But the opera itself was not performed until one year later, in 1873, when Dvořák had at length achieved fame for his "Hymnus". When the Czechish National Theater did think of producing it, and rehearsals had lasted four weeks, it was declared impracticable to produce. Smetana himself, who intended to conduct it, said: "It is a serious work, full of ideas imbued with genius—but I don't believe it can be performed." Dvořák's contemporaries helped to spread this legend.

The National Theater had not yet produced one of Wagner's works, it had not even given Smetana's "Libussa", and, moreover, Dvořák had conformed to the model of Meistersinger, first performed in Prague at the German Provincial

43

Theater in 1871. On the other hand, Dvořák, whose "Alfred" had never been heard on the stage, had not the slightest idea that he was exacting more of the singers than did those other composers whose works were being given at the Czechish National Theater.

In this comic opera, more than in any of his later works, Dvořák consistently followed the practice of using leit-motifs. The instrumentation is too heavy, overburdened with Wagnerisms. Dvořák is none the less on the road to self-liberation. There are eloquent signs of this in the score with its recurrent outbursts of folk-melody despite all the rustling harps and Wagnerian chords in ninths.

There was really nothing insurmountable in the way of its production, although it was difficult and, in contrast to the simple text, unnecessarily complicated. The story would have been effective in a marionette theater: King Mathias is lost while hunting and, unrecognized, enjoys the friendly hospitality of a charcoal-burner. His presence occasions a lovers' quarrel between the charcoal-burner's daughter and her jealous sweetheart. In reward for the kindness of his host, the King invites them all to visit him. Astounded to find out who it was they have sheltered, the lovers are re-conciled. All this, however, demands a great deal of beating about the bush for three acts, necessitating a lot of episodes and subsidiary characters who remain entirely in shadow.

Whatever the rights and wrongs of it, Dvořák, following upon a heated exchange of opinions at one rehearsal, with-drew his score and it was the general impression that, as was his habit, he had destroyed it. He kept silence. Among his posthumous works were found the Overture and a potpourri; the latter was published in 1873 as a supplement to the musical periodical, "Dalibor".

In 1916, a member of the German Provincial Theater in Prague bought the score from a Nuremberg theatrical agent. The purchaser had no idea it was the long-lost "King and Charcoal-burner", and, as it turned out, he had only acquired the first and third acts. In 1928 the parts for the entire three acts were found in the archives of the Czechish National Theater, and in 1929 Ostrčil produced it in this, its original form.

For Dvořák, it now appears, not only employed several of its themes at one time or another, in the E flat major Symphony, in "The Peasant Rogue", etc., but had also—something rare in the annals of music—rewritten and revised the entire opera. And it was only latterly that the work became known and performed in this final version, to which we shall refer.

Popular criticism, of course, kept demanding that both Dvořák and Smetana should leave off following in the footsteps of Wagner. One critic adjured him to return to writing songs. Perhaps it was this that moved him to compose settings to the cycle of poems, "In the May of Life" by Eliška Krásnohorská: "Memories", "Therefore", Obstacles", "Pondering" and "The Orphan". This last was dramatically effective. Later on, following the success of his Slavonic dances, German music publishers turned their attention to Dvořák. Three of the aforementioned cycle, in a German-text version by Srb-Debrnov, were published by

Schlesinger in Berlin as *"Lieder und Gesänge"*. Others have likewise appeared in print.

Success

IN COMMON WITH every young artist of his day, especially among those in the aspiring new generation of a people freshly aware of their national destiny, Dvořák longed to attain outstanding success. That success of which he dreamed, however, was not to come from his chamber-music, symphonic works, nor yet from his songs, and certainly not from his operas. Success, and with it fame, became the portion of the singer of his people, the comforter and awakener of national hopes. Nothing could retard nor dismay his tireless activity, his ebullient creative imagination.

On July 3rd, 1872, he completed the score of a Cantata for mixed choir and orchestra, entitled *"Hymnus"*, based on a poem, "The Heirs of the White Mountain", by Vítězslav Hálek. In 1620 the Czechish people, defeated on the White Mountain, were beaten back, forced into a decline and condemned to a silence which endured for centuries. But with the reawakening of the national soul, that silence was now broken for the first time. In solemn tones, the poet proclaims his passion for the suffering people, yet challenges them to love their native land so much the more, with a passion transcending that of any other people.

To this text Dvořák composed a music of great simplicity, power and impressiveness, beginning softly and solemnly, gradually descending into ever greater depths of lamentation and mourning, only to rise thereafter to ever greater heights of resolve. An abrupt change from E flat to C, a march-like theme, and, with this turning point, defiance and the will to victory are awakened. The style becomes rich and gay with iridescent modulations, employing all the artifice of counterpoint as in the masterpieces of classic choral literature, returning by way of a repeat to the principal key, now no longer symbolizing lamentation but rejoicing. In spite of every enticement, Dvořák seeks complete liberation from Wagner.

The first fruits of victory came to him with the performance of this "Hymnus" on March 9, 1873, sung by a choir of three hundred voices supported by a reinforced orchestra, conducted by his friend, Karel Bendl. Now at last, the clouds parted. From now on Dvořák stood in the full light of recognition, even of fame. The Hymnus was first published by Novello in London, 1885, as Opus 30.

Marriage and Further Compositions

SUCH RESOUNDING SUCCESS was of importance only to the young man in shaping his future plans. As far as the creative artist was concerned, any one of his works was just as valid as the other. He went on working. Once again chamber-music, songs and even opera! About this time Dvořák conceived the plan, which later matured, for his Oratorio based on the life of St. Ludmila.

Dvořák, now in his thirties, was entering upon a period—the Seventies of the Nineteenth Century—that bears the stamp of a reckoning with his own past, a thrashing-out of differences with Wagner and Liszt, in particular an evaluation of the new form they threatened to impose upon him, and, finally, a finding of his path to Brahms. This pathway did not lead him so much to the artist, whom he was at length to meet face to face as master to master, as to Brahms the man, the challenger, the epoch-making figure.

Certain works that followed may be cited in illustration of this. Such was his *Piano Quintet in A-major*, not to be confused with the later work of the same nature famed as Opus 81. This earlier work was composed in 1872 and remained in manuscript. It reveals strong indications of Dvořák's typical sureness of form once he had surmounted the Wagnerian crisis. Still there are occasional outbursts of "Sturm und Drang"; he is not yet the master of the wealth of his material and the flood of new ideas.

In the Third Movement, he cannot contain himself within the bounds of balanced harmonies such as he later came to observe. It takes him a long time to find a solution to the purely instrumental problem of writing for the piano. Here again it is noticeable, as in several other piano parts, that while composing for the piano he is actually thinking in terms of the violin. In the Quintet there are echoes of thematic material from the Hymnus; the pathos of the first and last movements is long drawn out. It takes him 140 bars to state a single theme of the Finale! There is no scherzo.

As evidenced in several of his youthful works, Dvořák found the scherzo quite a problem. He did his best with national coloring (masking) derived from the Polka, "Dumka" (Elégie), "Furiant", and for that very reason was decried at home as "a street-song writer". Brahms helped him to obtain clarity, as may be discerned from Dvořák's String Quartet in C, Opus 61. Dvořák most nearly achieved maturity in his slow movements, as in the Adagio of this Quintet. And now he has relinquished the attempt to comprehend the whole within the span of one movement or to link the entire work through interrelated themes. Here, all four movements are separate and distinct.

The Quintet was followed in the same year by two Song Cycles: one consisting of settings for Serbian folk-poems, the other of settings for the lyric poems in the "Königinhof Manuscript". As soon as Dvořák stands upon the firm ground of folk-poetry, folk-song and folk-dance rhythms, he is perfectly at home and at ease. He lays aside everything artificial and schematic, discovering within himself the primitive strength of the people. The Serbian verses were translated into Czechish for him. The melodies have nothing to do with Serbian folk-song but were Dvořák's own invention.

The verses of the Königinhof Manuscript were as if made to order for Dvořák. One of his settings, *"The Lark"*, was published in 1873 as a supplement to the musical periodical, "Dalibor". This was Dvořák's first published composition, followed shortly thereafter by the rest of the *Königinhof Lieder* (published by Stary, Prague, Opus 17). In 1879, Simrock published both the foregoing Cycles as Op. 6 and Op. 7, leaving out two of the Königinhof Lieder and printing the text only in German and English. In 1887, Novello brought together in one volume both cycles, including those Simrock had left out. Simrock reproached Dvořák on this account but was satisfied when Dvořák excused himself and made restitution by turning over to him *"Four New Songs"*, Op. 82.

In the same fruitful year of 1872, Dvořák wrote three more nocturnes for orchestra, likewise a violin sonata, all of which he later destroyed.

Of those he left intact, in 1912 Simrock published posthumously one of Dvořák's most interesting works, composed in 1873, the *Symphony in E flat*. Performed by Smetana in a Prague Philharmonic concert in 1874, and awarded the Austrian State Prize in 1875, this Symphony is the more remarkable inasmuch as here Dvořák shows himself to be absolutely possessed by Wagner. For the first time we find motives actually recalling Wagner, such as the first subject of the First Movement and the D flat major themes and

cries of lamentation in the Slow Movement, that is, the Second. There is altogether something of a mythical air about this Symphony; affinities with the world of Valhalla seem to arise spontaneously, accentuated by the dramatic instrumentation (harp, English horn, etc.). Notwithstanding, the instrumental apparel is magnificent, the invention superabundant, sometimes imbued with pathos, and the Third (and last) Movement—again no scherzo—rises to heights of sheer jubilation.

Dvořák especially loved this work and often turned its pages toward the end of his life. This is understandable when we recall that, particularly in his last years, he again felt the powerful appeal of Wagner. Nevertheless, in spite of all these affiliations, this Symphony falls within the orbit of the emotions and ideas generated by the Hymnus. It is, indeed, a Wagner in Slavic guise whom Dvořák employs to such effect.

The success of the Hymnus left its mark on the youth and the man. He felt himself at last sufficiently established, and married his beloved former pupil, Anna Čermák, in Prague, on Nov. 17th, 1873. They first lodged with the bride's parents and then moved into their own home in February 1874. Dvořák, after eleven years' service, gave up his place in the Orchestra and took the position of Organist in the Church of St. Adalbert, where he earned ten gulden a month.

There was but one shadow on their happiness, and that was the unfortunate failure at rehearsals of King and Charcoal-burner. Dvořák took it very much to heart, subjecting to merciless scrutiny everything he had ever composed and destroying the greater portion of what remained in manuscript. He is reported to have said: "I always had plenty of paper with which to build a fire." To those that were left he gave new Opus numbers, no longer valid today because the publishers later renumbered everything. At that time Dvořák called the Overture to Alfred, Opus 1; the Overture to King and Charcoal-burner, Op. 2; the Hymnus, Op. 4; the Piano Quintet, Op. 5; the Serbian Songs, Op. 6; the Königinhof Cycle, Op. 7; the String Quartet in F minor, Op. 9; the Symphony in E flat, Op. 10. All these opus numbers were later superseded.

The *Quartet in F minor* was composed on the eve of this numbering; an *A Minor Quartet* followed immediately thereafter. About this time, a new chamber-music organization had been founded, with the famous Anton Bennewitz (later Director of the Conservatory) as First Violin, and with Smetana as Pianist. In the hope that they would perform something from his compositions, Dvořák, as was his custom, immediately wrote these two string quartets, in sequence the Fourth and the Fifth. The first of these, that in F Minor, was finished before his marriage.

Published in 1929 by Breitkopf and performed for the first time in Prague, 1930, this Quartet is autobiographical, similar to the admittedly greater work by Smetana, "Scenes from my Life", but without the catastrophic climax. As in Smetana's work, Dvořák's First Movement is full of sullen melancholy; the Second, of slow, introspective flashes of illumination, a backward glance at earlier days and joys. The Third Movement is a still more melancholy waltz, but the Fourth turns effortlessly to what life has still to offer, and the national character of its gaiety is so striking that one is reminded of the later Slavonic Dances (particularly the Eighth).

Dvořák evinces a remarkable moderation in the style and sonority of this work, and this again is prophetic. The Andantino from this Quartet at some time or other was transformed into a *"Romance for Violin and Orchestra"*, Op. 11. Beginning with the second subject, this "Romance" goes ahead on its own, with very happy results. Published in 1879 by Simrock, the Romance is no ordinary concertpiece but fills out the full dimensions of the great sonata form.

The *String Quartet in A Minor*, Op. 12, was completed shortly after his wedding, in December 1873. It betokens Dvořák's last attempt to make one long movement out of four: in this instance he has merely joined together four clearly defined movements. Dvořák later indicated their limits and separated them. In the manuscript, several pages are missing at the end of the First Movement. Therefore it could not be printed or performed.

Two Comic Operas

IN THE YEARS from 1873 to 1875, Dvořák underwent a transformation that was to determine both the man and the artist and for the first time to establish his full individuality. Strange to say, his passion for Wagner was instrumental in this. Aware that he was obsessed by Wagner, it was only natural that he should scrutinize the difficult struggles of his great compatriot, Smetana, who was so often condemned because of his leaning toward Wagner. Notwithstanding, Smetana had already recognized his own peculiar mission; repudiating nothing that Wagner had given him, he devoted his entire art and energies to expression in the national idiom. Thus he had already composed "Dalibor" and "Libussa"; and, about this time, his gay folk-opera, "Two Widows", was performed.

This was the road for Dvořák to follow. There could be only one solution for him: from groping to seeking, from seeking to finding. Beethoven and Schubert, the guardian spirits of his earliest beginnings, must again hold sway; the fruits of this experience are to be seen in Dvořák's regained mastery of form.

This is readily perceptible from a comparison of his Symphony in E Flat with its sister work that now followed, the *Symphony in D Minor*, composed in the first three months of 1874. (Again not to be confused with the D Minor Symphony, Op. 70, of eleven years later!) In contrast to the soaring fever of the Symphony in E Flat, the D Minor of 1874 speaks of healing and spiritual convalescence. In the same year, Smetana conducted the Scherzo from this work and eighteen years later, just before his departure for the New World, Dvořák himself conducted the entire Symphony, which remained unpublished until 1912 (Simrock).

In their clear formulation, the themes themselves—except one from the last Movement—are a repudiation of "the endless melody" of the music-drama: everything here strives for definiteness and regularity. Naturally, this does not mean that Dvořák subscribes to any sort of Philistinism; he has too much that is interesting to say. Ideas rain down upon him, beginning with the first subject which exhales peace and a healing spirit. And now the song-theme overflows, swaying all hearts, as if sprung from the very soil of his native land.

In the Andante, there sings, still with some resemblance to Wagner, an almost classic melody, and here Dvořák

writes his first variations in the manner of the classics. This time he has composed a Scherzo, clinging to thematic affinities with the First Movement, and only the trio reminds one of Wagner (entrance of the Tailors in "Meistersinger"). The actual theme of the Scherzo Dvořák later reiterated in a concert-piece, *"In Troublous Times"*, from the "Bohemian Forest" cycle. With the exception of this Scherzo, Dvořák manages to get along with the Beethoven-orchestra. The Wagnerian demons are here deliberately permitted to resonate; the alien might of Wagner is felt, but in the last Movement, Dvořák makes a victorious assertion of his own rediscovered identity.

The pathway of companionship with Smetana inevitably led to lyric drama. Had Dvořák not already had the material for a folk-opera in his hands? Was not the reason it fell through really that these stage people had such pretentions to superior education whereas, in fact, they actually had insufficient knowledge of operatic stage technique? Could not the damage be repaired? On the basis of his recently gained experience, Dvořák thought it could, simply by translating folk-elements into national terms and treating them as such.

In the same year of 1874, from April to August, Dvořák showed his self-discipline by composing afresh the entire King and Charcoal-burner. Note for note was revised, not even a bar remains of the earlier version. Indeed, Dvořák himself had become quite another being. Whereas Wagner had formerly been his model, it was now Smetana, but, beyond and above him, Weber and Lortzing. Returning to the earlier German "Singspiel", to the folk-opera, Dvořák sought a new approach to the stage—that stage which had yet to be built in Prague. There are echoes of Meister-singer here, even leitmotifs, but only by way of reminis-cence. The scenes are more nearly self-contained as in the early German Singspiel and Italian opera. The real charm of each scene lies in the music for it, a rich harvest of spon-taneity, youthful vigor and intoxicating melody. There is a plethora of riches in the form of national rhythm and melody.

Both main themes of the Overture preserve this national coloring and the folk-dance influence. Lost in the forest, the king sings a ballad introduced by one of Dvořák's earliest themes that recurs throughout his entire later works (see page 38). A doodlesack-piper enters bringing with him a fragment of genuine Czechish folk-music, key-noting the whole opera. In the Second Act, Liduška, the charcoalburner's daughter, has her big aria. In the Third, a gavotte characterizes court-life; Jeník, the bridegroom, sings his aria, and the mood and style of comic opera are perfectly caught. The king's song in the manner of Lortzing's couplets fills out the picture. This act is enriched by exceptionally gay ballet-music, waltz and polka.

The libretto, nevertheless, remains a heavy liability. And so Dvořák began a long series of painstaking revisions. The 1874 version enjoyed great success, but after four performances was removed from the repertoire. In 1881, Dvořák revived and conducted it himself. This time there were only two performances. In 1887, V. J. Novotný, who had with marked felicity improved Smetana's Dalibor libretto, rewrote the Third Act of King and Charcoal-burner, and Dvořák composed for it entirely new music which, however, is in sharp contrast to the rest. In all, eight performances of this version were given. Then it was not heard again until 1914. It was finally published in Prague, 1915, in the definitive Czechish version arranged by Kovařovic, Opera Director of the Czechish National Theater, for its performance in 1914.

Immediately upon finishing his second version of King and Charcoal-burner, from the end of August to September 12th, 1874, Dvořák composed his *"Rhapsody" in A Minor* for large orchestra. (Published posthumously in 1912, it was listed as his Opus 15.) This Rhapsody is another stage in the transition from the free romantic form of a Wagner or Liszt to the established, closed sonata form in which Dvořák ever more clearly perceived his predestined and best-suited vehicle.

Externally, this Rhapsody nevertheless tends towards the type of symphonic poem created by Liszt. Although Dvořák later overtly christened it "Slavonic Rhapsody", this Opus 15 tacitly follows the national program. Its lyric pathos points to a glorious past, to the myths of the homeland. This time, moreover, it is Smetana with his "Vyšehrad" who is Dvořák's model. Dvořák withheld this Rhapsody and it was not performed until after his death, in 1904, by Nedbal.

A man of such creative powers as Dvořák is self-critical, yet he does not doubt nor despair; he goes on creating something new. Only twelve days after finishing the Rhapsody, Dvořák is again busy composing a *String Quartet in A minor*. In this work he shows himself capable of confident surrender to the severe style of chamber-music, without fear of its fetters. Indeed, he exaggerates the severity, lapsing almost into classic asceticism. His impersonal melancholy is remarkable. Even the Scherzo, which usually helps out the composer with at least all the devices of popularity, this time passes in review as a slow minuet. There are two themes, and no more, to each Movement; the movements are nevertheless here and there interrelated. The general effect is that of discipline and an unaccustomed restraint.

But perhaps this was to be explained by the fact that he had not yet altogether outgrown the Wagnerian crisis.

This Quartet, the sixth he had composed, was Dvořák's first chamber-music work to appear in print (published by Stary, Prague, 1875, and Bote & Bock, 1893). Fibich—cited by his compatriots along with Smetana and Dvořák as belonging to "the classic trinity of Czech music", but not so well known abroad—wrote an analysis of this Quartet in A minor, published in the musical review "Dalibor".

Swept along by the surge of creative activity, with the Quartet barely finished, on October 4th Dvořák began composing his second opera and completed it on Christmas Eve, 1874. The text was all ready for him, but, in that unreflective Wagnerian age, it seemed to him too simple, not "significant" enough. Dr. Josef Štolba, the second notary to write him a libretto, did better in his poetic avocation than had Guldener. His book is witty, providing plenty of opportunity for scenic effects. The title, *"Tvrdé palice,"* in the very poor German translation was "Dickschädel": i.e., *"The Numbskull"*. (A better translation would have been "The Obstinate Children".) The piano score, Op. 17, was not published by Simrock until 1882, one year after the première, postponed for seven years! The production was so execrably staged that, after one performance, it was taken out of the repertoire.

It certainly did not merit such a fate. The form alone is a great advance over anything in contemporary Czech opera, which had not yet done away with spoken dialogue and recitative. Dvořák had set the entire libretto to music of spontaneous good humor. With admirable delicacy, he had written a stimulating, ever-surprising musical comedy, full of charm, fascinating, moreover, because of its peculiar, almost symmetrical structure. Even in other countries, accepted in the right spirit, it should enjoy success.

Let us examine this almost marionette-like symmetry: a wealthy widower has a son, Toník, who, he avers, shall marry Lenka, the daughter of a wealthy widow. Godfather Řeřicha, doubting that these obstinate children will obey their parents' wishes, concocts a scheme. He tells Lenka that she must marry the wealthy widower, the father of Toník, who in turn is to marry her mother. Jealous of her mother, Lenka immediately confesses her love for Toník whom, out of obstinate pride, she has hitherto spurned. Řeřicha tells the same tale to Toník, who declares he would rather marry Lenka than let her marry his father. The alarmed lovers are driven into each other's arms, much to the satisfaction of their parents and neighbors in the village. Upon the successful outcome, the Godfather (obviously related to Kezal in the Bartered Bride), confesses his part in the affair.

High spirits, good humor and folksy accents, from the opening bars of the Overture, with its contrasting themes of love and obstinate denial (and for good measure a third theme not in the opera itself), carry everything before them. This one-act opera sustains the pace of contagious mischief and exuberant gaiety to the very end.

The Austrian State Prize

WHILE DVOŘÁK was working on this opera, a piece of great good fortune, far-reaching in its consequences, befell him: he received a yearly allowance from the Austrian State. After all, it seemed, Austria did think about those she was privileged to call her own. (Bohemia, at that time, still belonged to the Habsburg Monarchy.) And, in this instance, Vienna had accorded him recognition even before his more provincial compatriots.

The Austrian Commission for the State Music Prize made the award on the basis of a report from Eduard Hanslick, seconded by the Commission-members, Johannes Brahms and, presumably, the Imperial Opera Director, Herbeck. Dvořák had submitted to the judges his Symphony in E flat and, possibly, the Symphony in G minor, together with a chamber-music work. As Hanslick later recounted, the Commission was astonished by the great gifts herein proclaimed. The other competitors could also lay claim to youth and poverty, but there were few with real talent.

Dvořák thus received 400 gulden and, since he regularly submitted his works for consideration and the Commission as regularly made him the award, this continued for several years in succession. Not one of the Commissioners judged his work on the basis of personal acquaintance with him, but their decision made them come to know the man. This was the purely objective beginning of that bond between Dvořák and Brahms which, some years later, became an intimate and lasting friendship. This friendship opened up to

Dvořák the lands of German music, and thus he earned the admiration of such an one as Hans Richter, who likewise first came to hear of Dvořák in Vienna. In ever-widening circles, first England and then America became aware of Dvořák's music.

This was all a process effected by the years, however, years that in the long run were a period of ascetic renunciation of all joys except those in the family and in his work. Dvořák worked instinctively, creating as unconsciously as Mother Nature herself, yet at the same time with the highest artistic awareness, incessantly rounding out the formal structure of his works and as incessantly hammering out his own character. It is impossible to ascribe a particular significance to each successive work. Nevertheless, the entire panorama of his work circumscribes Dvořák's intensely individual and unique career. The sum total gives the sense of a dispensation, of a destiny, of a joyous growth and maturity.

When he received the Austrian State Prize, Dvořák was just composing a *Quintet in G major for two violins, viola, 'cello and double-bass*. Interrupting his work to take a short trip, a luxury he felt the circumstances permitted, he had none the less finished it by March, 1875. Performed in 1876, it was published, with slight revisions, twelve years later by Simrock—but as Op. 77!

From the rather theatrical flourish of the First and Fourth Movements, we perceive his recent preoccupation with opera; these two movements are related by thematic similarities and the thread of innuendos is woven even through the Scherzo. The ruling key this time comes to the fore in the Scherzo and the Andante that follows it. The second subject of the Scherzo, chromatically tinted, turns into the minor second, a modulation characteristic of Dvořák and derived from Moravian folk-song. The beautiful solo passage of the first violin lends an air of especial consecration to the Andante, making it seem even more significant than the work already is, thanks to the Scherzo. A peculiar feature is the writing for the 'cello in a high register, made possible by the deep double-bass of the ensemble.

As frequently happened, Dvořák was so impressed by the tonal picture evoked by this instrumental setting with the double-bass that he was not content with the possibilities afforded by one work. It must be followed as soon as possible by another: the *Serenade in E major for Strings*, Op. 22, composed in the first half of May, 1875. This is an especially beautiful work, rich in sonority, in complete harmony with the character of the serenade, all its effects as if intended for the open air, in now tender, now mischievous accents. In keeping with this mood, it is not weighed down with long-drawn-out thematic development but remains within the bounds of the three-part song without abjuring the artifices of style.

The first part is key-noted by a fanfare-theme demanding attention for the serenade. Then there is a waltz of somewhat complicated structure and subtle instrumentation, of which the trio voices an especially moving melody. In the Scherzo, there is again a trio, this time full of yearning. A particular gem is a Larghetto in the most dream-like mood, with an almost Schubert-like middle part. The Fifth (and last) Movement is more impassioned, quiets down in the middle, cites again the Larghetto, and finally leads back to the introductory fanfare.

This exquisite Serenade at once enjoyed a great success everywhere it was heard. That same year, it nearly turned out to be Dvořák's first composition to be performed in Vienna; but it was not to be. However, from that time forth, the keen attention of Hans Richter, Conductor of the Vienna Philharmonic Orchestra, was directed to the composer, Dvořák, and Richter certainly had intimation of what was yet to come.

Dvořák wrote two more chamber-music works in 1875. The first of these was a *Piano Trio in B*, composed in May. Played for the first time in 1877, with Ondříček as violinist, it was published in 1880 as Op. 21 by Schlesinger. A work full of passion, it has a tempestuous First Movement, a touching prayer in the Andante, a carefree Scherzo that seems to gather fresh strength in order to withstand the passionate attack of the Finale. The first three movements are in the mediant relationship so characteristic of Dvořák (B—G—E-flat); the trio of the Scherzo jumps to B major. The inventive genius of the master embraces wide melodic arcs, conceives especially ingenious harmonic turns and genuine surprises in handling the voices. This all indicates manly courage and, as far as pure artistry is concerned, a newly obtained perspective. So pronounced is this that the *Piano Trio in G minor* written the following year, in accordance with Dvořák's habit of composing in pairs, is a somewhat weaker work.

Close on the heels of the Piano Trio in B, came the *Piano Quartet in D*, Op. 23, composed in the last days of May and the first days of June. Here again he sets himself new problems of content and form, and out of the rich depths of a musician who has learned to think, Dvořák finds ever new solutions. The chief features of this work, however, are its greater intimacy and contemplative power. New, indeed, is the treatment of the first subject comprising merely two bars in the opening Movement and new is the wealth of fantasy in the sequence of ten variations in the Andante. The Scherzo, still cautiously approached, is linked to the Finale as one movement. The reserve evidenced in this work is in tune with its destiny: it was not performed until five years later in 1880, when it was published by Schlesinger.

Moravian National Poems—F Major Symphony—"Wanda"

THE FIRST FEW months of 1875 were sufficient to afford Dvořák another sortie into the mysterious land of success. For three years he had not composed any songs, yet he was aware that he need only follow up the vein of folk-song and folk-poetry to hit upon that form of lyric expression best suited to his temperament. Thus he came to compose the *"Moravian National Poems"* for soprano and tenor. He wrote these for two voices because they were intended for Johann Neff, a Prague wholesaler, and his wife, Marie, in whose home Dvořák gave piano lessons.

The youth and the maiden of these folk-songs are supposed to bill and coo and quarrel until finally they are one heart and soul; or else there is talk of absence and the pain of separation. The printed translations are not only stressed in conflict with the melody but they scarcely reproduce the sense of the original. Unfortunately, the Czechish text was not printed. Simrock did not publish this Opus 20 until the later-composed "Moravian Duets" were already known. (Incidentally, of the four Duets in this edition the Fourth, "The Last Wish", belongs to the later Opus 32, with which it was not printed at that time.)

The whole charm of the "Moravian Duets", which later so loudly proclaimed Dvořák's world-fame, may already be perceived in these "Moravian National Poems". One of their chief attractions is the magic of a melodic by no means simply plundered from folk-song airs but created by an original musician in the true spirit of folk-song. The "Moravian Duets", however, were written for two female voices, which heightened the melodic effect.

Thus Dvořák went on without pause, piling up manuscripts that were to be useful in a not-far-distant future. No sooner was the Piano Quartet finished than, five days later, he began a new *Symphony in F major,* composed in five weeks from June 15th to July 23rd. How many predecessors it had had! Yet this was the first one that really counted. It is the third of the five symphonies published in his lifetime. (The later-written symphonies in D, Opus 60, and D minor, Opus 70, appeared in print before this one.) Published by Simrock in 1888, it was known as Opus 76.

Considerable injustice was done to Dvořák through the fact that this came to be known as his "Third" Symphony, and was felt to indicate a retrogression in style, following as it did upon the other two later and riper works.

In the First Movement of this Symphony in F, idyllic mood and firm resolve seem to alternate, now one and now the other gaining the upper hand. The formal structure is beautiful, the harmony significant; there is a hint in the themes of the Czechish national character. In the Second Movement, a short Andante (a rare exception with Dvořák) almost achieves that kind of elegiac mood for which Dvořák later borrowed from another Slavic tongue the name, "Dumka", as designation. It is a melancholy serenade, breaking into passionate movement in the middle portion.

The Andante almost runs over into the Third Movement, the Scherzo, in which a peculiar knocking rhythm seems to portend the impact of exciting influences. These contrasts are accentuated in the Finale. Although thus far the chamber-music idyll has rather held the stage, just as it keynoted this work at the outset, now a genuine symphonic pathos has its say. The keys of F major and A minor are in conflict until F finally triumphs. This mightily expanding Movement indicates Dvořák's forward-striding and lofty aspiring within the limitations of the Beethoven-orchestra. After the feverish struggles of a searching soul, there is a return to the mood of peace of the beginning.

It is understandable that the dedication of such a work must have brought joy to the recipient. It was Hans von Bülow who thanked Dvořák in a characteristic letter, the terms of which were particularly appropriate at that time (1887):

"Most Honored Master:

"A dedication from you—next to Brahms, the most God-gifted composer of the present day—is a higher decoration than any 'Great Cross' from the hands of any ruler. With most heartfelt thanks, I accept this honor.

"With most sincere esteem,

"Your devoted admirer,

"Hans Bülow."

From June through December in 1875, Dvořák was busy composing a new tragic opera, "*Wanda*", from its inception apparently unblest. Probably it was the example of Smetana's "Libussa" that impelled Dvořák, after two attempts in the lighter genre, to try his hand likewise at an heroic opera based upon stories out of Slavic mythology.

"Wanda", however, is a Polish, not a Czechish tale. Messrs. Zákrejs and Beneš-Šumavský had fabricated a five-act libretto, based on a dramatic poem by a Warsaw professor, containing very little of a Slavic nature. Abounding in exaggerated situations, it reveled in a style of diction more often than not approximating involuntary parody. Dvořák's music, despite all his hard-won distance from Wagner, just succeeded in surmounting all these vicissitudes—but in that very act it died of inanition. More than this was hardly to be expected.

Wanda, something like Libussa, is a Polish Princess. Two neighboring rulers quarrel over her: the Pole, Slavoj, and the German, Roderich. Roderich, defeated by Slavoj, takes flight to the Witch, Homena, with whose aid he still hopes to win Wanda. (The witch, a typical appearance in Slavic fairy-tales, is a favorite figure in Dvořák's operas and symphonic poems.)

Again the rivals do battle for Wanda. Perceiving that she is the cause of so much suffering, Wanda swears to dedicate her life to the Gods if her own people are victorious. The victory is given to them and Wanda, after two interminable acts of leave-taking from followers, throws herself in the Weichsel River. The shades of French grand opera haunt this work, but at any rate it contains some beautiful music in those very scenes of leave-taking and in the choruses, and therefore it may justly be considered the forerunner of Dvořák's "St. Ludmila."

The "Stabat mater" Period

JUST AS DVOŘÁK finished composing the First Act of Wanda, about mid-September, his little daughter died. This afflicted him deeply: we shall soon see how this tragic experience evoked several compositions. Naturally, it had an adverse effect upon his writing of the Second Act of "Wanda". The première took place April 17th, 1876, but it was soon removed from the repertoire and was never revived. In 1881, Dvořák sold the score to Cranz in Hamburg, but the latter published only the Overture. In order to reanimate it, Wanda would have had to be entirely rewritten; nothing else could have saved it.

The death of his child thus cast its shadow on his first three works of 1876: a Piano Trio, a String Quartet and the

"Stabat mater". The *Piano Trio in G minor*, completed on January 20th of that year and published in 1880 by Bote and Bock as Opus 26, is similar to the Trio in B composed one year previously. But in this Trio, grief weighs down on both defiance and the joy of life. The keynote is passionate longing: everything is veiled except the profound lamentation of the Largo; even the Scherzo will not brighten up; only in the last Movement is there some trace of reviving spirits and the work ends on a D major passage. But the force of the earlier Trio in B, with its wealth of invention and formulation, was greater.

Begun on January 20th, the day the Trio was finished, the *String Quartet in E major* was completed two weeks later. One of the best-known and most appealing of Dvořák's works, it is remarkable if for no other reason in that, despite the affirmative bright key, it time and again sinks back into the mood of grief. It is almost monumental in its sheer perfection of form, apparently in tribute to Beethoven.

The mildness of the beginning swiftly runs over into the minor key; the second theme adds to this palette the national coloring. The Slow Movement, similar to that of the F major Symphony, is devoid of Dvořák's usual breadth. The Scherzo is a waltz in the melancholy manner of Chopin. In the Finale, the viola begins almost rhapsodically; it takes thirty-two bars to attain the main key, and then begins Dvořák's typical struggle between the parallel major and minor. The penultimate bar is in C sharp minor, and only the final bar returns to the E major of the beginning.

This minor-keyed mood lends to the whole Quartet, otherwise striving towards the major, a peculiar charm which, together with the gratifying instrumental setting, has made it especially beloved. Joachim played it for the first time in Berlin, but not until 1890; in Prague, the Bohemian Quartet played it on the occasion of its debut, October 22nd, 1892. Published in 1888 by Simrock, it was listed as Opus 80! This was a grave injustice to Dvořák inasmuch as, later on, people found fault with this work for its lack of maturity whereas, actually, it was one of his earlier compositions.

The most beautiful, outstanding, and touching memorial of his grief and consolation was Dvořák's "*Stabat mater*", written between February 19th and May 7th, 1876, but only in sketch form. The mood escaped him; he began other undertakings and it was not until the fall of 1877 that he resumed this work. There was tragedy enough to compel him: in September, his three-and-a-half year old son had a fatal accident, and in October he lost a second little girl. The very weight of grief turned his thoughts to the Stabat mater, which consumed the rest of October and was finished on Nov. 13th (published as "Op. 58" by Simrock, 1881).

Dvořák's life and work hitherto had been a simple and straightforward tale of want, meager victories and strenuous ascent. It was only natural, therefore, that his suffering and painful search for consolation in the Eternal, should be just as simple and convincing. This music was not written under the compulsion of any hollow piety and, although he follows a religious text, Dvořák is not restrained by convention. He is guided, out of his deep feeling for Nature, by an undeviating faith in the Creator of all things visible for the enjoyment of man and hence, just as inevitably, by his trust in the Dispenser of that which brings sorrow to man.

As a musician, he does not even attempt to measure his own powers against those classic composers who handled the same text, and he has no thought of writing a "spiritual opera". On the other hand, he does attempt to portray within the accepted limits of the form, the whole man that he is and his environment, at the same time depicting the national nuances of the community in which he lives. This national coloring finds expression in "Stabat mater," the first oratorio of modern Czechish music, in relation to which it is of the same importance as Smetana's operas to the Czechish stage. Dvořák's Stabat mater is particularly remarkable, as is all his religious music, for its freedom of treatment, defying convention. It is a dialogue between a sincerely devout man and musician, wounded to his very core, and the spiritual concepts commanding his faith. His blessed melody mediates between them. Death is the point of departure of this work; transfiguration is its conclusion.

In the orchestral Overture, the line leads from the lowest to the highest F sharp (B minor) as if the image of the Cross were magically illumined. In another plaintive tonal form, the line descends chromatically: beneath the Cross stands the Mother. There is an outburst of anguish, thrice repeated. In muted accents, the choir murmurs the first verse; the song of the solo tenor is accompanied by a consoling clarinet; but the contrasting and interweaving of the quartet of solo voices with the choir leads back again to the despair of the beginning and, once more, to tender consolation. In the second part, the solos are concerned with observations on the death of the Son and the sorrowings of the Mother, the whole in unison, very softly, as if to evoke the dying moments of the Savior.

In part three, the choir sings "Let us suffer with Thee!" and the description of Christ's suffering ends. Even more clearly than the text (one of the most magnificent in the world's literature, voicing all the passionate depth of the awakening Franciscan faith, the birth-throes of Italian mysticism), the music now turns from contemplation to prayer: "Let my heart be consumed with love for the Savior" sung by the solo bass (Part four). In much lighter tones, almost a pastorale, the choir now sings (5): "Share Thy pain with us." A sort of march intervenes, an outburst of song, with tenor and male choir alternating (6): "Let us stand with Thee beneath the Cross." The entire choir now sings (7): "Apportion unto us Thy pain." Solo soprano and tenor follow, with ever fuller melody, in (8): "We are submerged in Thy sufferings." Here the alto solo (9) permits Dvořák to let us enjoy to the full—and he is one of those rare composers who know how—the timbre of the feminine lower register in tragic supplication, in prayer to be identified with that supreme Destiny. The Finale (10) in the manner of the classic oratorio, ascends to even greater heights, in harmony with the poem, conducting the soul through suffering to the glories of Paradise. Once again the lamentation of the beginning resounds, to be dissolved, however, in consolation, rejoicing, and, finally, in the yearning of the Amen.

This work, with its instrumentation enriched by the experience of another year's achievement, certainly attains the greatest heights of any of Dvořák's compositions thus far. The very first performance in Prague, Dec. 23rd, 1880, made a profound impression. So it was again in Budapest, 1882; in Vienna, 1886; and—of especial importance to Dvořák—in London, 1883.

In London, there was an immediate demand for its repetition the following year, and Dvořák was invited to conduct it. This was in 1884, his first triumph in a country so far from home. In London, he found at his disposal an orchestra of 150 and a choir of 900. That same year, he again conducted his "Stabat mater" in Worcester Cathedral. And again the same year, it was twice performed in New York. The Anglo-Saxon world of music and America in particular had recognized Dvořák who, from now on, was to belong most especially to them.

In the following months, between the Stabat mater and a new opera, Dvořák composed a number of shorter works in a great variety of forms. Not one of these was without significance to Dvořák, but one of them with its sequels, in continuation of a genre he had once before attempted, earned him a phenomenal success, even more overwhelming than that of his Stabat mater. This was the appearance of his *"Moravian Duets"*.

His trail still lay unblazed before him: nobody yet knew what was to determine it, what was the goal, and, least of all, what the reward. He worked and was happy in his work except when one of his children died. Whenever he was unhappy, then he worked most of all.

He wrote Two Minuets for Piano, published as Opus 28 in Prague, 1879, and later in Berlin by Bote and Bock. Once again we feel the proximity of Schubert, and again Dvořák's own peculiar, national utterance is heard, especially in the Minuet's approximation to the "Sousedská", a Czechish dance in slow three-quarter time.

His next work was *"Four Songs" for Mixed Choir*, Op. 29: the first two, "Evening Blessing" and the delightful "Lullabye" were settings of texts by Heyduk; the remaining two, "I shall not tell" and "The Abandoned Girl" are based upon folk-poems. Dvořák simulates the melody, rhythmic structure and certain technical details of folk-song, but he borrows nothing, remains the master of his own invention. (In 1898, Kistner published a German-text edition of these choral songs.)

In 1877, he wrote several songs for male choir, brought out (in parts as Op. 43) by various publishers. He is always happiest when he can relax and lean upon folk-poetry. These choral songs are beautifully arranged, with rich tonal settings, interesting melody and unmistakable national coloring. One of the most fascinating is called "The Beloved as Poison-Mixer". The theme of seven bars in the chorus, "I Am a Fiddler", with its irregular periods characteristic of Dvořák's inventive faculty, appears later on in the Symphonic Variations, Op. 78.

Moravian Duets—Brahms—Simrock

ALL THESE SONGS for mixed voices were composed about the time of the "Moravian Duets", originally conceived for two sopranos. They sound better, however, sung by soprano and contralto. The earlier "Moravian National Poems", Op. 20, it will be remembered, were written for soprano and tenor. But two women's voices, with piano accompaniment, blend together more easily, and with less restraint. The second cycle, of Five Songs, which won immediate fame, was composed between May 17th and May 21st, 1876; the third cycle, of Ten Songs, between June 26th and July 17th; the second and third are noted as Opus 32.

The form is simple, in strophes or three parts, the melody in the style of folk-song, but Dvořák's own invention. The music betrays the peculiarities typical of Moravian folk-poetry and song: wide leaps in the melody, gliding of a motive in the interval of the major second, modulation in the minor second. All these features Dvořák thereafter adopted in his instrumental works. The charm of these great works in miniature is only partially explained by the delightful text, the peculiar interplay of the two voices, now imitative, now accompanying. Further commentary is superfluous: the listener surrenders to their spell.

When thirteen of the fifteen were published at Christmas, 1876, in Prague—the expense being borne in part by the wholesaler, Neff, to whom, with his wife, these songs were dedicated—their success was immediate and striking. For some unaccountable reason, two of the fifteen were omitted and thus only later became known. Of these, "*The Last Wish*" came out as the Fifth in the later-printed Op. 20, and "*The Soldier's Farewell*" was first published in 1913 as a supplement to the "Hudební Revue".

Dvořák, however, included these Duets the following year, when submitting his works for the Austrain State Prize he had already twice received. Thus they came to the attention of Brahms who, enchanted, immediately recommended them to his publisher, Simrock. This remarkable letter published in the Simrock Year-book for 1929, Vol. II, runs as follows:

"Vienna, Dec. 12th, 1877

"Dear Simrock:

"For several years past, in awarding the Austrian State Prize, I have been delighted with the pieces by Anton Dvořák (pronounced "Dvorshak") of Prague. This year he submits, among other things, a Cycle of Ten 'Duets for Two Sopranos with Pianoforte' that seem to me so perfectly charming they should be a practical publishing venture. He seems to have had this collection printed at his own expense. The text and titles are unfortunately both in Bohemian.

"I have urged him to send you these Lieder! When you play them through, you will be as delighted with them as I am, and as a publisher you will be particularly pleased with their piquant originality. But great care would have to be taken to provide a good translation. Some of the texts may already have been translated by Wenzig (recently deceased). Otherwise Dr. Siegfried Kapper in Prague might be secured. Dvořák has written all sorts of things: operas in Bohemian, symphonies, quartets and piano pieces. At all events, he is a very talented man. Besides, he is poor! I beg you to bear this in mind. These Duets will tell you everything, and they should be a good 'selling article'. His address is Prague II, Kornthorgasse No. 10.

"With best regards,

"Your J. Br."

In consequence of this letter, the Duets finally appeared in 1878 as "Airs from Moravia" ("Klänge aus Mähren"), one after another, in the not very happily-chosen German translations by Srb-Debrnov. The authoritative edition we have today was translated by J. V. Löwenbach. Dvořák received no payment. Two years later, following upon their great success foreseen by Brahms, all the Duets were united in one volume, in German and English. Simrock likewise became Dvořák's chief publisher; only in this way could Dvořák ever succeed in breaking through the provincial narrowness of Prague, where in those days there was very little publishing and that only for Bohemia.

Dvořák, who in 1877 had moved to Korngasse (or Kornthorgasse; Czechish, "Zitna ulice") No. 10, was at this time not so fortunate with the rest of his lyric creations. He composed his *"Evening Songs"* to texts by Hálek, and they were published in various editions with many different Opus numbers. They must have been close to his heart, for he returned to them again and again in varying arrangements. Composed between the Second and Third Cycles of the Moravian Duets, they did not have the same power to win through to popular favor.

About mid-June, 1876, he permitted himself four weeks' rest, a great rarity with him in those years. In August he began another work of bigger dimensions, the *Piano Concerto in G minor*, in four movements, finished in September. Dvořák wrote it for the pianist, Slavkovský, who played it for the first time on March 24th, 1878, in Prague, and to whom later on Dvořák dedicated several piano works. Op. 33: it was published by Hainauer, 1883.

Dvořák himself, although he was a good pianist, was by predisposition a violinist, as is noticeable from the fact that, in his chamber-music and symphonies the string parts are so well "fitted" to the violin-hand. He later wrote a Concerto for Violin and another for 'Cello, both of which show more regard for the soloist than the Piano Concerto; to compensate for their technical difficulties they afford the artist gratifying virtuoso effects. Not himself a virtuoso, Dvořák was not so successful in this Piano Concerto and hence it is comparatively little played. Maybe he would rather have written works for a 'cellist or violinist, but in those days he knew no-one who might have played them, whereas Slavkovský had begged his compatriot for a piano concerto.

Its structure is symphonic throughout and in each detail it reveals the style of a master maturing almost before our very eyes. In the First Movement, the somber mourning of the commencement of Stabat mater is again to the fore; the Second is melodically reminiscent of the Moravian Duets; in the Third, however, after long resistance, Dvořák's confidence in life returns victorious and with it his high humor that loves to play, not with the serious things of life, but with the abundant ideas of his own creative imagination.

The Piano Concerto is at any rate genuine, original Dvořák, particularly in its national intonation. At the same time its spiritual affinities with Brahms (in his D minor Concerto) are remarkable, the more so inasmuch as Dvořák at that time had never heard any Brahms. (The solo part of Dvořák's Piano Concerto in G minor has recently been arranged for the excellent young pianist, Rudolf Firkušný, who has played it in this version with great success.)

In the train of the Piano Concerto came shorter piano pieces. One of these is a *"Dumka"*, Op. 35, imbued with Slavic melancholy, interrupted in the middle by a presentiment of the "Slavonic Dances". A beautiful and valuable work is the *"Theme with Variations"* (eight of them), Op. 36. The theme, a sort of minuet, is characterized by its chromatic progressions, giving opportunity for rich and bold modulations, demanding a brilliant piano technique. The fourth, scherzo-like variation harks back to the Moravian Duets. The dream-like sixth variation is one of the most beautiful character-pieces of Dvořák. Here again he may lay claim to innate affinity with Brahms.

Finally, in 1887, Dvořák composed the "Scotch Dances" (deriving from Schubert) Op. 41, and Two *"Furiants"*, Op. 42, both for piano and dedicated to Slavkovský, who played them for the first time. These Furiants, however, do not yet employ the typical rhythmic ambiguity of the real Furiant, a folk-dance first introduced into the realm of art-music by Smetana in his earliest operas.

"The Peasant Rogue"

SPURRED ON BY Smetana's comic opera, "The Kiss", first performed in 1876, Dvořák had again, in 1877, turned to the theater. A highly gifted, but extremely eccentric young author, Josef Otakar Veselý, had given him a libretto that Dvořák, in his zeal, accepted without taking into account the fact that Mozart had already exhausted the possibilities of the story it told.

The only thing original about the book is the national coloring, with its praise of the patriarchal relations between landowners and their peasants. But even here, the cast of characters in the Bartered Bride is to a certain extent duplicated. Here again, we have the wealthy, stupid, Wenzel who, in *"The Peasant Rogue"* ("Šelma sedlák"), Op. 37 is the father's choice for his daughter, who, in turn, has set her mind on marrying another, the poor devil of a shepherd, Jeník. Wenzel's father comforts him with the promise that everything will turn out all right with his courtship because they are all from Domažlice, where only clever people live.

The maiden, Bětuška, tries to secure the necessary consent of the Count to marry the man of her choice. The Count, however, falls in love with Bětuška, promising she shall have her beloved, together with land and money, if she will first give herself to him. The Countess, learning of this, like her prototype, Figaro, attiring herself in Bětuška's clothes, goes to meet her husband, the Count, at the appointed rendezvous. Nothing of Figaro's trappings is lacking: the Count pining away for love, and the servant couple in the same predicament. There are pardons all around and Bětuška, of course, gets her Jeník.

To this text, Dvořák composed an effervescent music, almost as refined in accent as chamber-music but with a great deal of fresh invention, the whole paying its respects (as does Smetana) to Mozart. Dvořák's rhythmic originality is evident in the first bars of the Overture: two three-measure phrases, one four-measure phrase—and so on. However tragic the course of Bětuška's true love, nevertheless her entrance-motive is an appealing polka. There is a theme of peasant cunning and one of patriarchal devotion. There are gems in the arias and ensembles, but all the riches of opera are in vain if the text is inadequate.

Notwithstanding, at home in Bohemia the work was not unfavorably received. On January 27th, 1878, it was performed at the Interims Theatre. It attracted Jauner's attention in Vienna, but the German première was at Dresden, conducted by Schuch. Its success gained Dvořák all sorts of friends, as he wrote to Simrock, who published the score and a piano score arranged by Dr. Josef Zubatý. The Vienna Imperial Opera performance, on the Empress Elizabeth's name-day, November 19th, 1885, took place at a time of especially bitter strife between German-Austrians and Czechs. Demonstrating German-nationalist students had to be disciplined. The cast showed that there was not much enthusiasm about the production on the part of the management. There was only one more performance, and the critics wrote absolutely uncomprehending reviews.

Hugo Wolf, always a partisan and never too finicky about his choice of words, called the instrumentation "revolting, brutal, trite" and opined that it was enough misfortune to encounter Dvořák's music on the concert platform: "There may be people who are serious enough to find this opera comic, just as there are people comical enough to take Brahms' symphonies seriously."

How naturally effective was Dvořák's instrumentation at the time may be seen from the *"Symphonic Variations for Large Orchestra"*, composed in September, 1877. The theme is taken from his choral piece for men's voices, "Guslar" ("I am a Fiddler"). Its irregular periods and chromatic

course afford a wealth of possibility for variations, and Dvořák, with ever farther-soaring fantasy, passion and mastery, pursues them to the very end. He produces 28 variations and a coda in polka style. With this achievement, the macrocosmic world of music opens out to Dvořák, already perfectly at home in the microcosmic. And more—

the same experience is open to all who, with an understanding heart, listen to his works.

The first performance was in Prague, 1877. A decade later Dvořák sent this work to Hans Richter, whom he had gained as friend in 1879. Richter conducted it that year 1887, in London and wrote to Dvořák that he could not remember, in all his hundreds of concerts, having ever had such success with a novelty. Richter likewise conducted it at the Philharmonic Concert in Vienna, December 4th, 1887, on which occasion, it met with stormy applause. In token of his admiration for these Variations, Brahms gave Dvořák a cigar-holder. The Variations were published as Op. 78 in 1887 by Simrock.

The art of instrumentation acquired through the writing of these Symphonic Variations, stood Dvořák in good stead when composing the orchestra-part for his Stabat mater. In December, 1877, Dvořák also composed a *String Quartet in D minor*, Op. 34, published by Schlesinger and not by Simrock to whom Brahms had warmly recommended it.

Although there is much exuberant playing in this Quartet, it is overburdened with gloom. Its melancholy might be termed "Brahmsian" if it were not this time also "Dvořákian"! The national coloring leaves no doubt of this. The Scherzo idealizes the polka in the manner of Smetana's "Scenes from My Life", and the trio hints at the slow Sousedská. In the Slow Movement, a ray of illumination penetrates in D major (with muted strings!), but even this is extinguished in the restlessness of the Finale.

Dvořák and Brahms

THIS WORK was dedicated to Brahms, and from now on Brahms is the figure we shall encounter over and again in Dvořák's life. Here, at the outset of a new epoch in that life, we find two artists of the utmost disparity as to origins and experience, yet in some sense striving towards the same ends, who, with the assurance of predestination, meet each other. Their works speak for them to one another until they are finally drawn into close personal proximity. What Brahms means to us today hardly needs reiteration: what Brahms meant to Dvořák in those days was the great, outside world of music.

Ten years his senior, Brahms had been destined from his youth to be a musician: he was to achieve that which had been denied his father. When not yet twenty, he had entered upon the horizon of Robert Schumann who, in his famous essay, "New Trails", had proclaimed Brahms enthusiastically to the world. All the musicians of his time took note of him, and with many he enjoyed personal relationships.

Brahms' educational background was rich and continually being enriched. He had been about the world, lived in Vienna, was the object there, it is true, of much enmity and misunderstanding—he never could dispel the memories of those early failures, the Requiem and the First Symphony! Brahms was the name raised on the standard about which rallied many powerful forces in music, particularly those who held him to be the prime antagonist of Richard

Wagner. And that was no small matter. Even though the role was unsuited to him, he went through its paces or at least did not deny its implications.

A North German and a Protestant to his very core, yet with the German yearning for the lands of the South, Brahms enjoyed the established forms and the atmosphere of the Viennese classic composers as much as he enjoyed the gusto of Austrian life. In Vienna, it was easier to strive for that southern creative facility of, say, a Schubert. Brahms' own particular gift, however, was the severe logic in his work and in his construction.

In striking contrast to all this we have Dvořák, the simple being of the petit bourgeois, in almost rustic and certainly provincially narrow surroundings, wrapt up in the joys and sorrows of his family, never completely fulfilled except when composing. (The joys of family life were something that Brahms wished for and then again did not wish for: at any rate, he never experienced them). Dvořák derived from the inexhaustible musical resources of a people just awakening; and those forces, physical and spiritual, which Brahms had had to seek elsewhere, were everywhere about Dvořák, his close and staunch support.

There is not the slightest question that Brahms was above all impressed by Dvořák's wealth of invention. Brahms declared that another musician might well shape his themes out of those that Dvořák let fall by the wayside. As an absolute musician and companion pilgrim along the way of classic music, Brahms often found his own confirmation and justification in Dvořák. It was no mere trifle in those days to take one's stand in the face of such revolutionary convulsions as those that emanated from Wagner. Now then, here was a Dvořák to set over against a Bruckner! The adherents of the anti-Wagner party saw this very clearly, at least, they believed they did.

Was Dvořák, on the other hand, really immune to the Wagner contagion? We know how seriously the experience of Wagner had obsessed him; the danger it carried for him had only recently been exorcised; it could (and would) return. It was not without reason that Brahms was fearful of this and ever and again tried to entice Dvořák to Vienna; he wanted him to become a Conservatory instructor there. (For Bruckner was teaching counterpoint at the Vienna Conservatory. We have only to read Kalbeck's biography of Brahms to grasp the meaning of this.)

When Dvořák, much later, objected that he could manage to live with his family in Prague, but certainly not in expensive Vienna, Brahms repeatedly offered to place his fortune at Dvořák's disposal, reiterating this offer shortly before Dvořák went to America. Brahms was afraid that his friend might betray the artistic convictions they shared together if Dvořák was to be so far away from the canons of musical taste prevailing in Vienna. As it turned out, in America, Dvořák, after his own fashion, actually did undergo a transformation.

Brahms was a magnanimous friend. He not only recommended Dvořák to his own publisher, but he also corrected his proofs for him when it turned out that Dvořák had not yet learned how to do this. While Dvořák was in the United

States, Brahms alone did his proof-reading for him. Entirely without envy, he earned the lifelong devotion and reverence of that simple man, Dvořák. It goes without saying that Brahms exercised a beneficent influence by strengthening Dvořák's confidence in himself. Even such a soundly established character as Dvořák had need from time to time of confirmation from outside. Thus they both gave to each other, though at first it seemed as if, in an external sense, Brahms was the only giver.

Were they influenced by each other's works? In a certain sense, yes. As far as their individual creative powers were concerned, at the source, no. When reading his proofs, Brahms had written to Dvořák calling his attention to missing accidentals and at the same time stressing the necessity for clean copy in score-writing. This admonition had a good effect on Dvořák and the following generation of Czech musicians.

Soon Dvořák and Brahms were studying each other's works, and thus there came about involuntarily some slight similarities and "reminiscences". (By those who would attempt to "establish" the influence of Brahms on Dvořák's earlier works, however, it must be borne in mind that Brahms' compositions were unknown in Prague until the early Seventies.) Of course, they had in common some of the same models as for instance Beethoven and, in harmony, Schubert.

As to the syncopations and suspensions found in the works of both, it must be remembered that Brahms derived them from the Gypsies, Dvořák from Slavic folk-music.

The music world, however, came to know of Dvořák later than Brahms and therefore presupposed such "influences", whereas a knowledge of the true sequence of events shows this to be out of the question. Brahms never permitted such misconceptions. He saw in Dvořák his sole rival among the living, but above all he saw in him his friend.

The period of national seclusion for Dvořák had now come to an end. He began to hear of the success of his works in foreign lands. In 1876, he had given up his position as organist. In 1877, he leased a larger apartment in the same house (in the Korngasse), and this apartment he maintained for the rest of his life. Now, for the first time, he was able to work without interruption, strengthened and encouraged in the pursuit of his own creative vein by the knowledge that his works were being disseminated everywhere by a large foreign publishing house.

Dvořák at Twenty-Seven

CHAPTER II

BEYOND THE CONFINES OF BOHEMIA

Slavonic Rhapsodies and Slavonic Dances

THE MAN who had thus transcended the narrow circle of his immediate environment and penetrated into the outside world, was to go farther and farther afield. Dvořák's continually growing success, signalized by Simrock's acceptance of the Moravian Duets, had helped him to overcome the last effects of personal bereavement. He remained a man of great simplicity, almost middle-class in tastes and inclinations, but he carried a world of art within him. He was certainly not simple-minded nor lacking in ideas. On the contrary, he did everything in his power to control, restrict and discipline his teeming wealth of ideas. He constrained himself to preserve the constructive forces of form rather than to dissipate his energies in fresh experiments.

Of extreme sensibility, he went through all phases, from the keenest enjoyment of life and good humor to dreamlike melancholy, and then again to pathos or confident exaltation. This sensibility of his, saving him from self-satisfaction, kept alive his aspiration. Although on the whole he enjoyed an exceptionally happy life, many of his wishes never were fulfilled, as for instance that of a decisive operatic success abroad, or his modest desire to visit Italy, especially to see Rome.

His genuine, profound piety remained unchanged, likewise his love of Nature, his homeland and his people. As time went by, the national coloring in his work became more pronounced. He liked to use the word "Slavonic" in his titles, and was at pains to see that foreign publishers reproduced his works not only in their own tongue, but in his original Czechish. (And he retained the Czechish form of his name: "Antonin". But in English-speaking countries, the usage of the more familiar "Anton" became firmly established.)

Fate was kind in preserving him from any further losses in his family. His parents attained a hale old age, and he and Anna had six more children. Living modestly as he did, with the imposing amounts he was gradually receiving for his works he was able to take care of them all. In a short time, he could afford to disregard the hints and wishes of his publishers.

The new apartment in the Korngasse (his fifth and last in Prague) consisted of only two rooms and a kitchen, enough for his needs. The chief pieces of furniture in his work room were his piano and desk, above which hung a picture of Beethoven. He went for a walk each morning, preferably to the nearby Franz-Josef (Wilson) Railway Station, where the life of the yards fascinated him. With deep seriousness, he studied the locomotives and tried to make a note of their numbers and the names of their drivers.

Later on, when he was teaching at the Conservatory he

used to send his pupils to find out which locomotive was to take out the express-train on a particular day. One of his messengers was Suk, a favorite pupil, at that time engaged to Dvořák's daughter. But when Suk returned with the number—he had absolutely no understanding for railways!—Dvořák, the practiced connoisseur, at once branded it as incorrect. Suk was roundly scolded: it was not the number of the locomotive, but of the coal-tender. And Dvořák reproached his daughter: "So that's the kind of man you want to marry!"

He also loved to walk in the Karlsplatz Park because there the birds sang so beautifully; and he usually wound up in a near-by café where he attentively studied the newspapers.

The first work of this new period is the gay *"Serenade in D minor"*, Op. 44, for two oboes, two clarinets, two bassoons, one contra-bassoon, three horns, 'cello and double-bass. There is nothing more of melancholy to be found in this work; with the exception of one movement, full of love's tender emotions, it is in the jolliest good humor. It is a deliberate attempt to revive the old-time cassation style of band-music for the open-air.

The First Movement almost parodies the old-fashioned village-march. The Minuet takes on the guise of a Sousedská, its trio has the rhythmic character of the Furiant. There follows the romantic Slow Movement and a lively Finale which, like the String Serenade, cites in conclusion the opening theme. The whole work is rich in fine craftsmanship and beautiful tonal quality. Composed in the first weeks of January 1878, it was performed the same year, conducted by Dvořák, and published the next year by Simrock. The dedication expresses his thanks to the German critic, Louis Ehlert, who so enthusiastically advertised the Slavonic Dances.

In the latter half of January, rehearsals for "The Peasant Rogue" began, and again the wish bestirred Dvořák to write another opera. This time he was fortunate in finding a libretto by a real poet, Julius Zeyer, entitled "Šárka". For three years, Dvořák held on to this book with the intention of using it. Then in 1881, he received "Dimitrij" and decided to give up "Šárka", which the poet thereupon turned over to Leoš Janáček. (Janáček completed his opera, "Šárka", in 1887.)

"Three Slavonic Rhapsodies" for Orchestra Op. 45, composed in 1878, were indeed happily inspired. The First, in D major, builds up an idyllic theme to grandiose heights,

following an undisclosed program derived from heroic Czechish sagas. This idyllic theme is interwoven with another suggesting a joyous knightly tournament in a delightful rondo. The *Second Rhapsody in G minor* has the same knightly character with its lovers' idyll in the second theme. The *Third Rhapsody in A flat* tells of the hunt, of tourneys and the service of fair ladies. Its theme is first introduced in solemn tones by the harp alone, as in Smetana's "Vyšehrad". The same theme immediately reappears as a dance, taking on several forms and variations until the ceremonial tones of the beginning resound once more in conclusion.

The gorgeous and natural invention, the masterful and delicate treatment of this theme, demand a special place for this composition among Dvořák's works. From the very first it was a pièce de resistance. Its triumphs began in Prague, in 1878 (when only the First and Second Rhapsodies were heard). The third Rhapsody in A flat was given at a Berlin Symphony Concert by the Royal Opera Orchestra. Further performances in Germany and Budapest followed. In 1879, the Vienna Philharmonic under Hans Richter performed the Rhapsodies as that work which had found most favor among novelties submitted.

Dvořák enjoyed a personal triumph in Vienna: the audience called him out again and again, and Richter himself, carried away with enthusiasm, dragged him out onto the platform. As Dvořák wrote to a friend at home, Hanslick turned up with the score at the general rehearsal, declaring his intention of writing a lengthy article on Dvořák. There ensued any number of performances in Germany, England and the United States.

Another composition that year garnered almost the same success as the Moravian Duets and the Slavonic Rhapsodies. Simrock (on the suggestion of Brahms, it is said) indicated to Dvořák that he would be the very man to compose some "Slavonic Dances" in the style of Brahms' Hungarian

Dances. This was his cue; Dvořák had already employed the Polka, the Furiant and Sousedská in his works.

On March 18th, 1878, Dvořák composed the first Slavonic Dance, and then, in rapid succession, seven more (like Brahms' Hungarian Dances, arranged for four hands). There are two Furiants, Nos. 1 and 8, two Skočná (Jumping-Dance), Nos. 7 and 9, one Polka, No. 6, and two Sousedskás, Nos. 3 and 4; in addition, there is one Serbian Dance, No. 2. In these pieces, Dvořák idealized the folk-dance, but only in its rhythm. The melodies and harmonies are his original invention, whereas Brahms confined himself to actual Gypsy melodies. There is something utterly elemental about these Slavonic Dances, like a natural phenomenon, so that the listener is entirely unaware of the artistry and craftsmanship that have gone into them.

All the good qualities of Czechish folk-music seem here realized in the most intelligible manner, but it is the genius of Dvořák that leads them on to their ultimate triumph. Such a discovery as this of Dvořák's could only be made by a man who was singled out, to whom the call had come from the people. At the same time that he was writing the score for two pianos, he also undertook the arrangement for orchestra, with which he was no less successful.

In August 1878, the *"Slavonic Dances"* were published by Simrock as Op. 46, and Dvořák received 300 marks in payment. Simrock made a fortune out of them. According to Šourek, however, this was at that time a suitable price to be paid to a composer still comparatively unknown. A second series of Slavonic Dances, Op. 72, ordered in consequence of the tremendous success of the first, was reckoned at 3000 marks.

Upon the appearance of the first series, Louis Ehlert, the critic on the Berliner Nationalzeitung, sang the praises of the "heavenly naturalness" of this music, which he declared should be advertised precisely as if one had found a jewel in the street. The orchestral version was soon heard in concert-halls all over the world. Countless arrangements of the Slavonic Dances were made. In 1901, on Dvořák's 60th birthday, the Prague National Theater even staged the Slavonic Dances as ballets.

In the same year, 1878, Dvořák likewise composed the *"Bagatelles"* ("Malickosti"), Op. 47, for the intimate musical evenings at the home of his friend, Srb-Debrnov; these Bagatelles were set for two violins, a 'cello and harmonium. During the first weeks of May, he was composing dances and Bagatelles, one after the other. These five Bagatelles, arranged as a suite in Five Movements, are definitely chamber-music. Their masterly voice-leading led him on to write further chamber-music works. There is a remarkable identity of themes in the "Lullabye" (the second piece) and the Scherzo (the third). The Minuet and Polka are warmly imbued with national coloring.

It was inevitable that he should follow the delicate Bagatelles with the beautiful *String Sextet in A major*. Begun two days after completion of the Bagatelles, May 14th, 1878, the Sextet was finished in two weeks. Dvořák won and held many friends by the rich sonority of this particular work, in his lucky key of A major. Connoisseurs are enchanted by the transparent interweaving of the six voices as much as by the natural, spirited burgeoning of all phases in this glorious music. Its affinity with the Slavonic Dances and Bagatelles is emphasized by the Dumka as the Slow Movement and the Furiant in the Scherzo.

This Sextet, published by Simrock in 1879 as Op. 48, is Dvořák's first chamber-music work to be performed abroad before it was heard in Bohemia. Joachim played it in his Berlin home before invited guests, and thereafter performed it for the first time publicly with his Quartet in Berlin, Nov. 9th, 1878; soon after, they gave it its London première.

Dvořák was invited to Berlin for that first private performance in Joachim's home. The fact that Joachim himself was giving a soirée in his honor left him nonplussed; he could not believe that he, Dvořák, should all at once be the guest of honor among such famous people; to top everything, Joachim straightway demanded of Simrock that he let him have Dvořák's very next composition.

Dvořák's daughter, Ottilie, was born, June 6th, 1878.

The joyous feeling that his efforts as a composer were now about to bring their own reward impelled Dvořák about this time to turn his attention to that instrument he had hitherto neglected, although it was the one most natural to him,—the violin.

Curiously enough, of the "*Concert Piece for Violin with Piano or Orchestra*" ('Capriccio') only the solo-part for violin with piano accompaniment has been preserved—nor was the work published during his lifetime. An arrangement by Günther Raphael, published by Breitkopf, only ap-

98

peared in 1929. From the opening bar of this brilliant virtuoso piece, its affinity with the immediately preceding Slavonic Dances is apparent.

A concert of Dvořák's compositions having been planned,
he composed in August *"Three Modern Greek Songs"* with
texts by Nebeský, Op. 50. The first of this cycle relates in
dramatic accents the exploits of the rebel Kolias. The second
is an idyll far removed from thoughts of war: the shepherd,
Jannis, resists the blandishments of the Nereids. This is the
first time any elemental spirits appear in Dvořák's works.
The third song is an heroic dirge for the fallen city of Parga,
betrayed into the hands of the Turks. All three songs are in
the minor key. Without any deliberate striving for "modern Greek" effects, Dvořák does attempt by means of peculiar alterations to give them an exotic character. This
unique work was published by Hainauer in Breslau, 1883.

The concert actually took place November 17th, 1878
and, to the gratification of orchestra and public alike,
Dvořák made his bow as a conductor, acclaimed as a worthy
successor to Smetana. He conducted his First and Second
Slavonic Rhapsodies and his Serenade for Wind Instruments. Slavkovský played both the piano Furiants; and Lev,
the baritone from the National Theater, sang the Modern
Greek Songs. This concert was a triumph for the composer.

Five Chorals for Male Voices, of much the same charm
as his earlier songs in this genre but especially attractive for
the folk-music quality of their invention, were published in
1890 as Op. 27. (This opus number should really have been
given to the String Quartet in E, erroneously listed as Opus

80.) These Chorals were sung for the first time by the Vienna Slavic Choral Society. The manuscript bears the remark: "Composed December 12th, on the way from Prague to Vienna."

Dvořák made this journey to visit Brahms and present in person the score of the Quartet dedicated to him. He poured out his thanks to the elder master for his part in awarding the Austrian State Prize, which Dvořák had now received for the fifth time. The warmth of their meeting was heartfelt on both sides.

On his return journey, Dvořák enjoyed another warm reception at the hands of the twenty-four-year-old composer Janáček who, for two years past, had been conducting the Brunn Choral Society. While a pupil at the Prague Organ School he had met Dvořák and later said of him: "You know how it is when some one takes the very words out of your mouth? Well, Dvořák has taken the very melodies out of my heart!" This remark gives a deep insight into the character of Janáček, whose art appears to have had its origins from quite a different source than that of Dvořák. At all events, a great man and a great musician in his own right, Janáček gave impetus to a tremendous celebration in Brunn (Brno) in honor of Dvořák.

Kremsier and Olmütz, to Dvořák important centers in Moravia, received him with open arms. Kremsier boasted a choral society, "Moravan"; and in Olmütz the Roman Catholic Vicar, Heinrich Geisler (later Prelate), was President of the "Žerotín" Choral Society. Geisler and the Kozánek family in Kremsier soon became his very dear friends.

Dvořák, moreover, already had a warm place in his heart for Moravia, whose folk-music meant so much to him.

Dvořák's close friend was the Moravian, Alois Göbl, secretary on the estate of Prince Rohan in Sychrov near Turnau. Every winter Göbl accompanied the Prince to Prague, where Rohan frequently requested him to sing at his Palace. Possessor of a beautiful baritone, Göbl used to receive a first copy of each of Dvořák's published works. In return, he sent Dvořák all kinds of things that could be used about the house. He became godfather to several of Dvořák's children, and the youngest daughter was christened Aloisia after him. The greater part of Dvořák's extant correspondence consists of his letters to Göbl, to Judge Anton Rus in Písek, to Simrock and to Hans Richter.

Besieged with Orders

THE YEAR 1879 brought to Dvořák such great success with his published works that from that time on his material circumstances were bound steadily to improve. On his trip to Berlin in the late Autumn of 1878, he had sold Simrock the Serenade for Wind Instruments, the Slavonic Rhapsodies and the Bagatelles; and Bote & Bock had taken the Piano Variations Op. 36 and the Two Furiants for Piano. Most of these were published in February 1879, and two months later the first printings were exhausted.

The same publishers, and others too, demanded new works, but they wanted only shorter things, easily playable, easily saleable. Because he had none, Dvořák tried in vain to interest them in his earlier works: operas, symphonies, and chamber music. Nevertheless, on a second trip to Berlin, in March 1879, he did succeed in placing the Serbian Songs, the Königinhof Lieder, the Moravian Duets Op. 20 and 38, the Violin Romance, the Mazurek, the Sextet, a newly composed String Quartet in E flat, and the overture to The Peasant Rogue. Simrock secured an option on all his forthcoming short pieces, some of which Dvořák, in the intoxication of his success, had already promised to other publishers. In addition, he received all sorts of orders from choral societies, conductors, and chamber-music societies.

It speaks worlds for Dvořák that, although he was able to fulfil most of these demands upon him, he never lost his inner poise or the faculty of self-criticism, and he always kept his own goal in view. In all his works written to order, his wealth of inner resources enabled him invariably to produce something worthwhile and often to give of his very best. From July 1879, it took him a full year to catch up on all these orders.

Jean Becker, first violin of the famous Florentine Quartet, wanted a "Slavonic" work. Dvořák began the *Quartet in E flat major*, Op. 51 but due to interruptions, did not finish it until March 28th, 1879. Joachim played it for the first time, in his own home, together with the Sextet, on July 29th, 1879. Becker introduced it in November on his concert tournée and played it repeatedly, particularly in Switzerland. One of Dvořák's most brilliant works, especially in the spirited counterpoint of the First and Last Movements, it is rich in tonal coloring and full of ravishing melodies. It contains two slow movements, the first of which, "Dumka" (Elégie), has a fast, dance-like middle portion employing the same theme in the style of the Furiant; this middle section is heard again at the end of the Movement. The Third Movement, "Romance", is a tender, song-like melody. The gay Allegro finale assumes the character of the Skočna or jumping-dance. Becker had asked for something genuinely Slavonic and he certainly got it.

The Prague Choral Society, "Hlahol", under its new conductor, Knittl, also got the new choral work ordered for its Spring Concert in March 1879. "*The 149th Psalm*", arranged for mixed choir, was published by Simrock in 1888 as Op. 79. Here again the underlying trait is joy and clarity. Dvořák's models were obviously Händel and his own "Hymnus", which it recalls without attaining a like significance. This work is remarkable for its reminiscences of Gluck (Overture to "Iphighenia in Aulis") and of a theme in Meistersinger; it is also remarkable for the alternating voices against a background of sustained chords in the strings.

Simrock received the violin work for which he had asked. A "*Mazurek*", Op. 49, for violin and small orchestra, it was a kind of Slavonic Dance with two richly expressive contrasting themes. The solo part, dedicated to Sarasate, is violinistic but not easy. It was performed in Prague on March 29th, 1879, on the same occasion as the world première of Smetana's "Scenes From My Life".

In February 1879, Dvořák composed a *Festival March*

in celebration of the Silver Wedding of the Emperor and Empress of Austria. Written for a gala performance at .he Czechish National Theater, it was published as Op. 54. About the beginning of April, Dvořák was writing a *"Czechish Suite in D"* for small orchestra, Op. 39. This low opus number was the perpetration of a pious fraud on Simrock, who had obtained an option on all his future works, whereas, on the other hand, Dvořák had to satisfy Schlesinger, another publisher who clamored for his works.

Published in 1881 simply as "Suite", in five movements, three of which are dances in character, this is one of Dvořák's most exquisite compositions. The modest means employed are perfectly in keeping with the idyllic mood. Following upon a pastoral introduction, a Polka is heard, succeeded by a Sousedská in the guise of a minuet. Clarinets and bassoons make their entrance just as in village music in Bohemia. The flute and English horn recount by turns the Romance. Finally, there is a highly effective Furiant, elemental in its drive. The Czechish Suite was heard in Prague that May, and soon after in London, Vienna and other European capitals.

May and June granted a slight respite from his work. In the meantime, Dvořák's friend, Dr. Zubatý (the orientalist and later Professor at the University of Prague), undertook to arrange the various piano scores demanded by Dvořák's publishers. Incidentally, we have Dr. Zubatý to thank for the first biographical sketch of Dvořák, published in German by Hug Brothers in Leipzig, 1887. He also later wrote some valuable memoirs of Dvořák.

About this time, Dvořák wrote a *Polonaise for 'Cello and Piano in A*, followed by another *Polonaise with Orchestra in E flat*, the latter especially written for a ball. The former, whose theme is heard again in the C Major Quartet, was long unknown and remained unpublished until 1925 when, edited by Wilhelm Jeral, it was brought out by the Vienna Universal Edition. The latter Polonaise gained immediate popularity and has been much played.

In July, Dvořák went to stay with his friend Göbl on Prince Rohan's estate at Sychrov in order to work undisturbed on the *Violin Concerto in A minor*, Op. 53, which he was writing at Joachim's request. The score, finished in September, he sent to Joachim. The latter, however, in the years that followed, suggested several changes, both in the solo part and in the instrumentation, and Dvořák dutifully made them. Joachim, nevertheless, in the friendliest fashion, made still further objections. Finally, in 1883, Simrock bought this Violin Concerto in A minor for 1000 marks. The Czech virtuoso, Franz Ondřiček, played it that autumn in Prague and again in December with the Vienna Philharmonic Orchestra conducted by Hans Richter. On this occasion, Dvořák enjoyed another personal triumph.

Compared to the Piano Concerto, this Violin Concerto shows a great advance. The solo voice takes its place as usual in the symphonic structure, but the soloist has much freer sway; it is true, he must possess an exceptional technique, especially of the right hand. In three movements, the form of this work is in detail extremely individual, often rhapsodic, reminding one of a spirited improvisation. Thus, the recapitulation in the First Movement is restricted to a citation of the first subject whereupon the tempo suddenly relaxes and the transition to the Adagio is accomplished. (Simrock wanted Dvořák to indicate clearly the demarcation between the movements, but he would not do so.) In this Slow Movement, the lyric essence of the concerto is perfectly revealed, the national melos has its say. In the Finale, the jubilant syncopation of a Furiant is interrupted by the Dumka.

For the publishers, moreover, Dvořák was now writing five collections of short piano pieces. The first to be completed, composed in October and November, were twelve pieces entitled *"Silhouettes"* Op. 8. When they appeared under the imprint of Hofmeister in Leipzig, Simrock had to be content with the assurance that they were old ones. Actually, they were merely old themes from his youthful Symphonies in C and B and from the "Cypresses," now employed afresh. Hofmeister, much to Dvořák's satisfaction, commissioned Theodor Kirchner to write a four-hand piano arrangement.

In November, the Sextet and the new Quartet met with great success when played by the Hellmesberger Quartet in Vienna. Ehlert wrote from Wiesbaden, prophesying world-wide success for these two works. With tireless enthusiasm, Gustav Walter sang Dvořák's songs. Jean Becker, Joachim and Ondříček were playing Dvořák everywhere. And the Vienna performance of the Slavonic Rhapsody brought about Dvořák's personal acquaintance with Hans

Richter who, from that time forth, whenever possible, placed one of Dvořák's works on his programs.

Furthermore, about the turn of the decade (1879-80), Dvořák produced eight three-part *Piano Waltzes*, Op. 54. Here was displayed an astounding wealth of variety in mood, in the wholesome Musikant manner, far removed from the refinements of such a composer as Chopin. Two of these Waltzes, arranged by Dvořák for string quartet, have often been performed.

From January 18th to 23rd, 1880, Dvořák wrote *"Seven Gypsy Melodies"*, songs to words by Heyduk based on folk sources. In these songs, voice and piano are better related than in any of Dvořák's earlier works, the voice clearly taking the lead. These are Slovak Gypsies, Gypsies through and through in their ironical outlook on life, much the same as Lenau has depicted them. But adamant they are in one thing—their insistence upon Gypsy freedom. The exquisite *"Songs My Mother Taught Me,"* fourth of these songs, is especially beloved in America.

Immediately thereafter, from the end of January to the beginning of February 1880, Dvořák wrote the *"Four Eclogues for Piano."* Simple three-part idylls (all his piano works of this period are in three parts) they were not at once published; Dvořák used some of their themes for his later Mazurkas and one of them for his Ninth Slavonic Dance.

His next work, a *Violin Sonata*, completed on March 17th, 1880, and published as Op. 57 that same year, has a fresh second subject, somewhat in the national idiom, in the First Movement, and a gay Polka melody in the last of the three movements. The later "Sonatine For Violin", Op. 100, certainly has more to say to us. The price Simrock paid for these Sonatas, Piano Waltzes and the Gypsy Melodies, altogether 2,800 marks, gives us some idea of Dvořák's earnings at this period.

In May 1880, he planned a new series of "Scotch Dances", of which the sketches were first published in 1929 as *Albumleaves*. Only four of the *"Six morceaux pour piano"*, composed in June, were published without any collective title in 1881 by Hofmeister as Op. 52. These are perhaps the finest, most carefully executed piano pieces of that period, not a little influenced by the pianistic poetry of Schumann.

Finally, *"Six Mazurkas"*, Op. 56, published in the fall of 1880 by Bote and Bock, bring to a close Dvořák's series of piano pieces composed more or less to order. Now gaily animated, now drenched with melancholy, they are among the finest inspirations of Dvořák's temperament, unequivocally national in purport.

July and August were a welcome interim after such unremitting labors. Dvořák spent this short holiday in part on the estate of his brother-in-law, Count Kaunitz (married to Josefa, sister of Dvořák's wife), at Vysoká near Příbram and the rest of the time with Göbl in Sychrov. From here he went to Wiesbaden, where he was warmly welcomed as a guest at Ehlert's summer-place.

D Major Symphony—Legends

THIS BRIEF SUMMER-TRIP may be taken as a symbolic prelude to the ensuing decade of the Eighties, years of peregrination for Dvořák, who exchanged the narrowness of Prague for citizenship of the world. Nevertheless, the man who confronted this world was a unique being. In the midst of a people awakening to political reality, a people striving for the unattained and as yet unattainable, Dvořák in his own realm was striving to overcome romanticism and to achieve a new classicism. Along with this, he introduced the idiom of his native land, not as a curiosity but as a contribution of his essential being, at the very least a color that would be missed if left out of the palette of a future "world-music".

For more than a year now, he had been writing music "to order". It was high time that he return to himself and compose only that which urged him to utterance. For the first time in five years, he was to write a large symphony. (There was always the chance that now such a work might be marketable.) After conducting a concert in Zlonitz on September 26th, 1880, in order to raise money for a memorial to his teacher, Liehmann, Dvořák returned to Vysoká where, from the end of September to mid-October, he composed the *Symphony in D major*, Op. 60. Dedicated to Hans Richter and published in 1881 by Simrock, this was the second symphony of those which were printed in his lifetime.

This particular Symphony seems strikingly akin to

Brahms, in some way corresponding to the latter's Second Symphony composed in the same key. Nevertheless, Brahms' airy gaiety was not achieved with a light heart, whereas Dvořák's Symphony in its entirety is the outpouring of a joyous spirit intoxicated with the world.

The first bars are a fanfare in praise of the homely contentment pervading the fruitful, idyllically peaceful landscape of Bohemia. This serenity sings and day-dreams in the First Movement, sometimes rising almost to heroic heights, yet above all remaining perfectly happy within the charmed circle of its own thematically colorful retreat. In the Slow Movement, a theme of passion is heard in conflict with another that seems to breathe the peace of the summer night. The Scherzo is a genuine Furiant, as if derived from the Slavonic Dances, with a middle section broad and calm, pointing to the classics. In the trio, the brief motive in the piccolo is positively grotesque. The Movement closes in a passionate frenzy of the dance. The Finale, immediately recalling the first movement, returns to the mood of careless gaiety; the second subject in the clarinet seems the bearer of greetings from a Bohemian country-fair.

Craftsmanship, the gift of discovery, and invention, are united throughout this naturally spontaneous work. The style and sonority indicate a master who, drawing upon the sources of the soil, ascends to ever more blissful heights. At the same time he does without several instruments, such as the harp, for which he had a special fondness, and even renounces trombone and tuba in the Second and Third Movements.

Dvořák took the piano score to Vienna in November and played it through for Hans Richter who after each movement embraced him. Richter wanted to perform it that same December in Vienna, but his programs were already made up. Thus the world première took place in Prague the following March 1881, under the baton of Dvořák's tried-and-true friend, Adolf Čech; its instant success was so tempestuous that the Scherzo had to be repeated.

In March 1882, this Second Symphony was performed in London under the English conductor, Mann; and a few weeks later, on May 15th, Richter conducted it in one of his London concerts. Richter wrote to Dvořák of his own enthusiasm and that of the orchestra at rehearsals. There soon followed various performances in Germany, but it was not until 1883 that Gericke conducted the Second Symphony in Vienna before the Society of the Friends of Music. The same year, Theodore Thomas, a particular admirer of Dvořák, presented the work before a New York audience.

After the Second Symphony, there was a sort of interlude while Dvořák composed a cycle of short pieces for two pianos. But this time Dvořák was not merely being driven by publishers; he tackled this work with a special affection. These Ten "Legends", Op. 59, were composed in

Prague and Vysoká from February to March 1881. In three parts each, they begin in the idyllic mood, but with the Fourth rise into the atmosphere of myth and epic, attaining a climax in the Fifth and Sixth. In the Sixth, Dvořák cites a theme from the Adagio of his early Symphony in E flat major. The Seventh Legend effects a transition to the more idyllic Eighth and Ninth, returning in the cycle. The Tenth is an almost wistful epilogue.

It is a source of sheer delight to perceive with what great harmonic and contrapuntal ability and with what inventive artistry these brief Legends attain significance. Their success with the public was immediate, scarcely less great than that of the Slavonic Dances. Brahms wrote, full of enthusiasm, to Simrock; Hanslick, to whom they were dedicated, sang the praises of one after another of these Legends; Bülow declared they had "hit the mark"; and the publishers wanted them orchestrated as quickly as possible. Dvořák wrote the instrumentation in November and December of 1881, the piano version having already appeared that summer.

"Dimitrij"

In October and November, at the request of Simrock, Dvořák orchestrated five of Brahms' Hungarian Dances (Nos. 17-21). Though he appears to have achieved little in those fall and winter months (1881-82), otherwise his best time of year for working, this was chiefly because his mind was preoccupied with plans for a new opera. The Czechish National Theater was to be inaugurated in 1881 and, of course, every creative and interpretative artist felt himself bound to place his services at the disposition of such a great enterprise. Dvořák was moved by the same impulse and, moreover, the revival of his King and Charcoal-burner in January 1881 had reawakened his passion for opera.

He had not yet given up the idea of composing an opera to the text of "Šárka". But about this time, through the Theater Director, Maýr, he received a libretto by Marie Červinková, daughter of the elderly Czechish statesman, Rieger. This was once again the tale of the False Dimitry, seen on the stage so often and in so many guises. But the "*Dimitrij*" intended for Dvořák begins where the "Boris Goudunoff" of Pushkin and Moussorgsky leaves off. Marie Červinková knew Schiller's fragmentary story and she had also read a Czechish drama about "Demetrius". Her own version is written in emulation of this Czechish play, particularly the leading female role.

Dimitrij and his armies are outside the gate of Moscow. Boris has been murdered and only his daughter, Xenia, is left alive. The people doubt that Dimitrij is really Czar Ivan's son and rightful heir to the throne. Nevertheless, Marfa, widow of Boris, bears witness supporting Dimitrij's claims, with the object of securing his aid in revenge upon her enemies. Amidst the acclamation of the people, Dimitrij enters the Kremlin as Czar. (End of Act I.)

Dimitrij is married to Marina, daughter of that Polish nobleman from whose stronghold Dimitrij had set out against Russia. But the Poles and the Russians quarrel, and the Polish soldiery even threaten Xenia beside the grave of her father, Boris. Dimitrij rescues her and they fall in love at first sight without Xenia's knowing that her savior was her father's deadly enemy. Concealed behind the gravestone, Dimitrij overhears some conspirators plotting his death. He makes himself known and the plotters are dispersed by the people running to his aid. (End of Act II.)

The conspirator, Shuisky, has been condemned to death, but the Boyars and Xenia plead with Dimitrij for mercy. For her sake, Dimitrij pardons Shuisky, and in that instant Xenia, recognizing the Czar as her rescuer, faints. In her jealousy, Marina reveals to Dimitrij that he is not Ivan's heir, but the son of a peasant, Grischa Otrepjeff. But Dimitrij, feeling himself born to rule, declares that the betrayal is the crime of the Poles who thought to use him as their tool against Russia. Realizing that she is spurned, Marina swears revenge. (End of Act III.)

Dimitrij decides to divorce Marina and marry Xenia; but Xenia refuses to become his wife, and is thereafter assassinated at the behest of Marina. Marina, confessing her crime, reveals to the Boyars the secret of Dimitrij's birth. Marfa is once more called upon to swear that Dimitrij is Ivan's son. Dimitrij, however, prevents her, despising a people who are only concerned with royal birth and descent. He is about to abdicate when he is shot by Shuisky, and the people break forth in lamentation over the death of their wise and just ruler. (End of Act IV.)

Such a text demands a great opera in the style of Meyerbeer; it would have been just the thing for Verdi; it is the kind of story Moussorgsky might have handled in the same manner as his Boris, at that time unknown outside of Russia and certainly unknown to Dvořák.

Dvořák proceeds to treat this libretto in his own fashion as the truly great and natural musician he is, a composer of innate genius, unhampered by the limitations of form. Very few leitmotifs—one for Dimitrij, one for Xenia, one to symbolize the decree of Destiny—are interwoven in this music. Without going back to the old scheme of musical scenes complete in themselves, this is plain and simple operatic music, in tonal illustration of the situations, rich in melody, richly endowed, too, with ensemble and chorus. Apart from the conspirators' scene at the grave of Boris, and a few similar incidents, there is little in this music to recall operatic conventions of the past; but it has glowing arias and a convincing style of its own, as in the love-duet of Dimitrij and Xenia.

Dvořák's vision of a suffering and oppressed people (like Moussorgsky's) inspires him to compose, out of the depths of his Slav feeling for the brotherhood and unity of man, music of a soul-shaking intensity; and, like his Russian contemporary, he has the same sense of the solemnity and exaltation of the Czardom, its mission, responsibility and religious consecration as typified in the Kremlin, the patriarchate and the whole Byzantine-Greek-Orthodox tradition.

The essential differences between Moussorgsky and Dvořák are, however, immediately apparent: in Moussorgsky, practically everything is a matter of intuition and inspiration, cast in the mould of genius with most profound dramatic penetration; in Dvořák, it is a matter of brilliant ideas and invention, mastered and articulated by means of a disciplined sense of form, nevertheless without any loss of the dramatic.

In Dimitrij it is not difficult to perceive the deficiencies of the text and of the dramatic sequence of events. But they will not weigh in the balance with those able to enter into the spirit of that world of ideas out of which such a work was conceived. Here and there we observe Dvořák employing some of the means that Verdi had used (as in Aida); for suitable harmonies, Dvořák made a study of Russian ecclesiastical music; the Poles he characterized by their national Mazurka, in much the same manner as Moussorgsky.

Be that as it may, for the first time Dvořák really turned his knowledge and ability directly to the solution of dramatic problems. Since composing Dimitrij, he was no longer exclusively a writer of "absolute music" and a rather unhappy lover of the stage: he had now become a composer for the theater and his consuming passion was to remain one. Dimitrij is a turning-point not merely for him but for the entire evolution of Czechish opera.

Dvořák was well aware of this transformation in himself, yet the work in which he had placed such great hopes was condemned to a veritable "pathway of sorrows". The tale of these misfortunes begins with the actual labor of composition in the spring of 1881. On June 11th, the Czechish National Theater was provisionally opened with the production of Smetaná's "Libussa"; the official opening was to take place the following autumn. In August, this edifice, built at the cost of so much sacrifice on the part of the nation, burnt to the ground. It would have been impossible to produce Dimitrij in the small Interims Theater. By October, Dvořák had completed the composition in outline.

Then came all sorts of interruptions. Hellmesberger in Vienna wanted a string quartet; the Prague "Hlahol" Society wanted a new choral work; the Theater wanted incidental music for a play; Simrock demanded the instrumentation of the "Legends". Thus, inside of three months, Dvořák composed the String Quartet in C, the music to "Josef Kajetán Tyl" and the choral pieces for mixed voices, "In Nature's Realm".

At last he could return to the work on the opera. On August 16th, 1882, he finished the score. On October 8th, the première took place in the so-called "New Czechish Theater", the provisional home of the Czechish National Theater. Simrock and Hanslick were both present. Dimitrij met with great success, but Hanslick declared that the scene depicting the murder of Xenia was too crass and would have to be changed if the work were ever to be heard in the outside world. The text was therefore altered so that Xenia, before she can be hindered, swears upon the Cross of the Patriarch to take the veil, whereupon Marina and Xenia are reconciled. This is hardly a happier solution.

The music to this version was composed in two weeks in July 1883. Dvořák wrote on the score: "Revised up to this point at the request of Dr. Hanslick in Vienna." This revised Dimitrij was produced as the third gala performance in the new National Theater, Nov. 20th, 1883. Crown Prince Rudolf and Crown Princess Stefanie, both of whom were seriously interested in Dvořák, appeared on the occasion of the second performance. Despite the change thus made, however, and despite every effort to that end, Dimitrij was not produced in other countries. In Vienna, as may be deduced from a letter of Bülow's, it was allegedly not given on the grounds of nationalistic resentment against the Czechs.

In 1885, Dvořák inserted some brilliant music for the ballet, a "Polish Ball", at the beginning of the Second Act. In 1894, he undertook an especially thorough revision of the entire work. The Wagner-adherents demanded greater profundity. So Dvořák, by that time in America, under the influence of such a Wagner-disciple as Seidl, gave in, eliminating all repetitions and pointing up whole scenes into lengthy recitative. His opera had now become a music-drama. But as soon as he heard this latest version, he sorely missed the beauties of the earlier Dimitrij.

On May 1st, 1906, the second anniversary of Dvořák's death, Kovařovic, Opera Director at the Czechish National Theater, revived the 1883 version. And it was the new piano-score of this version, with Czechish text only, which was published in 1911 by the "Hudební Matice". No translation ever having been made, Dimitrij has remained unknown to the outside world.

In November, 1881, Dvořák had written to Göbl: "I see in the papers that on December 15th Hellmesberger is to perform my new quartet that does not yet exist. There is nothing left for me to do but compose it." Actually ready on time, this *String Quartet in C major* was published, with a dedication to Hellmesberger, as Op. 61.

Here we have a work of classic maturity. On the other hand, apart from the third theme of the opening movement, it is the least nationally colored of all Dvořák's chamber-music. Even the Scherzo manages this time without a national tone; and only the last movement returns to his habitual folk-vein. Beethoven is more than ever his model and in the Slow Movement, Schubert, too, is in his mind. Notwithstanding, Dvořák had long ago become his own model, and this time it is particularly evident.

After revising Four Lieder of the Cypress collection, published as Op. 2, Dvořák again returned to the theater. From December 1881 to January 1882, he was working on the incidental music to a drama by Šamberk, *"Josef Kajetán Tyl"*. This comprises nine pieces: an Overture, two inter-mezzos and some melodramatic music for each act.

Tyl was the first organizer of the Czechish Theater, and the play portrays the tragedy of his struggles to achieve something with very meager financial means, always in conflict with prejudice and missed opportunities. It contains some effective humorous scenes along with a great deal of sentimentality and bombast. The beautiful music of the Overture, the most important part, includes after the repeat an apotheosis of the song composed by Škroup, the text of which was by Tyl, "Kde domov můj" ("Where is my Native Land?"), that later became the Czechish National Hymn. Simrock published the Overture under the title of *"My Home"* as Op. 62.

Dvořák was moved to write impressionistic descriptions as vocal settings for some of Heyduk's poems, *"In Nature's Realm"*, *Five Chorals for Mixed Voices*, Op. 63. Whatever Dvořák composed that was singable was nearly always published at once. About isolated piano pieces there was not so much haste. In 1916, twelve years after his death, the publishers "regretted" that such a composition as the "Impromptu", an exquisite work composed about 1882, should not have appeared until then.

Clouded Skies—Defiance

A FEW DAYS after the première of Dimitrij, Dvořák wrote to Marie Červinková, author of the libretto: "It has turned out well, but I should like to talk to you about a new subject." One opera alone was not enough; he would have preferred to compose another immediately. Schuch of Dresden and Jauner of Vienna had both let it be known that they would like to produce an opera by Dvořák. This would have been the long-dreamt-of stage-success in the outside world. But they were quick to say that they did not wish anything Slavic and certainly no Czechish-national story. Yet Dvořák knew that only such a libretto could do him justice and, furthermore, he could not accept any dictates in this matter. On the other hand, he would have been only too glad to see an opera of his performed in some foreign theater. This meant much more than laurels on the concert-platform, no longer a novelty.

He would have been satisfied with a story something like Carmen, he also thought of doing a musical version of

"The Broken Jug" by Heinrich von Kleist; and he seriously considered whether or not he should try his hand at one of the two German texts sent to him by the General Manager of the Vienna Opera, Baron Hoffmann.

Here was a real dilemma for a simple artist. In addition, dark clouds of grief and melancholy descended upon him when his mother died on December 14th, 1882 in Kladno. All this, however, aroused in him fresh powers of resistance. In the ensuing months, he went through all the phases of doubt, defiance, silent grief, resignation; and they are indicated in the Piano Trio in F minor, the Scherzo capriccioso, the Hussite Overture and the Symphony in D minor.

Composed in February and March 1883, and published the same year by Simrock as Op. 65, the *Piano Trio in F minor* is a work of wide-embracing spirit; it almost bursts the bounds and transcends the content of chamber-music, passionately striving to merge into the symphonic. In keeping with its blustering defiance, the very first theme of the opening movement is virtually a reiterated outcry of "Why?" answered by the march-like: "Go ahead at all costs!" A bridge-passage of the exposition cites the song, "The Cuckoo", from the Königinhof Manuscript (Op. 7, No. 3). The development and the repeat luxuriate in affirmations of the mood. In the Scherzo (Second Movement), the mood of defiance becomes capricious and the

Allegretto grazioso

theme, with its peculiar accentuation, assimilates still another national overtone; piano and strings seem breathlessly
to snatch it from one another. In the trio, a quiet reverie
holds sway. The Slow Movement restores calm but not
peace, for the modulations appear to jar against one another.
In the Finale, a theme related to the First Movement introduces the very spirit of revolt. Defiance may also be seen in
the length of the development. At the very end, however,
the contrasting theme, with a turn to the major, brings back
at least a mild and peaceful, smiling mood.

Almost immediately, a very few days later, Dvořák gave
full vent to his fine frenzy in an orchestral work, the
Scherzo Capriccioso, Op. 66 (Bote and Bock), finished in
April, 1883. Here rage is transmuted into the fantastic.
Several motives testify to its relation to the Trio in F-minor.
Ghostly lights and shadows are hinted in the very instru-
mentation: the atmosphere is achieved by using the harp,
English horn, bass-clarinet, piccolo, tuba and percussion
instruments.

The work is in the traditional form: Scherzo and Trio
with two themes each, return of the Scherzo. Notwithstanding, thematic, modulatory and contrapuntal details are
especially rich and new. The whirling motion is incessant,
no calm here. On the contrary, after a cadenza in the harp,
a very quick stretto images the last breathless career of the
hunt. It is an uncommonly effective piece, not easy to perform, but effective in every concert-hall. After the performance, in 1883, conducted by Adolf Čech, at the Prague
New Czechish Theater, Dvořák himself conducted it the

following year in London at the Crystal Palace. Richter and Nikisch liked to place it on their programs.

Things were now so far advanced that, after further great sacrifices, the Czechish National Theater could be opened. For the forthcoming festivities, at the request of Director Šubert, Dvořák wrote his *Hussite Overture* ("Husitska"), intended as prelude to a Hussite dramatic trilogy that never got farther than the first act. Composed from August 9th to September 9th, 1883, in Vysoká, it was published by Simrock in 1884 as Op. 67. In his conflict with the world-citizenship in music expected of him, Dvořák thus decided once and for all in favor of his own national character. His own suffering is metamorphosed into heroic defiance by the spirit of that people to whom the Hussite idea held forth the promise of liberation. Musically, he describes the growth of this national movement, its struggles towards freedom and its trending towards peace.

The introduction of this Overture in the classic form culminates in a triumphal theme: the pride of those openly declaring their faith in a great religious idea. The first few bars of the old Hussite choral appear together with a motive from the ancient Czechish Catholic Song of St. Wenceslas, showing that Dvořák considers that his subject transcends the denominational. In the Allegro, the legend becomes the battlecry, and two new themes sustain the mood. In the development, the Hussite choral ominously roars. Finally, the true victor is revealed: peace, as symbolized by the National Hymn from the introduction. Admirable is the grasp that encompasses all this with every energy of melody and rhythm; no less admirable are the orchestral colors.

As planned, this work was first performed, on Sunday, November 18th, 1883, at the gala opening of the new Czechish National Theater, following Smetana's Overture to Libussa and an address by the poet, Vrchlický. In 1884, Dvořák conducted it in London and Berlin; in 1892, Richter conducted it in Vienna.

It was precisely this Hussite Overture that convinced Bülow of Dvořák's art, which he had at first opposed. Bülow, conducting in Prague in 1884, turned over the baton to Dvořák to lead his own "Overture to Tyl". Moreover, as was his habit, he welcomed Dvořák in a few words of Czechish especially conned for the occasion.

When in 1886 he was again to conduct in Prague, Bülow was violently attacked by German-Nationalist papers on the grounds that he was conniving at the suppression of the Prague Germans! His inclusion of the Hussite Overture on his program was especially held against him because it contained "inflammatory Bohemian songs". Bülow's answer was, first and foremost, to place the Hussite Overture on his program in Hamburg and then to accept another concert engagement in Prague. He used it more and more in his concerts, and soon became interested in other works by Dvořák. Finally, he wrote to the concert manager, Hermann Wolff, that he considered Dvořák to be, next to Brahms, the most important composer of his time. Dvořák, on his part, dedicated his F major Symphony to Bülow.

It was high time to do something more for his publisher, who incessantly begged him for easy piano duets, but

Dvořák did not feel much like composing any just then. On a visit to Mme. Červinková in Maltsch (Maleč) in southern Bohemia, he complained that Schumann had used up all the good titles for piano pieces! When she replied that the music was what mattered, he angrily declared: "I've got the music—but I have no titles!"

Out of the sum of his impressions gathered that summer of 1883 on several trips to the Bohemian Forest, in the company of Janáček, he finally hit upon the requisite title with the help of Mme. Červinková. In the last few months of 1883 and the first days of January 1884, he composed six "character-pieces" for four hands, entitled *"From the Bohemian Forest"*, dedicated to his patrons, Crown Prince Rudolf and Crown Princess Stefanie. The titles of these pieces are something new for Dvořák: the path of his trend to program music may be traced from them to the Symphonic Poems. But with him the program was invariably based upon his own inner musical experiences.

These pieces "From the Bohemian Forest" resemble the Legends in that they have as a rule the same three-part structure, the same beautiful piano sonority, the same never-failing freshness of invention. "In the Spinning-room" is a simple, graceful song to "spinning-wheel" accompaniment. "On the Black Lake" is perhaps the most profound in mood of the lot. "Witches' Sabbath" is a wild dance that, starting with many, finally dwindles away into one lone, evanescent phantom. "At the Stand" is a hunting piece. "Forest Peace" is one of Dvořák's most beautiful melodies, later arranged by him for the 'cellist, Wihan, with piano accompaniment, and very often played. The last piece, "In Troublous Times", with its march-melody, recalls the uprising of the free border-peasants against the landed gentry who wanted to make them pay tribute. In the middle section, Dvořák cites a bit from the Scherzo of the D minor Symphony of 1874. Here again, and throughout this work, there is that defiance typical of the composer at this period. "The Bohemian Forest" is really the landscape of that country described by the Austrian poet, Stifter, but seen with Czechish eyes.

About the beginning of October 1883, Dvořák went to Vienna to visit Brahms. Brahms, in unusually high spirits, heartily welcomed him and played over his new F-major Symphony. Dvořák much admired this new work and, somewhat later, wrote enthusiastically about it to Simrock. On December 2nd, Ondříček played Dvořák's Violin Concerto in Vienna, on the same program with Brahms' new Symphony, in a Philharmonic Concert conducted by Hans Richter. Afterwards there was a banquet at Faber's to which, besides Brahms, Dvořák and Richter, were invited Billroth, Brüll, Goldmark, Hanslick, Hellmesberger and Simrock.

England

AT THE OUTSET OF 1884, he received bad news: Ehlert, in Wiesbaden, who had done so much to make Dvořák known in Germany, died on January 4th. This was the loss of a true friend although Dvořák certainly no longer needed to be heralded abroad as he was known and esteemed in many lands. That same year, he was to win a place in the hearts of English music-lovers.

At one time fatuously called "the land without music", this England was and is a music-loving country. Apart from any of its own creative and artistic achievements, if it had done nothing more than offer a genuine hospitality to Händel, Weber, Mendelssohn and many a great interpretative artist—and, in Dvořák's day, to Hans Richter—it would have had every right to claim a proud position in the annals of music. And we must not forget what England, thanks to her comparatively great prosperity, was able to offer such an outstanding genius as Beethoven. England is the land of great choirs, of mighty oratorio performances, of tremendous music festivals and excellent orchestral concerts.

Close upon the heels of his great successes in Germany, Dvořák's works found their way to England. First of all, the Slavonic Dances were heard there in 1879. Almost at the same time the String Sextet was performed, and only a little later the Third Slavonic Rhapsody and the D major Symphony, both conducted by Richter. Oskar Berlinger had played the Piano Concerto. But Dvořák's greatest success was that of "Stabat mater" in London, on march 10th, 1883, conducted by Barnby. Now, however, people demanded Dvořák's personal appearance, and it was hoped to win him over to participate somehow in English musical life. The Philharmonic Society invited him to conduct a concert in London, and the Albert Hall Choral Society engaged him to conduct a performance of Stabat mater.

Accompanied by his friend, Heinrich von Kàan, piano

instructor in the family of Prince Fürstenberg, Dvořák left Prague on March 5th, 1884, and, after making stops in Cologne and Brussels, arrived in London on March 8th. He was met at the station by the proprietor of Novello's Music Publishing House, Mr. Littleton, with his son, and the pianist, Berlinger, whose guest Dvořák was to be. He was to conduct three concerts; the first of these included Stabat mater, and of this event he wrote home as follows:

"On Monday, March 10th, the first rehearsal was held in Albert Hall, which can easily hold 12,000 persons. As I came up to the conductor's stand, I was greeted with long, sustained applause. When I finally should have said something, I was so deeply moved I could not speak a word. Everything was excellently prepared. On the second day, I rehearsed with the orchestra in the morning and with the soloists in the afternoon. . . . Don't be frightened when I tell you there are more than 800 voices in the choir and 24 first violins in the orchestra. The effect of such numbers is really overwhelming.

"Tuesday, Littleton gave a big dinner in my honor. There were 150 persons present, among them the leading artists and critics. Everyone welcomed me most heartily. Only my compositions were played: three choruses from Stabat mater, four Gypsy Melodies, an aria from 'The Obstinate Children', the Piano Trio in G minor, two Lieder, and the Moravian Duets (!). We were up together until 2:30 in the morning. Littleton is charming and his house is furnished in princely fashion. . . ."

The performance took place on March 13th. "As soon as I appeared, I received a tempestuous welcome from the audience of 12,000. These ovations increasing, I had to bow my thanks again and again, the orchestra and choir applauding with no less fervor. I am convinced that England offers me a new and certainly happier future, and one which I hope may benefit our entire Czechish art. The English are a fine people, enthusiastic about music, and it is well known that they remain loyal to those whose art they have enjoyed. God grant that it may be so with me!"

Dvořák's success was sensational: at one stroke he was the hero of the hour. The papers wrote enthusiastically about his work and his conducting. They praised the unostentatious, simple and yet assured manner of his cues to the players; they acclaimed the deliberation of his conducting which shed a new and significant light on the full content of his work. Another soirée made Dvořák personally acquainted with the leading critics.

The remaining concerts took place on March 20th in St. James Hall and on March 22nd at the Crystal Palace. The program on the first evening comprised the Hussite Overture, the Symphony in D, the Second Slavonic Rhapsody and, accompanied by Dvořák at the piano, several Gypsy Songs. At the Crystal Palace, he conducted the Scherzo capriccioso and the Nocturne for Strings, Op. 40. Each concert was a brilliant success. There was another reception at Littleton's and a banquet given by the Philharmonic Society at which Dvořák, acknowledging the enthusiastic toast in his honor, made his first speech in English. A few days later, he said good-bye to his hosts and, on March 29th was back again in Prague.

He came home in the best of spirits. Material success coincided with the honors he had received. Just before his trip to England, Simrock had paid a very good price for the Hussite Overture and the piano-pieces, "From the Bohemian Forest". And Novello had offered him 2000 Pounds for a new oratorio—20,000 Gulden, for him an absolutely fantastic sum!

Now at last he could realize an old dream and buy a piece of land in Vysoká. This residence, ideal for him, was beautifully situated among hills and forests, about one-and-a-half hours' walk from the mining-town of Příbram. The foothills of the Bohemian Forest may be seen to the south on clear days. Partially inhabited by Příbram mining-folk, it is a typical old-world village.

Dvořák acquired a one-story building, formerly a granary, and had it done over and furnished as a summer place. His sleeping-quarters were in the largest room on the ground floor. By day, this was also the dining-room. On the first floor was his work-room, equipped with a small piano, a desk and, a further requisite to composing, a window commanding the lovely countryside. Dvořák was perfectly happy in the midst of Nature. He laid out the garden and began to breed pigeons. Pigeons were a favorite topic with him, and whoever liked to talk about them found in him a patient listener. If a host unwittingly served pigeons at dinner, he would leave the table.

From 1885 on, this simple country-house in Vysoká became his second home and a haven of refuge. As soon as spring came, he moved to Vysoká and did not return to Prague until winter began. It was not only Nature that enticed him; he was fond of the people in Vysoká and became much attached to them. In the evenings he would sit among the folk at the local inn, listening to their conversation, and now and then interjecting some remark.

Particularly when he came home from America, he had to tell them all about it time and again. The villagers, very loyal to Dvořák, always used to serenade him on the eve of his name-day. Each time he returned from America, there was a gala parade and a great celebration in the village inn. And, of course, Dvořák was always a welcome guest at the near-by Castle of his brother-in-law, Count Kaunitz.

The Spectre's Bride—D Minor Symphony

Upon his return from London, Dvořák wrote to Simrock from Vysoká that he was listening to the birds and not even thinking of composing. Yet, somehow or other, he must have felt the urge to get back to work. He wanted to write a Czechish oratorio, and he had promised a new work for the Birmingham Music Festival of 1885. Novello was keenly interested in acquiring a big choral work, no matter what kind, but of course Dvořák did not wish Simrock to know this. A newspaper report that J. V. Widmann of Vienna wanted to send him a new libretto, based on Shakespeare's *Twelfth Night*, was not substantiated.

Since he could not find the text he needed for an oratorio of a national character, he began working on a choral ballad. *"The Spectre's Bride"* ("Svatební košile"), based on a ballad by the Czechish poet, K. J. Erben, whose work had companioned and stimulated Dvořák's creative activity throughout his career. Begun in June, the sketches were finished about mid-July; the score was completed by the end of November, 1884. Novello published the piano score, arranged by Kàan, with the German text, as Op. 69.

The similarity of The Spectre's Bride to analogous folktales in other lands may be seen at a glance. In German, there is a similar poem in "Des Knaben Wunderhorn" (The Boy's Magic Horn); its kinship with Bürger's "Leonore" is evident. But the Czechish version has its own features, especially appealing to Dvořák. For instance, it is thanks to her piety that this Spectre's Bride suffers no dishonor from her terrible adventure with the phantom bridegroom.

A pious maiden has spun and hemmed the marriage-blouses (according to Czechish peasant custom), and has waited three long years for word of her beloved. At the witching-hour, she prays fervently that he may return. He comes— she must leave at once with him. In the midst of their wild career on horseback, he snatches away her prayer-book, rosary and cross. Finally, they arrive at his abode—in the cemetery. For this was an evil spirit sent to drag virtuous and trusting maidens to their doom! The maiden calls upon all the saints and angels and is saved—as the phantom vanishes.

An exceptionally vivid theme, oft reiterated, is allotted to the uncanny 'bridegroom' in his mad career. The chorus, now and then interrupted by the solo-baritone, tells the story. The maiden (soprano) and the bridegroom (tenor) have their solos. The tale is in three parts. Dvořák has hit upon the exact tone of the ballad: the grotesque terror of the Czech folk-tale haunts the entire work. At the same time, his great spiritual fervor is not to be denied and, even in the apparition of The Spectre's Bride, remains victorious. This choral ballad came to be of great importance to Dvořák; it opens out a perspective on a great many things in his later works. Taken as a whole, The Spectre's Bride calls forth our admiration for the resonance of its choruses and the powerful appeal of its execution.

This uncommonly gratifying work was performed about the beginning of 1885 in Pilsen, and in Olmütz by the "Žerotín" Choir. The same year, Dvořák conducted it in England with a chorus of 400 voices and an orchestra of 150. Even at the general rehearsal its success was extraordinary. The Spectre's Bride was scheduled to be heard again the following season, and there was no less enthusiasm in London when Mackenzie conducted it in 1886. It was performed in Milwaukee in 1885. In 1907, Richard Wickenhauser revised and improved the German text.

In 1884, while still working on the score of The Spectre's Bride, Dvořák made his second trip to England, which had showed itself so hospitable to him that spring. On August 13th, accompanied by V. J. Novotný, he left Prague to attend the Worcester Cathedral Jubilee celebrations. Arrived at Dover, Dvořák was met by Littleton, with whom he was this time to stay.

In London, between rehearsals of Stabat mater and the

D major Symphony for the forthcoming festivities, Dvořák composed a "Dumka and Furiant" (Op. 12) and a "Humoresque", both for piano. While in London, he met the American composer of sacred music, Dudley Buck, who urged him to undertake the journey to America. Dvořák, until recently accustomed to the narrow confines of Prague, did not exactly say no. But it was not until eight years later that he was to cross the Atlantic.

After a week in London, Dvořák went to Worcester where, for five days, the Music Festival held the entire surrounding country spellbound. At noon on September 11th, he conducted his Stabat mater in the Cathedral, and, in the evening, his Symphony in D major. Again the enthusiasm was tremendous. From Worcester, Dvořák immediately returned to Prague, where he conducted his new Symphony. Shortly after, on November 21st, 1884, in Berlin, where the Symphony was again performed under his baton, he made his conductor's debut in Germany.

The exalted mood engendered by his success in England now stimulated him to compose two new big works: a symphony and, he hoped, the oratorio on a national subject, "St. Ludmila". This work, commissioned by Novello for the princely sum we have stated, was to be performed at the Leeds Music Festival.

Meanwhile, on June 13th, 1884, the London Philharmonic Society had elected him an Honorary Member, at the same time requesting a new symphony. This decided him to undertake that composition he had secretly planned ever since he had heard Brahm's Third Symphony. Composed from mid-December, 1884, to mid-March, 1885, *The Symphony in D Minor*, Op. 70, undedicated, was published by Simrock, 1885.

For once Dvořák was aiming at the stars. He intended this symphony to be a large-scale, representative work, in marked relation to his own classic ideals, as he wrote to Simrock and especially to his friend, Judge Rus in Pisek. (Rus was a man of great musical talent who had only lacked financial means for its development. From the depths of his heart devoted to Dvořák, he received and cherished many letters from him.)

In deference to such universally human and at the same time highly personal ideas, Dvořák practically renounced the national idiom, which is only to be found in the last movement where it gives just the right note of color. Symphonically, this work is once again a thrashing-out of all those problems, magnified to titanic dimensions, which beset his soul.

The reminiscences of Beethoven's Ninth Symphony are neither fortuitous nor disturbing. Only a believing spirit such as Dvořák's does not despair but holds tenaciously to the conviction of an auspicious ending as it is here forecast. Musically and technically, everything is on the biggest scale, the greatest diversity combined with overwhelming logic; Dvořák, the composer, has mastered his own idiom and the entire materials of his art.

Violas and 'cellos indicate the gloomy first subject of the First Movement, expressing restlessness, passion and pain. An intermediate passage plainly hints at the Allegro-theme of the Hussite Overture, composed not long since (1883) and in the same spirit of defiance. This is followed by a gentle, pacifying song-theme from the flute and clarinet, in character reminiscent of Brahms. In the brief development, eloquent pauses, such as Beethoven loves, are contrasted with powerful outbursts. The repeat suggests an ideal picture: that symphonic conformation to which Beethoven succumbs in his fateful D minor; this is abruptly terminated, leaving a great deal to be said by the mighty coda. An ascetic mood, indicated even by the instrumentation, pervades the whole of this Movement. Horns and trombones relinquish their independence and become, as in the earlier days of the orchestra, merely voices to complete the harmony. (This is the only piece of work by Dvořák in which some conductors have from time to time retouched the instrumentation. It is the only one in which they could find anything to retouch.)

In the Second Movement, Poco adagio, there is an introductory episode that appears again at its close. The first subject begins as a touching plea for peace, soon transformed into a passionate confession of faith. There follow intimations of this peace; the mood becomes gentler, rich modulations seek their culmination only to relapse ever and again under the spell of somber grey.

The Scherzo, once more in D minor, is characterized by a theme that surges forward, yet as if "dragging its chains along" (Kretzschmar-Botstiber). No matter how often this Movement attempts to relax into gaiety, the joy of the

dance cannot lift its head. Only the G major trio is an
awakening in Nature, as if after a bad dream. Nevertheless,
the Scherzo obstinately returns, but variated in the instrumentation.

The first subject of the Finale, more D minor than ever,
immediately links up with the motive of Hussite defiance
already cited in

the First Movement. The national coloring intensifies just
as the song-theme in A major brings light into this long-
drawn-out gloom. From here on, the upward flight is decisive, a syncopated horn-rhythm prepares the way for the
struggles of the development; a tremendous climax, but with
no cheap fireworks, is attained. The work closes with a ma-
jestic declaration of spiritual dignity.

Simrock immediately wanted to acquire this Symphony,
but complained that Dvořák's other big works did not sell.
He offered 3000 marks, at the same time demanding a new
series of Slavonic Dances. But Dvořák was no longer the
obscure, hard-pinched Musikant of former days. His letter

to Simrock reveals a consciousness of his own worth and at the same time a feeling of his own responsibilities:

"(1) If I let you have the Symphony for 3,000 marks, I shall have lost about 3,000 marks because other firms offer me double that amount. I should very much regret it if you were, so to speak, to force me into this position;

"(2) Although such big works do not at once achieve the material success we could wish, nevertheless the time may come that will make up for it; and

"(3) Please remember that in my Slavonic Dances you have found a mine not lightly to be underestimated;

"(4) If we look at this from a common sense point of view, reconsidering all you have indicated in your last letter, it leads to the plain conclusion: that I should write no symphonies, no big vocal works and no instrumental music; only now and then perhaps a couple of 'Lieder', 'Piano Pieces' and 'Dances' and I don't know what sort of 'publishable' things. Well, as an artist who wants to amount to something, I simply cannot do it! Indeed, my dear Friend, this is how I see it from my standpoint as an artist. . . . Please remember that I am a poor artist and father of family. . . ." (Simrock Year-book, Vol. II, p. 109.)

Simrock came round to his point of view, inviting Dvořák to visit him in Karlsbad. Dvořák received 6,000 marks, but had to promise to deliver further Slavonic Dances the following year "if he felt like so doing". On his part, Dvořák demanded that the titles of his works should be printed in Czechish as well as German. His first name should be given as "Ant.", which could mean either "Anton" or "Antonín". Simrock thought this was petty, but Dvořák replied to him from England, attempting to explain national conditions in Bohemia at that time. In a later letter, Sept. 1885, he expressed regrets that Simrock obviously only had one-sided information on these matters. He continued:

"After all, what have we either of us to do with politics? Let's be happy that we can consecrate our services to the fine arts alone! And let us hope the nations that possess and represent the arts may never go under, no matter how small they are. Forgive me for this digression: I was only trying to explain that an artist also has a homeland in which he must have firm faith and to which his heart must always warm." (Simrock Year-book, Vol. II, p. 111.)

(In spite of this exchange of letters, the Symphony in D minor was again published with only the German title, and his name again printed as "Anton".)

On April 16th, 1885, Dvořák made his third trip to England, this time accompanied by Professor Zubatý, who had helped him arrange the Symphony in D minor for piano four hands. Again Dvořák stayed with Littleton. The three concerts he was to conduct were so scheduled that he had to spend a whole month in England. According to Zubatý, the tenor of Dvořák's daily life was simple enough. In the mornings, he went to town where he saw what there was to be seen: the Abbey, the Galleries, the Zoo, etc. Then he would lunch with Littleton and his son at the Criterion. Afterwards, he would resume his strolls, returning to

Sydenham in the late afternoon. In the evening, he dined with Littleton and his guests.

At the General Rehearsal of the new Symphony, he had besieged and won all hearts, both public and critics. The performance by the Philharmonic Society on April 22nd in St. James Hall was a triumphant success. The success was as frenzied and the criticisms were as enthusiastic as they had been for Stabat mater. Dvořák's D minor Symphony was compared with Schubert's C major Symphony and extolled above Brahms for its immediacy of appeal.

In January 1887, Richter conducted it in Vienna, where it was not received with as much warmth as might have been expected. Richter himself wrote that it was his favorite work of Dvořák's thus far, but he felt that only a Wagnerian schooled in the theater could conduct this Symphony so as to bring out all there was in it. The taste of the Vienna Philharmonic public was sometimes unaccountable. . . .

Bülow's conducting of the Symphony in Berlin, 1889, was a victorious assault and capture; Dvořák could not take enough bows to satisfy the audience. Bülow wrote to his wife, describing Dvořák as "a genius who looks like a tinker". Dvořák had let his hair and beard grow a bit longer, and that was enough for Bülow to call him "Caliban". One month later, Bülow performed the Symphony in Hamburg. Nikisch brought the D minor Symphony to America where, in Boston alone, he conducted it three times in 1891.

At the London concerts on May 6th and 13th, Dvořák's Piano Concerto and his Hymnus, which Novello had just published, were performed. On May 14th, he returned to Prague. Probably the strongest impression, outside of music, he retained from this visit was that of seeing Parliament in session. Among Dvořák's posthumous works were found two songs written during this London stay. Both are delightful, especially the first, a *"Lullabye"*, the exact motive of which returns at a significant moment in his later "Jacobin".

At home, he found a great deal to be done, everything was ready except the text of "Ludmila", about which he had been negotiating with Vrchlický for the past year. He made some revisions of his earlier works, wrote a new Overture to the Second Act of Dimitrij and composed a *Ballade for Violin and Piano*, Op. 15, published by Urbánek, Prague, 1885. The passionate allegro middle-section of this Ballade demands attention; and the pain expressed by the whole composition gives rise to the supposition that in this work he was employing a sketch intended for, but not carried out in, the Second Movement of the D minor Symphony.

To satisfy the request of a relative, he composed a short *Choral* for Four Voices and Piano Four Hands, extolling Czech peasant-life. Otherwise he "lazed about" as he put it, only taking an interest in his household and his garden.

On August 15th, 1885, he again traveled to England, for the fourth time, this time alone: "just to see how it goes", as he put it. He went straight to Birmingham where, received with exceptional hospitality, he conducted rehearsals for The Spectre's Bride. Then he visited Littleton at his

villa in Brighton. On August 25th began the Birmingham
Festival, lasting four days, with eight concerts from four to
five hours in length—a test of endurance which Dvořák
found "simply terrible".

On this occasion, Dvořák celebrated a triumph which put
in the shade the attractions of another novelty, the "Mors et
vita" Oratorio by Gounod. On August 31st, Dvořák traveled straight home to Vysoká. He did not intend to put off
his own Oratorio any longer. Based on an incident related
by the historian, Palacký, describing the conversion of the
Czechs to Christianity in the Ninth Century, the text had at
last arrived.

"Ludmila"

THE ORATORIO, "ST. LUDMILA", falls into three parts. In the
Court of Melnik Castle where Ludmila reigns, the image of
the heathen goddess, Bába, is displayed. With idyllic, rustic
ceremonies, Ludmila's subjects are about to decorate it with
wreaths and flowers when there appears the anchorite,
Ivan. With words of fire, he condemns this idolatry and
extols the Christian Cross, finally destroying the image of
Bába. The people are stunned, speechless at seeing him un-
visited by any punishment. Ludmila is shaken to her depths.
The recognition of the Light dawns in her awakening soul;
she becomes a disciple of the anchorite.

The Second Part takes place in the Woods of Beraun in
front of Ivan's cave. Driven by the hunger in her heart and
soul, Ludmila seeks refuge in the forest. Here she meets
Prince Bořivoj who, enchanted by the radiance that ema-

nates from her, wants to take her home to be his wife. But the anchorite permits their betrothal only on condition that Bořivoj become a convert to Christianity. The Prince agrees.

In the Third Part, Ludmila and Bořivoj, with their retinues, assemble before the Church of Velehrad in East Moravia (since regarded by all Slavs as a consecrated spot), where Bishop Methud, the great Slav apostle, baptizes and marries them. At the same time, their subject peoples accept the Christian Faith.

From September 7th, 1885, to May 30th, 1886, Dvořák worked on this Oratorio, its poetically beautiful text certainly the best he had ever had. In the fall of 1886, Novello published it as Op. 71, with the title "Saint Ludmila— Oratorio", in two editions, an English and a German-and-Czechish. Karel Weis, who later composed the opera, "The Polish Jew," was responsible for the piano score. Ludmila is dedicated to the "Žerotín Choral and Music Society in Olmütz".

While composing it, Dvořák did not permit himself to be disturbed either by the failure of his comic opera, "Peasant Rogue" in Vienna, November, 1885, nor by the success of his Stabat mater in that same Vienna (and in Melbourne, Australia, too!), and, indeed, only broke off once in order to conduct the première of his D Major Symphony in Prague on November 29th, 1885.

Among Dvořák's entire compositions, Ludmila is musically something altogether new. This music streams forth like something elemental, surging with tremendous power, its inspiration derived from Dvořák's hearing of the splendid English choirs for which it was intended. With great force he has developed the contrast between paganism and Christianity in conflict with each other; he has found the perfect tone both for the dauntless anchorite, Ivan, and for the tender maiden, Ludmila. Needless to say, Dvořák is absolutely at home in his music depicting the forest wilds about the hermit's cave. Each musical episode is independent in itself, rich in melody, handled with admirable technique and artistry of style. There are several "memory" motives bound up with the leading characters, and to these the ear returns with the effect of repose: a motive to characterize the new Faith, one for the Cross and one for the love of the Prince.

It is evident that Händel was Dvořák's model: the choral crescendos by far excel anything Dvořák had hitherto attained, and Ludmila is happily far removed from any influence of the operatic stage. But for the grandiose climax of the Third Part, Dvořák is indebted to the enduring remembrance of ancient Slavic sacred music beginning with the age-old choral, "Hospodine pomiluj ny", intermingled in the final chorus with an old Czechish hymn. Here, as proven by its effect on audiences ever since, the elemental power of this Oratorio is most distinctly felt.

On October 1st, 1886, Dvořák went to England for the fifth time. He was to conduct the première of Ludmila, which each great English city was trying to snatch ahead of the rest. But he had promised it to Leeds and had already received word that it was there being rehearsed with enthusiasm. This time, too, he was Littleton's guest.

The great event took place on October 15th. The audience had come together from all over England, many having traveled all night to get there in time for the performance at noon. In Dvořák's words, the choir of 350 voices and the orchestra surpassed everything he had heard before in England. Both singers and listeners were swept off their feet. The whole affair culminated in such ovations as Dvořák, who certainly could not complain of England in this respect, had never experienced. When he was finally able to express his thanks in a few words of English, the storm once more broke loose.

On October 29th and November 6th, in London, Dvořák conducted two further performances of Ludmila. On February 25th, 1887, Prague followed, with Dvořák again conducting. In 1901, Ludmila was produced in costume with scenic settings at the Czechish National Theater.

His journeys to England had brought to Dvořák both honors and riches. That great and powerful land of music, whose choirs and orchestras had inspired Dvořák to create new works, had been won for a composer until that time little enough known. This was of benefit, as he himself had hoped, not only to him, but to the whole of Czechish music. Indeed, Dvořák's works had brought the first intimations of its existence as a separate entity.

He remained the plain and unassuming person he had always been, of profound humility, especially in his own work and when confronting fresh tasks. Once, when a choir conductor in the country wrote him a letter exuding too much devotion, he replied: "You are not speaking to a

Demigod! I am a very simple person, to whom such expressions of exaggerated modesty as yours are entirely inappropriate. I remain what I was: a plain and simple Bohemian Musikant."

In the years succeeding, the career of this master (he had long since earned that title!) went on ascending to ever-new heights, and the sphere of his influence widened perceptibly. England had given him his feeling for the outside world, and he knew that this was not the only portion of the world he had still to see. He embarked on the writing of several larger works of considerable importance. His approach to them, however, was more deliberate; he was now in his mid-forties. Every once in a while, he would return to his own sources, rediscovering the un-revised works of his youth which could now appear as the product of a famous man. The fifth decade of his life was coming to a propitious close; thereafter, his life was to enter upon what was to be its most remarkable, and perhaps most important, phase.

Slavonic Dances (Second Series)—The Mass in D— Piano Quintet in D

IN A PERIOD of such spiritual and creative expansiveness, Dvořák naturally began to think again of composing another opera. Since the beginning of 1886, the libretto of "Jacobin" had been ready and waiting for him, but he would much rather have done something else. The National Theater was again after him, this time for a ballet; that, too, was little to his taste. And as usual the publishers were clamoring. Novello got his Oratorio in short order, but Simrock, as soon as he read about it in the papers, likewise wanted to have it even when it was still unfinished.

Dvořák had to admit that he had promised it to Novello, whereupon Simrock reminded Dvořák of his earlier contract by the terms of which Simrock claimed an option on everything new he composed. There was a spirited exchange of letters in an ever less friendly tone. It was apparent that Dvořák was being paid on quite a different scale in England and, also, that he was rather tired of hearing how poorly some of his longer, and certainly more important, works were "going". Furthermore, he did not care to hear the eternal requests for new and "popular" pieces, if possible in the same genre as the earlier ones.

Simrock was very little interested in symphonies, operas or certain earlier works that Dvořák from time to time offered him; what the publisher wanted was new Slavonic Dances or even Lieder. It took some time for Dvořák to make up his mind to compose anything of that nature, and the work of composition did not proceed with such ease. Nevertheless, about the beginning of July, 1886, he did have ready "*Eight Slavonic Dances*" (Second Series) for four hands, published three months later as Op. 72. As soon as he had seen the manuscript, Simrock wanted the dances orchestrated. Dvořák took another six months to do this— and the instrumentation "sounds like the devil", as Dvořák himself declared.

Dvořák knew perfectly well why he was so dilatory at this work and why it was so "damned difficult" for him.

A genuinely great artist does not again attempt to dig out of an empty lode; he cannot be sent back at command to find the same treasure twice. In this second series of Slavonic Dances, Dvořák does something which suffices to insure our admiration for his artistic intelligence: he does not write any more naive melodic pieces like the first. Whenever he returns to the use of Czechish dance melodies, what he really does, without at all emulating Czechish originals, is to write dance-poems in a similar style. In further demonstration of his altogether greater perspective, he now actually composes a series of dances typical of the various Slav peoples.

The Second of these dances is a Polish "Mazurka" with all the finish of Polish elegance and melancholy; the Sixth is an idealized "Polonaise"; the Fourth introduces the voice of the Ukraine; the Seventh is the tempestuous Serbian "Kolo". The First Dance is a no less wild, and then again wistful, "Odzemek", such as one could find danced in Slovakia. Pure Czechish is the Third, the "Skočná", but in this instance Dvořák has deftly delineated the form rather than produced anything of an elemental nature that he really experienced.

There is a special circumstance connected with the Fifth Dance, "Špacírka", which Dvořák is said to have learned from the young people in Vysoká. They used to dance it with great energy in the open air: it is a hand-in-hand striding-and-stepping that gradually becomes faster and faster. Finally there is the Eighth and last, a "Sousedská", a reminiscence of his lost youth by a mature, resigned spirit. This was definitely and irrevocably the last; after that, there could be for Dvořák no further Slavonic Dances.

In the long run, the external necessity demanding shorter forms apparently corresponded more and more to Dvořák's own desire. Simrock wanted to have more songs and Dvořák gave them to him, though not until September; the publisher hastened to bring them out before Christmas. Entitled "In Folk-tone" (literally, "*Im Volkston*"), Op. 73, these four songs are Dvořák's own invention although three of them emulate Slovak models, and one reproduces the spirit of Czech folk-poetry. Like the foregoing Slavonic Dances, all four seem to be tinged with a light melancholy. The piano accompaniments are in themselves works of art. The German text version is by Ottilie Malybrok-Stieler.

October and part of November, 1886 were occupied by his fifth trip to England: Ludmila's performances in Leeds and London; the D Major Symphony in Birmingham; and two performances, at which Dvořák was present, of The Spectre's Bride, conducted by Richter, on November 1st and 11th. On this last day, Dvořák returned to Prague, having just received news of his several successes in Germany where, in particular, the Hussite Overture was coming into its own.

In January 1887, he composed two works of an especially personal nature which were, however, not without larger implications: the "*Terzetto*" for two Violins and Viola, Op. 74 and "*Four Romantic Pieces*" for Violin and Piano, Op. 75. The first of these, it seems, he had written for the benefit of amateurs. But he soon saw that it would turn out to be too difficult and therefore re-wrote it, without the viola, as a suite of four pieces for violin and piano. In the simple piano setting we find traces of the String Trio as originally planned.

The First Movement of the "Terzetto" is united to the slow Second Movement, of a similar structure, by means of a few modulating chords. This slow Movement is a song in romantic accents. The Third Movement is a complete Scherzo, and the Fourth contains variations on a theme from the First. Dvořák's master-craftsmanship is sustained in the smallest details of this work. The "Romantic Pieces", though labelled with rather programmatic titles, reveal the same good taste: "Cavatina", "Capriccio", "Romance" and "Elégie".

His period of reflection and recollection continued. About this time, he received offers from England for a new oratorio. He declined, even though Cardinal Newman sent him his poem, "The Dream of Gerontius", as a text. (It will be remembered that "The Dream of Gerontius" was thereafter composed by Sir Edward Elgar.) Instead, Dvořák began the revision, convenient at that time, of his earlier works. He painstakingly corrected and improved, eliminating recognized errors, tiresome stretches and exaggerations of expression. He was spurred on to do this by the unexpected success of his Symphonic Variations, composed ten years previously, which Richter now included in the repertoire of his English concerts.

In this manner, Dvořák revised his String Quintet in

A minor of 1861, his Quartet in A major of 1862 and the "Cypress" Lieder of 1865. In April, 1887, in Vysoká, he re-arranged some of the Cypress Songs for String Quartet. Believing the first version to have been lost, he likewise completed the second version of "King and Charcoal-Burner" of 1874.

In spite of its large dimensions, the *"Mass in D"* for mixed Choir and Organ, is of an intimate character. Commissioned by a wealthy patron of the arts, Josef Hlávka, for the consecration of a chapel on his estate, the Mass in D was composed from March to June, 1886, in Vysoká, and Dvořák himself conducted it for the consecration ceremonies on September 1st. The first public performance took place in 1888 in the Pilsen Municipal Theater.

Since it was so successful, Dvořák offered the Mass to Simrock, but the latter hesitated. Before sailing to America in 1892, Dvořák completed the orchestration and gave it to Novello, who published a piano score of this version as Op. 86. (It should have been Op. 76, but Simrock had already given that opus number to the F major Symphony, actually Op. 24.)

In its simplicity and colloquial idiom, this Mass in D is like a veritable voice of Nature, speaking from Vysoká. It certainly has nothing in common with the so-called "Cecilian movement", at that time a powerful factor in the attempted reform of ecclesiastic music. Dvořák has his own way of letting God speak through music. Of course, he does not forget the necessities of good style and contrapuntal art in sacred music. Perhaps a citation of the nationally-accented theme in the "Credo" will be revealing:

The "Credo" and the "Agnus Dei" are the most important sections of the Mass. In the "Credo", the alto recites the Creed ahead of the rest of the choir. Too idyllic to be compared with his Stabat mater or with the Requiem, this sacred music is nevertheless the spontaneous utterance of Dvořák's heart.

That August, two days after having written Simrock that he was not doing anything new (probably in order to put the publisher in a frame of mind favorable to his earlier works), Dvořák began to write one of the most beautiful compositions of his entire career and of chamber-music in general: the *Piano Quintet in A*. Actually Op. 77, it was published by Simrock as Op. 81. Possibly Dvořák was moved to its composition, while revising the works of his youthful period, because he thought his A major Quintet had been lost. The joyful declaration of his own inner being, expressed in the Quintet in A, would seem to indicate this.

Several of his best friends have maintained that this Quintet provides a virtually life-like, full-length portrait of Dvořák: his joy in Nature and his love of melody, his feeling of communion with the world, his quickly changing moods, that faint melancholy and anxiety, swiftly dissolved again in the consciousness of his own power. Certainly we find ourselves completely under the spell of Dvořák's joyful singing and romancing. This is true from the very first theme of the First Movement, held to be a particularly good likeness of the man. Full as it is of alternating joy and reflection, profound intuition and, again, the release of melody, the First Movement includes other equally beautiful themes, inventions arising out of the sonata form.

In the Second Movement, through the metamorphosis of one and the same motive, the melancholy of the Dumka is made to alternate with that gaiety peculiar to Dvořák. Entitled "Furiant", the Scherzo, though not exactly a real Furiant, nevertheless possesses the dance-joyousness, primal, rhythmic energy and tonal sensuousness of that form. This sensuousness arises out of a contrapuntal reminiscence of the "portrait-theme" in the First Movement. The work ends with the same ravishing exaltation with which it began. In form and content, the Piano Quintet in A is one of the most intoxicating chamber-music works of all literature, comparable only to Schubert. It may well be likened to his "Forellen Quintet".

That autumn was devoted to still further revision. About the end of October, he went to Berlin to see Simrock, who on this occasion acquired the earlier Symphony in F, the Symphonic Variations, the String Quartet in G (with Double-bass), The 149th Psalm and the new Piano Quintet. For this entire group, Dvořák received 6,000 marks. Simrock wrote to Brahms: "It is extraordinary what a lot of music that man has in his head and, in spite of his silence (in Prague, his wife tells me, he is called the 'Bohemian Moltke'), he is a charming fellow. . . ."

About this time, Dvořák made two trips to Vienna, where, on December 4th, his Symphonic Variations were being performed. In mid-January, 1888, the last of his revised manuscripts, ready for printing, were mailed to Simrock. At last Simrock met Dvořák's request: the titles were printed in German and Czechish and Dvořák's name was abbreviated in the form of "Ant." (i.e., "Antonín" or "Anton"). Dvořák was much pleased at this.

He was much less pleased with the opus numbers that Simrock, often arbitrarily, without asking him, gave these works. The F major Symphony, actually Op. 24, appeared as Op. 76; the String Quintet, actually Op. 18, as Op. 77; the Symphonic Variations (40) as Op. 78; 149th Psalm (52) as Op. 79; the String Quartet in E (27) as Op. 80; and his latest work, the Piano Quintet in A, as Op. 81. Anyone who did not know would naturally think that these were Dvořák's latest works. The composer protested in vain.

He had a further reason to be upset. As already mentioned, Novello had published an Album of Dvořák's Lieder, the rights to which he had purchased from the Prague publishers, Urbánek, and Starý. These songs comprise

"Ballads", Op 5; "Five Lieder", Op. 31; and "Four Lieder", Op. 2; and, finally, four other songs that Starý had published as Op. 17. Dvořák had turned them over to him, receiving no payment, and, in his own words, had forgotten the whole matter. But Simrock had, at that time, published the same songs as Op. 7. As will be recalled, Dvořák had promised to make amends.

In order to save the trouble of making German translations, he therefore composed four songs to German verses by Ottilie Malybrok-Stieler from her book "Lyric Poems and Translations based on Bohemian Literature and Folk-Poetry". Three of these Lieder, Op. 82, "Leave Me Alone", "Spring Time", "By the Brook", are songs of love and the longing for Nature, the first of which has been widely popularized. The Fourth "At Her Embroidery", is a song of work. As it turned out, Simrock had demanded and he now received a beautiful work. Dedicated to Frau Sophie Hanslick, these Lieder are of great emotional intensity and lyric finish.

"Jacobin"

BY THIS TIME, Dvořák was so much rested, and had found such inner repose that, after much reluctance and hesitation, he could begin that opera, "Jacobin", the text of which had been lying ready for him the past five years. Were his doubts of the story and text justified? Their deficiencies he certainly did not ignore, having already had enough experience of inadequate librettos. On the other hand, he was irresistibly captivated by the voice of his homeland and the scenes of his youth as the background for a story taking place amidst historic events.

As indicated by the title, the action takes place during the French Revolution, but in Bohemia: in a country with its Castle and its ruling Count, with an art-loving schoolmaster and choir-conductor (at once he recalled his teacher, Liehmann), and finally, with its country people, simple, old-fashioned and good, subservient to, yet protected by, their masters. In several of Dvořák's opera-texts the kindly relations between gentry and tenants are portrayed, yet he does not hesitate to depict the people's resistance to every abuse of traditional feudal rights. (In his later "The Devil and Kate", Hell itself is mustered out against misrule.)

The plot is as follows: Bohuš the son of Count Haras (Harasov), returns incognito to Bohemia with his wife, Julie, whom he married in Paris. His family have never forgiven him for venturing into the outside world, for his hunger after freedom, and for marrying without consulting them. His uncle, Count Adolf, has done his best to keep alive this resentment knowing that, with Bohuš out of the way, he would be the next heir to the prosperous estate.

At home again in the little town at the foot of the hill on which stands his father's Castle, Bohuš is reminded of the goodness of his mother, who has died, and broods over the quarrel with his family. It is Sunday and a Fair Day, and the townspeople, coming from church, foregather on the Square. The arrogant Administrator of estates for the Count pays court to the beautiful Terinka, daughter of the schoolmaster, Benda. She, however, loves George, a young man of the vicinity. George makes fun of the Administrator in a song, and the latter threatens to have him impressed to the soldiery—one of the few remaining feudal rights. Bohuš learns that the old Count has disinherited his son, from whom he has not heard and whom his Uncle, Adolf, has represented as being a "Jacobin". His father intends to install Adolf in his place with appropriate ceremonies. The act closes with the appearance of the benevolent old Count, joyously greeted by his people.

In the Second Act, rehearsals are being held at the Schoolmaster's for the serenade to be sung on the occasion of Adolf's investiture. Terinka and George are the soloists and, in the time-honored manner of musical comedy, they take advantage of the music-parts they are reading, to confess their love for each other. Benda catches them at it and is anything but pleased since he would much prefer to see his daughter married to the Administrator. Bohuš and Julie appear, asking for lodging as traveling Bohemian artists, and the art-loving Benda is delighted to put them up. Neither he nor the others recognize his once favorite pupil, Bohuš. No-one else would give them lodging because the rumor has gone the rounds that there are Jacobins in the neighborhood. Taking advantage of this, Count Adolf, who has recognized the young "artist", denounces Bohuš as a Jacobin and has him thrown into gaol so that he cannot interfere with the forthcoming ceremonies. There is no way out of Bohuš' predicament unless Benda can reach the old Count, which, as a fellow artist, he agrees to do.

In the third act, George attempts to tell the Count the

whole story, but does not succeed. However, Benda and an old servant smuggle Julie into the room of the dead Countess, the mother of Bohuš. Adolf has just shown the old Count a newspaper-clipping stating that Bohuš has been executed by the "Girondistes" in Paris. The Count, all his love for his son reawakened, is shocked to his depths. At this moment he hears singing in the room of the dead Countess: the Lullabye she used to sing to her son. Opening the door, he discovers Julie, who explains everything. The Count exiles Adolf and installs Bohuš and Julie as his heirs to the estate. Terinka and George are betrothed, and there is general rejoicing over the happy outcome.

Obviously, this libretto employs the tried-and-true intrigant, or traditional operatic villain. On the other hand the Count and his son are not very distinctly delineated. The types of town and country, the teacher who only lives for his daughter and his music, the young lovers, the Castle officials, the dignitaries of the town and the people themselves—these are all far more successful. Perhaps Dvořák was aware that he was again composing an opera only for home consumption and not for production in the outside world, where he so dearly longed to meet with success. In any event, we can believe him when he writes Simrock that he has decided to compose this opera for his own enjoyment. And that is what he does.

It took him a year to write, from November 10th, 1887 to November 18th, 1888, and was first produced in Prague on February 12th, 1899, conducted by Adolf Čech. The old

Count was played by Karel Čech, brother of Adolf and a friend of Dvořák's youth; the Administrator, by Wilhelm Hesch; Julie, by Berta Foerster-Lauterer. (Both the last-named later became members of the Vienna Imperial Opera under Gustav Mahler.)

Of course, it was a success, but Dvořák knew that it would be the usual Prague success. In 1897, he attempted a complete revision, the text of which was furnished by Rieger, father of the poetess, Marie Červinková, who had died. In this version it was produced in Prague in 1898. In 1911, "Hudební Matice" published a piano-score with Czechish text, retouched with excellent taste by Kovařovic. In 1932, Adolf Heller conducted the first German version, "Der Jakobiner", his own translation, in the Municipal Theater of Teplitz-Schönau. In 1934, the Prague German Provincial Theater staged the second non-Czechish production, conducted by Georg Széll. But "Jacobin" has never been produced outside of Bohemia.

More than ever this music seems to spring from Dvořák's heart. Once the story with all its types and motivations had taken possession of his imagination, it could hardly have been otherwise. What could be closer to his own being than these contrasts: love of the homeland and adventure in the outside world, paternal and filial love, and the old-fashioned, countrified gaiety that cannot endure false pride? When Bohuš sings his song of greeting on returning to his native land, from which he has been so long away, it sounds almost like a premonition of Dvořák's homesickness later on in

America. The first theme of the opera, one of those themes, primal and native with Dvořák, compels the heart:

This theme is used in the manner of a leitmotif and sounds most beautiful in the Lullabye (the one that Dvořák had composed in London!) that Julie sings, thereby convincing the Count of the prodigal son's return. A second leitmotif, in the style of reminiscence, is Benda's serenade; a third, though of less importance, is George's song making fun of the Administrator.

Otherwise, there is throughout this work the usual opulence and matter-of-course variety of invention. Futile to argue whether it is dramatic, symphonic or lyric: there it is, like Nature, as liberally given and as freely to be enjoyed. In reply to the criticism, often made when this opera has been performed, that Dvořák's world is certainly not that of the stage, it is safe to say that a great deal of music, far less adapted to the stage, has nevertheless substantiated its right to a place in the theater solely on the grounds of its inner richness and beauty.

Piano Quartet—G major Symphony

ONCE AGAIN, Dvořák was back at his work of revision. This time he rewrote eight of the "Cypress" Song Cycle, and they were published as "Love-songs", Op. 83. The changes he made have to do with the key, rhythm and harmony; the piano part is simpler and fuller in tone. Otherwise the character of the songs has scarcely been touched.

Simrock was not so pleased to have these songs as Dvořák had hoped. He found them attractive enough, but regretted that he had no German translation and would therefore have to have one made. This would cost money and so he could not pay as much as Dvořák asked. Dvořák demanded the return of his manuscript; but finally they came to an agreement, and Mme. Malybrok-Stieler undertook the German translation.

About the beginning of the year 1889, the "Society for the Furtherance of Music in Bohemia", offered Dvořák a professorship at the Prague Conservatory (the following year to be merged with the old "Organ School"). At the time he felt that, in view of his activities as composer and his travels abroad, he must decline. He feared the bonds of obligations such as those from which he had suffered in his youth. Two years were to elapse before he would feel inclined to accept such an offer.

On the first Sunday in April, 1889, immediately after a successful concert in Dresden, Dvořák returned to his birth-place, Nelahozeves-Mühlhausen. What a world of memories was quickened into being! In the afternoon he visited the girls' boarding-school, now housed in the Lobkowitz Castle; there he sat down at the piano and improvised for a long time on motives from "Jacobin". He was back in the very atmosphere of that work.

This experience inspired him to write thirteen *"Poetic
Mood-Pictures"*, for Piano, Op. 85. He wrote to Simrock
that, although "13" was supposed to be an unlucky number, he had once written Thirteen Moravian Duets, and
they had been sung all over the world. He called this a sort
of "program-music", but only in the manner of Schumann,
who, too, was content to use merely programmatic titles.

Seldom has Dvořák so happily evinced his mastery of
small forms, such as he himself had developed. These pieces
contain an abundance of music in poetic mood, from the
Dance (Furiant) to the religious exaltation of the last piece,
"On the Holy Mountain". (This Mountain was a place of
Pilgrimage near Vysoká.) Simrock again complained that
this work would be expensive to bring out: he liked the
pieces very much, but he felt sure that such a Collection
would not find as wide a market as the earlier ones. He was
mistaken: these "Mood Pictures" turned out to be Dvořák's
most popular piano work.

He had taken up the spring with their composition, and
now the summer of 1899 (one of his most fertile years),
was to be devoted to a new chamber-music work, worthy
to rank with the Piano Quintet. Dvořák wrote it while
several members of the family were recovering from illness.
Under these circumstances, the recognition accorded by the
Austrian Government through the award of the "Order
of the Iron Crown" was certainly not unwelcome. Brahms
who had himself just received the still higher "Order of St.
Leopold," wrote to congratulate him. And Dvořák pro-

posed that they meet in Ischl (where the Emperor spent the summer) to parade their decorations.

The Piano Quartet in E flat, Op. 87, came as if in answer to the long-entertained and oft-expressed wish of Simrock. Dvořák, of course, knew quite well why he was fulfilling that particular wish at this time. Since composing the Quintet, he now had a far better knowledge of how to handle the piano and was therefore better equipped.

This Quartet is in no sense inferior to its earlier sister-composition as regards sonority and fertility of ideas. (Ever and again we are confronted by Dvořák's duality in the exploitation of moods, techniques and ideas!) It is to be distinguished, however, from the Quintet by its unity of form in contrast to the constantly changing moods of that work, and by the striking masculinity of its expression. The opening theme of the First Movement is a key theme running through the entire composition. The slow Second Movement expands the three-part form of his broad Adagio-singing into a kind of four-part form which is, however, something more than a merely constructive enrichment.

In the Scherzo, a simple, old-fashioned dance, soft and slow, alternates with a yearning melody almost Oriental in its coloring. In its impetuous, manly, and then again nostalgic way, the Finale resembles the First Movement. Not until the repeat does he introduce this very similar main theme in the principal key, and, as for the rest, he seems to revel in the style of a conqueror, taking every sort of harmonic and modulatory liberty. Published in 1890 by Simrock, the Piano Quartet was performed the same year in Prague.

Once again, it had been a good year. In August Dvořák had written Göbl that his head was so full of ideas—if only he could write them all down! What a pity that the hand required so much time! At all events, close upon the Piano Quartet, Dvořák began sketching another great orchestral work, the *Symphony in G major*, the fourth of those that were published. On November 8th, the score was ready.

Here again there is great variety of mood, great introspection in the ideas and a highly personal form. Kretzschmar goes so far as to deny the symphonic character of this work, placing it among the programmatic "Symphonic Poems" or, at any rate, among the "Slavonic Rhapsodies". Perhaps it is actually lacking in the true character of the symphony as we are accustomed to think of it. On the other hand, it holds the imagination because of the problems it poses and the wholly subjective expression of every solution it finds. The national coloring is unmistakable, but, as in the Second Series of Slavonic Dances, it transcends the merely Czechish sphere.

In the First Movement, after the "masking" typical of the sonata form with Dvořák, the first subject itself appears, and it could scarcely be more personal and self-willed:

Almost a movement complete in itself, this theme expands with a wealth of other thematic material—rather more contrasted, perhaps, than developed.

The Second Movement reminds us of one of the Piano Mood-Pictures, "In the Old Castle", but there are also traces of the choral theme from the Hussite Overture. In the delightful Scherzo, the trio recalls a folk-song sort of theme, the aria of Toník in the "Obstinate Children". One peculiar feature is the counterpoint of the oboe and bassoon, in a virtual Cossack dance, to the theme of the coda, which changes from triple-time to duple-time.

The Finale is introduced by a fanfare, the first subject of which undergoes four variations (as in the last Movement of Beethoven's "Eroica"). The second theme is practically a further variation, but in its peculiar harmonizing it has something of a positively East-Slavic nature.

This Symphony never became so well known as the others, very likely because it was published by Novello, as Op. 88, but not until 1892. Dvořák himself conducted its first performance in Prague, February, 1890. Richter wanted to follow suit, but Simrock insisted that he must first acquire the work (and therefore, would, of course, receive the royalty from Richter's performance).

The negotiations were long-drawn-out, Simrock again declaring that he did not earn anything from the publication of Dvořák's larger works, likewise scarcely anything from the smaller ones! Thus, for the time being, there were no further performances, neither in England nor Russia, whither Dvořák soon went on a concert-tour. The correspondence with Simrock finally became heated.

It appears that Simrock wanted to acquire the Symphony for only 1000 marks and, as if in compensation for such generosity, kept on demanding "short pieces" although he maintained that he could not even find a market for these. Whereupon, in October, 1890, Dvořák wrote that he was simply not going to offer Simrock any more of his big works. For, if he did, other publishers would want to know why Simrock had refused them. His smaller works would then assuredly lose their value and he would get less for them. Furthermore, he had at present "a lot of ideas for big works in mind". What could he do if no ideas for Lieder or short piano pieces occurred to him? "I shall simply do what God imparts to me to do. That will certainly be the best thing."

Simrock, at once alarmed, replied that their contract of 1879 was still valid, and, thereby, Dvořák must first offer to him every new work he composed. Dvořák did not reply. Novello acquired the Symphony, and Dvořák wrote for him the four-hand piano score.

In December, 1889, Dvořák and his wife went to Vienna where he was to be received in audience by the Emperor Francis Joseph in order to express his thanks for the Order of the Iron Crown. They stayed with Count Kaunitz, Dvořák's brother-in-law. The Emperor asked after his personal circumstances and that of Prague's artists in general.

"Requiem"

IN THE LAST DAYS of 1890, Dvořák, still swept along by the full flood of ideas, made his first jottings for a new choral work, destined to be his last and his best: a "Requiem".

166

There was no external occasion requiring him to write a Mass for the Dead; he simply felt that he had arrived at that time when he was equipped to do it and had the leisure. Notwithstanding, there is nothing merely constructed or cerebral about his Requiem.

A different character from Brahms, he is no pessimist, not even in this Requiem. It would have been foreign to his nature to cry out that all flesh is as grass, all is vanity and it shall pass away. This temporality is no grim conclusion to him but, whenever he admits it, brings genuine pain to his heart. He loves Life and is saddened by the thought that it must end. Only his profound piety, rejoicing in his own existence, can help him. He avoids as much as possible descriptions of a punitive "Justice".

Significant of the whole work is a leitmotif that he uses throughout, in all sorts of places, but with perfect consistency:

Dvořák's Requiem is in Two Parts, the first ending just before the "Offertory". The different sections are linked together without breaks. Solos and choir alternate in taking up and continuing the thread so that there is no opportunity for big solo arias. At the outset, the leitmotif is stated in the form of a motto by the 'cellos. (Suk employs it in his Symphonic Poem, "Asrael", dedicated to the memory of Dvořák, his teacher and father-in-law). Modulations and a soprano solo, lend a personal stamp to the very beginning of this work.

The "Dies irae" recalls us to the traditional sequence of the Requiem. Above the tempest in the orchestra, the choir bursts out in a cry of terror, and the sense of impending doom turns to tender-hearted mourning. Instead of pathetic orgies in the brass, the alto solo sings the lament in the "Tuba mirum". The theme denoting Judgement is more expressive of sublimity than of fear. The solo quartet sheds the beauty of its melody over the "Quid sum miser". The "Recordare" recalls Dvořák's "Quis est homo" in "Stabat mater". One theme is the inversion of the other. And throughout the work the leitmotif plays a leading role.

In the Second Part, the soul turns from the horror of Death, the Judgement and hopes of Salvation to a general expression of confidence and faith in God. An unusual feature is an old, traditional Slav hymn to the words of the text, "Quam olim Abrahae". Despair and confidence still alternate; the "Benedictus" seems to illumine all that Bliss to be found after death. In the stirring "Sanctus", B flat is contrasted with B, thus permitting Dvořák's peculiar chromatic ascent to the next-higher step.

Once again, the "Agnus" reveals Dvořák's diffident contemplation of death and, at the same time, the reconciling certainty of his unshakable faith. Rich in sonority, Dvořák's work is one of the most beautiful, original and worthwhile settings of the Mass for the Dead. It belongs to our picture of Dvořák to perceive how well he succeeds with religious choral works that are the very expression of his most sacred feeling for God. For, in Dvořák, unity of the spirit with God is just as genuine as his affirmation of the world.

In February, 1890, his composition of the Requiem was interrupted by a journey to Moscow, St. Petersburg and, thereafter, by another to England. From June to October, he continued and completed the Requiem, published by Novello as Op. 89. With great success, it was first conducted by Dvořák at Birmingham, October 9th, 1891. It was not until 1901 that Ferdinand Löwe conducted it in Vienna, but then it seemed to have earned an even greater triumph.

In Russia, great honors were heaped upon Dvořák when he conducted his orchestral works in Moscow. In St. Petersburg, after his concert, at the banquet in his honor, he was presented with a silver loving-cup.

In mid-April, on his sixth trip to England, Dvořák conducted his G major Symphony. There followed his triumph with the same work in Frankfort where his music was much loved, the Hussite Overture having already been performed there three times. Conducting his Hussite Overture himself, he is said to have taken the tempi twice as fast as the Frankfort conductor, Karl Müller. In the same "Museum Concert" in which he appeared as conductor, Eugen Gura sang Lieder by Schubert and Karl Löwe, and Clara Schumann, then seventy, played Chopin's Piano Concerto in F minor.

The year 1890 brought to Dvořák two further distinctive honors. The Czech University of Prague conferred on him the Honorary Degree of Doctor of Music. But the

Austrian Minister of Education, Baron Gautsch, failed to confirm the Degree because there was no Doctorate of Music at Austrian Universities. There was no way out except to give Dvořák the Degree of Doctor of Philosophy, honoris causa. This was conferred on March 17th, 1891. But even before that occurred, Cambridge University had made him a Doctor of Music. So that, willy-nilly, the Vienna Ministry of Education had to follow suit.

Dr. Antonín Leopold Dvořák also finally accepted a Professorship at the Prague Conservatory for Composition, Instrumentation and Form. He received a salary of 1200 gulden a year, and only had to teach seven or eight months a year. He was to begin his activities as instructor on January 1st, 1891, and his fiftieth birthday was approaching.

The Teacher

Dvořák, now sufficiently schooled by life, and sometimes "schoolmastered", too, suddenly found himself a teacher. He had hesitated long before accepting this responsibility. It was certainly sensible for the Conservatory and Organ School to become one institution, and this was thanks to the excellent Dr. Josef Tragy, who was on the boards of both institutions. But the Conservatory was famed for its classes in instrumental music, especially the violin class of Anton Bennewitz, and Dvořák doubted that he would be able to raise the class in composition to the same high level. He was to conduct the Master Class, and he was determined that it should earn that name (which, incidentally, it finally did not receive!).

170

On the other hand, as a condition of his acceptance, the selection of the most gifted students had been left to him. He took over the tuition of fifteen of the most brilliant pupils of Professor Stecker (provisional member of the faculty), among them Suk and Nedbal. The following year, Novák joined them. These three names alone would have sufficed to characterize the school of Dvořák, so important for modern Czechish music.

Dvořák, however, did not restrict himself to outstanding talents alone; with the greatest seriousness and tireless conscientiousness, he devoted his time, knowledge and ability to all whom he considered worthy of his instruction. Numerous testimonials and reminiscences of his students record his personality, the naturalness of his appearance, always slightly folksy, slightly demonic. All this instilled respect. Very soon, however, respect changed to affection. There was, furthermore, his fame at home and abroad.

The students knew that this sometimes strangely disgruntled and grumbling master was at the same time their comrade. He lived in and with them, let them participate in everything he felt, and himself partook of their cares. What else were the intermissions good for? And then, too, they could walk home with him! He did not pay much attention to study-periods or planned instruction. Supposed to teach from 8 to 9 A. M., he would stay the whole forenoon if he thought it necessary.

His common sense born of life's experience, his sincerity, his goodness that shone through every outburst of rage, his colloquialisms, and the way he would recommend some course of action—all this won their hearts. He could as easily have commanded rather than suggested: they would have obeyed him. In spirit he was just as young as they and there was a certain childlikeness about him often greater than their own. "Sometimes he's a comrade; then, again, he's a God!" Nedbal said of him. He talked about his plans, by no means despised advice from others, and was always ready with sound counsel if required. And he did not merely give advice: help was sure to follow.

One of his pupils, Ludmila Vojačková Wetche, writes of her days under his tuition in Prague ("The Etude", March, 1919): Dvořák's lessons used to last three hours in the morning. (This was after the more systematic regime he had himself inaugurated in New York.) But there were pauses when he would sit there, his thoughts far away, so that nobody dared disturb him. Or he would suddenly be transformed into a fellow-student, chatting of this and that, but most especially talking about America. For although he had said farewell, he still thought a great deal about this country. He insisted that things should always be as they were in America, where the millionaire and the baggage-porter called each other "Mister". The only thing that differentiated them was money; otherwise, they enjoyed the same rights. In Dvořák's eyes, this was as it should be.

Harry Patterson Hopkins, writing in "The Etude", May, 1912, tells how he wrote saying he had arrived in Prague, but for two weeks did not hear anything in reply. Dvořák's picture was in every house he entered. Suddenly, one morning, Dvořák came to his lodgings at 7 A.M., accepted Hopkins as a pupil and took him with him on the next train to Vysoká. There Hopkins was treated as a member of the family, having his lessons daily in Dvořák's work-room where at the same time the children played and shouted. Rarely Dvořák would become irritated, roundly scolding them; not that it made the slightest impression.

Dvořák's extreme sensibility was shown by his fear of thunderstorms: he would have all the window-shutters closed and play the piano as loud as he could. At meal-times, he always had a good appetite, drank a great deal of coffee and smoked so-called "Virginia" cigars. In the evening, after dinner, there was music, and Hopkins had to play four-hand piano scores with one of Dvořák's daughters. Many guests would drop in, bringing their instruments and music.

In Prague, Dvořák loved "window-shopping", but always preferred to buy from peddlers and the market-people, with whom he would pass the time of day. On his walks, Dvořák would frequently hear arrangements of his own music being played in cafés: if the playing was bad, he would fly into a temper.

Hopkins studied instrumentation with Dvořák and was amused by his drastic comments, in excellent English, on the nature of various instruments. Other students found that he required a lot of work, many sketches and long developments. "Otherwise, you are no composer!" Severe in his judgment, whenever he refused to teach untalented pupils, he would say: "It hurts you now, but later on it will save you much suffering." Once he roared: "This is miserable stuff—you're a donkey!" The offending pupil picked up his coat and went out, but Dvořák ran after him: "Come back! You're not a donkey!" The pupil as quietly returned.

On one occasion, some of his class were accompanying him home. It began to rain, no-one had an umbrella, their note-books were all wet; Dvořák apparently was unconcerned. Finally he said: "Now home you go! I believe a few drops have begun to fall." (Pellegrini, "Memoirs", Neue Muzik Zeitung, 1914.)

With regard to the work itself, Dvořák gave gifted pupils as free a hand as possible. In the less talented he attempted to inculcate at the least the fundamentals of technique. And no matter how much irony he employed, he was always fair and intelligent. Suk used to say that Dvořák would almost drive you to tears, but you learned a great deal in the process.

Dvořák's instruction was basically practical. His pupils did not always immediately understand what he meant, but his very being and the intuition that he took for granted and knew how to convey to others—all this bridged over every incompatibility. If, for instance, he declared: "I'm very fond of Chopin and Schumann, although I can't bear them!", they knew exactly what he meant.

According to Pellegrini, Dvořák said the art of composition meant to make a great deal, a very great deal, out of very little. For his teaching, he had two axioms: An artist must be capable of much, therefore he must learn a great deal. And he must be new and original. Dvořák did not consider invention any special credit to the student, but held that it came from God. Most important, however, was what the student was capable of doing with his ideas. Therefore, he demanded an exact knowledge of classic forms although he was not at all convinced that, as such, they could be forever perpetuated. To Dvořák, logical construction and intelligibility were fundamental premises.

Despite all this, he was anything but conservative or reactionary. Whenever anybody brought him "revolutionary things", he was received with abuse or with jokes, yet Dvořák much preferred such efforts to a well-behaved tedium. He himself never ceased to be interested in new works, such as those of Bruckner and Richard Strauss, at that time decried as completely revolutionary. Dvořák bought the latter's scores and carefully examined them.

His own models, of course, were Bach, Händel and the early Italian Masters, yet he was prepared to recommend such contemporaries as Wagner and Liszt. His grasp of musical literature was extraordinary, and he played everything at sight on the piano, even orchestral and operatic scores.

Naturally, his class was always crammed to the doors: it had become the goal of many foreign students and certainly was in no sense behind the Prague Conservatory's class in instrumentation. Dvořák found that he took an unexpected pleasure in giving tuition and, until the end of his life, continued to do so. From 1891 to 1892 he taught in Prague; then, three years in America; and, again in Prague, from 1895 to 1904.

On May 13th, 1891, his class was ready to give a concert

recital, and on this occasion a Piano Quartet by his seventeen-year-old pupil, Suk, evoked much comment. Soon, too, Novák was attracting the general attention. Thus it came about that, when their master was ready to leave Prague for America, people were already speaking of "The Dvořák School".

Dumky—The Program Overtures

DVOŘÁK, however, was not the man to be wholly consumed by his teaching activities. Just a few weeks after the Requiem, in February, 1891, he had finished what was to become one of his best known works, the *"Dumky" Piano Trio*, Op. 90 (Simrock, 1894). On April 11th, it was performed for the first time, Dvořák himself taking the piano and Hanuš Wihan, a brilliant 'cellist, his colleague at the Conservatory, playing the 'cello. This difficult and important part he had mastered out of his great affection for Dvořák.

In this work, Dvořák is still under the spell of the Requiem and its elegiac mood; the Dumka ("Dumky" is the plural) is well-suited to such feelings. Whether or not he was really acquainted with the Ukrainian Dumka is unknown. There is an anecdote to the effect that, shortly after having composed several Dumky, he was chatting in a café with the explorer, Kuba, whom he asked, "What actually is a Dumka?" This is beside the point. One thing is certain: to Dvořák the Dumka was a symbol of Slavic ways and it offered him an excellent vehicle for the expression of his own Slavic sentiments.

This trio consists of Six Dumky, all of them, like his earlier works, characterized by abrupt transitions from slow to fast tempi. The first Dumka has a theme that is perhaps most characteristic of the whole:

Lento maestoso

This same theme in D is taken over in the section in fast time, graced with spirited and jolly figurations, a perfect example of the multiple meaning of so many ideas that came to Dvořák. In the Second Dumka, there are two plaintive themes in the slow part, to which the fast section replies in passionate accents with a new, though related theme. The mood becomes calmer in the Third Dumka. Only the fast theme, in the minor, is again impassioned, though otherwise similar to the slow one.

Until this point, the whole work reveals a unified, almost self-contained construction, and the first three Dumky could almost be considered as an introductory movement, in a sort of rondo-form, or even as an attempted fresh interpretation of the sonata-form. In that event, the Fourth Dumka would be the slow movement, thematically reminiscent of the First Dumka, in the minor key, with the fast section in the major, the whole culminating in a surprising D major. The Russian character of the melody is remarkable: a melancholy song in four strophes is played on the 'cello. The Fifth Dumka may be called a Scherzo: its rhythmic energy does not abate until the end. The Sixth Dumka would be the Finale, with a vivace-theme surging forward to the conclusion.

Common to all these Dumky is the rhapsodic execution, the passionate dance-character of the fast movements, and the harmony of mood in spite of every change of scene. They are the "Slavonic Rhapsodies" or, if you will, the "Slavonic Dances" of chamber-music literature, show-pieces of instrumental sonority, written for virtuosos or players of real temperament with an understanding of the Slav nature.

If there is any program to these "Dumky", it is this: melancholy and the delirious joy of life combined in the same being. None the less, we perceive Dvořák, since the "Poetic Mood-pictures", being swayed by impulses extraneous to music, influences that were finally to lead him to compose symphonic poems according to an exact program. This reveals the extraordinary wrestling of a born musician, who is nothing else but a musician, with the ideas of his time— ideas seeking in vain to be liberated from Wagner and Liszt. Even such a genius of form as Dvořák is ever in search of something new and is not to be pacified with the ever-fresh, re-found securities afforded by tradition.

In the next few months, this predestined phase of programmatic experiment became all the more distinct through Dvořák's composition of a cycle of *Three Overtures for Orchestra*. Originally intended to be called, "Nature, Life and Love," they finally bore the separate titles of: "*In Nature's Realm*", Op. 91; "*Carnival*", Op. 92, and "*Othello*", Op. 93.

Dvořák was busy with their composition from the spring of 1891 to the beginning of 1892. All sorts of titles came to him, some of which are to be found in the manuscript and in the program of the first performance, under his baton, in Prague, April 28th, 1892. They were published, each separately, in 1894, after his reconciliation with Simrock. "In Nature's Realm" is dedicated to Cambridge University; "Carnival", to the Czech University in Prague.

One thing they have in common: all three Overtures employ a pastoral motive:

This is the opening phrase of the First Overture, "In Nature's Realm".

On a summer evening, a solitary wayfarer finds himself in the midst of Nature. He hears, at first dully and almost unconsciously, then more and more distinctly, and finally with jubilant rejoicing, the multifarious voices of Nature's mighty forces—forces that strengthen him within. Contained in the frame of the classic sonata, here is a wealth of alteration and diminution of the many motives denoting the joy of life. The beautiful pastoral motive of the opening phrase is transformed into a choral, but the ending remains introspective, contemplative.

In the Second Overture, "Carnival", the solitary wayfarer returns from this new-found security in Nature to the tumultuous joys of common humanity. He tastes these joys to their uttermost. Emptiness! And once again the contemplative mood returns, stronger than ever, in a lyric passage. The thinker recalls that Nature is the actual dispenser of all joys. In an Andantino, incorporated in the exposition of the themes, the clarinets reiterate the opening pastoral motive. The following development recalls the themes expressing joy but now as if twilight-veiled; in the repeat, however, they are once more released in the full radiance of their color. Here, too, the sonata form has been retained.

The Third Overture, "Othello", is rather freer in its treatment of the sonata. There is no compulsion to think of Shakespeare's play though one may do so. This music portrays the conflict between love and jealousy—a consuming and destroying passion. The slow introduction is eloquent of love's happiness; the motive of jealousy crashes upon it like a fanfare. The conflict is resolved in a delirious and tempestuous Allegro. Here again the introductory pastoral, though distorted, plays a great role. It seems as if we were swept away to the very scene of the murder. Whoever cares to trace their characters may easily find Iago, Desdemona and Othello in this Overture whose passionate drive is, as it were, impelled by all the Furies.

While still working on these Three Overtures, Dvořák had two of his most talented pupils, Suk and Nedbal, prepare the four-hand piano scores for publication. As it turned out, they were more easily playable than earlier such versions, even those he had done himself. In order to keep his eye on their work, the master invited his pupils to Vysoká, Suk to work on the First and Third Overtures; Nedbal, on the Second.

Suk was his favorite, but Dvořák did not then suspect that the seventeen-year-old boy was not only enamored of music but also of his fourteen-year-old daughter, Ottilie. Or maybe the master saw and knew more than he betrayed. At all events, poor Suk was daily locked in the porter's room at Vysoká so that Dvořák could be reasonably sure he would finish the appointed task!

Suk and Nedbal were likewise pupils in Bennewitz' violin class. Wihan organized a Conservatory String Quartet with Suk, Nedbal, the violinist Karel Hoffmann, and Otto Berger, a student from his own 'cello class. Their playing aroused the admiration of the whole school, and they remained together. This was the original "Bohemian String Quartet" which, without yet taking that name, made its first public bows in a concert on October 22nd, 1892.

The Bohemian Quartet played an important role in popularizing Dvořák's works. They loved his music and their playing of it established the world-wide fame both of Dvořák's compositions and the Quartet. In 1897, Wihan took the place of his pupil, Berger, who had died. Nedbal later left the Quartet, being replaced by Herold; and, finally, Zelenka took Wihan's place. Meanwhile, the second violin, Josef Suk, had become a great, creative master in his own right.

Cambridge

DVOŘÁK's COMPOSING and teaching were interrupted by the necessity of traveling to Cambridge to receive his Honorary Degree as Doctor of Music. The solemn investiture took place on June 16th, 1891. On this occasion, as if in place of the usual thesis, he conducted the Symphony in G and his Stabat mater, that work which had won him the favor of the English public. The Dean alluded to this when presenting the candidate, addressing the Vice-Chancellor of the University in Latin flavored with flattering references to Dvořák's chief works.

Dvořák described the affair as "frightfully solemn". He was last in line of those new doctors to be honored, among them Metchnikoff. The University Choir presented him with cap and gown. (A photo of Dvořák in his Cambridge doctor's robes, is a favorite among his countrymen.) Of course, there was a gala banquet. But what most pleased Dvořák was an appreciation of his life and works, by Sedley Taylor, published in the University Review.

Dvořák was so deeply moved he scarcely knew what was happening to him. Ceremonies in general made him feel "on pins and needles". But this was worse: "Nothing but ceremonies and Deans, all solemn-faced and apparently incapable of speaking anything but Latin. When it dawned upon me that they were talking to me, I felt as if I were drowning in hot water, so ashamed was I that I could not understand them. However, when all is said and done, that Stabat mater of mine is more than just Latin."

An epidemic of ceremonies began with September 8th, 1891, Dvořák's fiftieth birthday. Newspapers carried columns in tribute, the Prague National Theater staged a gala performance. Dvořák did not put in his appearance; instead he went strolling through the forest at Vysoká. He wrote in advance to thank the National Theater Director, declaring he intended to spend this birthday as usual with his family. If they were going to perform his opera, he hoped they would not announce that it was in celebration of a festive occasion. His wish, however, as might have been foreseen, was not respected.

CHAPTER III

THE NEW WORLD

Invitation to America

HE HAD GONE straight home from Cambridge in June, 1892, his journey hastened by important news: a definite invitation to come to America.

His music was well known in this country: the Slavonic Dances and Rhapsodies, the Legends, Stabat mater and the D major Symphony. In 1884, when he was in England, the American composer, Dudley Buck, had told him how highly esteemed he was in the United States and urged him to make his personal appearance over here in order still further to encourage American appreciation. To him the project at that time seemed almost fantastic. Now, however, he would have conceded that it was a clever idea on the part of the Americans to go the English one better by offering an engagement to this odd Bohemian musician who had such a reputation. Furthermore, the Americans seemed to want him permanently.

Mrs. Jeanette M. Thurber, founder of the National Conservatory in New York, had made up her mind that Dvořák must become the Director of that institution. She felt that his name and achievements would have more drawing-power than the National Conservatory had hitherto been able to exert. Her ill-fated attempt to establish an English-language opera-house in competition with the Metropolitan had cost her, within two years $1,500,000. She was more than ever determined that the Conservatory should be built up to a place of distinction. She had to have a famous European musician.

Mrs. Thurber therefore turned for advice to her friend, Adele Margulies, a Viennese who had come to this country and was then teaching piano at the New York National Conservatory. Miss Margulies tells how she asked her own teacher in Vienna, Anton Door, for his expert opinion as to who might be the best person to win for this position in America.

Door suggested two composers of rank: Dvořák and Sibelius. (At that time, because he had studied there for a while, Sibelius was better known in Vienna than later on.) Miss Margulies knew that she would have to deal personally with the composer finally chosen, and she preferred to seek out Dvořák in Prague or Vienna, where her family lived, rather than to travel as far afield as Finland, whither Sibelius had returned. So the two friends decided upon Dvořák.

In 1919, Mrs. Thurber's memories of Dvořák were published in "The Etude". With great feeling, she pays tribute to the modesty of Dvořák who on December 12th, 1891, when writing his final acceptance of her offer, had said: "I do not know whether I shall be just what you want in all particulars, but I rely upon your goodness and forbearance."

In the spring of 1891, the first cabled offer arrived in

Vysoká. Dvořák would not hear of it. But on June 6th, Mrs. Thurber wired him from Paris. He began to waver. He wrote Göbl, asking what he thought of the plan: two years in America as Director of the Conservatory; to conduct ten concerts of his own works; eight months' official duties and four months' vacation; $15,000 a year. That was 30,000 gulden in all. What should he do? He begged Göbl for an immediate reply. . . . The Prague Conservatory was paying him only 1200 gulden a year.

These were excellent terms, insuring a safe future for Dvořák and his loved ones. On the other hand, he was a family man, impassioned lover of his native land, unhappy when he had to leave home even for the few days' trip to England. He did make one concession: he would be willing to conduct the series of concerts in America. But Mrs. Thurber did not give in, telegrams rained, until finally he received a contract merely requiring his signature.

He was to arrive in New York, September 28th, 1892; half his salary to be paid in advance that spring (1891), the rest on a monthly basis in New York. All his other conditions had been accepted. There was nothing else for him to do but say yes. Furthermore, the Prague Conservatory gave him two years' leave from the fall of 1892.

That December (1891), the decision having been made, he felt inwardly more calm, and returned to the writing of his Overtures. But, again he had to break off their composition. Together with the violinist, Lachner, and the 'cellist, Wihan, he was offered a concert tour through Bohemia and Moravia. The chief feature of their repertoire was to be

Dvořák's "Dumky" Trio they had played before. For his partners in the Trio he would have to provide further instrumental works. There were the "Mazurek" and several other arrangements for Lachner, but he had nothing for Wihan.

About the end of 1891, Dvořák finished composing a *Rondo for Piano and 'Cello*, Opus 94. (The piano part was later also set for small orchestra.) Imbued with the melancholy of his approaching leave-taking, the Rondo is closely associated in his mind with thoughts of the homeland; so much so, that, later on in America, Dvořák was impelled to dedicate his 'Cello Concerto in B minor, full of nostalgia and joyful anticipations of the homecoming, to his friend Wihan, whose playing haunted him. For the Moravian tour, Dvořák rearranged for 'cello the Eighth Slavonic Dance and his "Woodland Peace" from "Scenes in the Bohemian Forest". (Both piano parts were likewise later arranged for small orchestra.)

The tour lasted from January 3rd to May 29th, 1892, Dvořák returning now and then to Prague. Hearing of the American negotiations, Simrock repented his part in the conflict with Dvořák and wrote to say he wanted to publish immediately the Dumky Trio and the Three Overtures. Dvořák, in no hurry, finally replied that he would rather wait until next season.

There he sat peacefully in Vysoká and was not even to be enticed away for the Prague National Theater's performance of his "Dimitrij" on June 2nd, during the Vienna International Music and Theater Exposition of 1892. It was the same memorable guest engagement that brought forth the triumph of Smetana's "The Bartered Bride", launched on its world-wide career.

It was no light matter to follow up the very next evening with "Dimitrij", especially as in Vienna they were obviously bent on placing in competition Dvořák, the friend of Brahms, with Smetana, "the Wagnerian." Notwithstanding, Dvořák's opera did not fail to leave a profound impression. He himself was far more affected by the mining catastrophe in Příbram on June 15th, in which many lost their lives, particularly as Dvořák in Vysoká was in daily contact with the townspeople of Příbram.

He had received a letter from Mrs. Thurber saying that he was expected to sail from Bremen on September 17th, bringing with him a new work to be performed on October 12th in commemoration of the Fourth Centennial Celebration of Columbus' discovery of America. He was promised that he would shortly receive the required American poem. Since it did not arrive, and as he did not want to appear with empty hands, he spent the month of July composing a *"Te Deum" for Soprano and Bass Solos with Mixed Choir and Orchestra* (published by Simrock, 1896, Opus 103).

The Te Deum was not performed until October 21st, a few days after the Columbus Celebration, together with the Three Overtures, in Dvořák's first concert in America. The work is an open-air paean of praise with joyful choruses and moving solo parts; this magnificent music, although intended for America, is not without some Bohemian national coloring. It is in four parts, like a symphony, the conclusion reverting to the material of the beginning. Due to the usual erroneous opus number, when the Te Deum became known in Europe it was listed among his "American" compositions; people tried to read into it harmonic and instrumental peculiarities characteristic of that period.

As soon as he had finished the Te Deum score, the promised American text arrived: "The American Flag", a poem by John Rodman Drake who died in 1820 at the age of 25. With only six weeks left before sailing, Dvořák nevertheless wanted to show his good will and sketched out the work; the score, begun in New York, was not finished until January, 1893. The poem, recalling in patriotic terms the War of 1812 and the ultimate triumph and freedom of the United States, is to be found in American school-readers.

"The American Flag" is especially fascinating by reason of its infectious gaiety and, above all, its ringing appeal to the spirit of freedom so close to the heart of Dvořák. Its form is similar to that of the Te Deum, with the conclusion the same as the beginning, only with Dvořák's typical chromatic ascent (A flat to A). The contralto, tenor and bass solos frequently sing the choral parts ahead of the choir.

The Flag of Freedom, born of the stars and the rising sun, is entrusted to the Eagle, sovereign of mountain-heights. There is an Hymn to the Eagle and an Hymn to the Flag, sung by the brave fighters—infantry, cavalry and marines—who gather round it. This is followed by a poetic apotheosis of the Flag that shall become a symbol of Freedom to the world. The March introducing the soldiers' oath of allegiance to the Flag is remarkable for its Czechish national coloring; it sounds almost like a polka, a message of greeting from Bohemia to the New World.

Its spirit of fraternal affection and unstrained naturalness certainly made an impression when it was first heard, but that was not until May, 1895, when Dvořák had already left America, for the last time. It seems that the composer himself had forgotten all about this work. His wife finally prevailed upon him to show it to Schirmer, who published it in 1895 as Opus 102 and saw to its performance.

Some time before leaving for America, Dvořák made the acquaintance in a Prague music-shop of a young Czech, Joseph J. Kovařík, from Spillville, Iowa, son of a music-teacher from Protivín in Bohemia who, emigrated to the United States, had become the choir conductor in Spillville's St. Wenceslas Church. Young Kovařík having just completed his violin studies at the Prague Conservatory, Dvořák begged him to postpone his return to America until the fall when they could travel together. In the meantime, he invited Kovařík to stay at Vysoká. Kovařík was naturally of great help in preparations for the journey.

Dvořák decided to take his wife and two of the children, Ottilie and Anton. It was hard for him to leave the rest at home; on the other hand, he was certain to be seeing the children and all his friends the following summer. This was his last word to them as the train pulled out of the Prague Railway Station on September 15th, 1892.

His ship, the S. S. "Saale" weighed anchor from Bremen

on the 17th. From Southampton, on the 18th, Dvořák wired the family in Vysoká to say they were all well. The crossing lasted nine days. They had one day of bad weather when practically everybody on board was ill. Not so, Dvořák, the sole passenger to appear in the dining-saloon.

On the 26th, they dropped anchor in New York Harbor to await the Quarantine. (There was cholera raging in Europe.) Not until the next afternoon were they allowed to set foot on American soil, to be welcomed by the Secretary of the Conservatory and, especially gratifying to Dvořák, by a delegation of Czech-Americans. The first thing he did was to telegraph the children in Bohemia, telling of their safe arrival.

Music in America in the Nineties

DvoŘÁK was not only in a new country but in a new world of music. There were still very few American composers who could have written music in consonance with this newness. There was no real artistic center and scarcely any organized musical life in most of the cities and states farther West. Interpretative music, on the other hand, especially in New York, was of a respectably high standard. There was plenty of money to attract European artists of reputation.

The Metropolitan Opera, founded in 1883, was an instance of this, having at its disposal conductors and singers of such a calibre that it could produce in the original tongues the chief popular works of an international repertoire. The Philharmonic Society, founded in 1842, gave a season of 16 concerts conducted by Anton Seidl; the general rehearsal of each concert was also open to the public. Seidl likewise conducted in Brooklyn. Another orchestra, the New York Symphony Society, was conducted by Walter Damrosch; it was not merged with the Philharmonic until the season of 1928-29.

The famous Boston Symphony Orchestra was at that time conducted by Artur Nikisch. Choral works were performed by the Brooklyn Academy of Music under Dossert, the New York Oratorio Society under Damrosch, and other leading choral organizations. The outstanding chamber-music organizations were the Kneisel Quartet and the Beethoven String Quartet in which Dvořák's friend, Kovařík, (from 1895 onwards violinist with the Philharmonic Orchestra) later assisted. There was certainly no lack of solo recitals; in 1892, for instance, d'Albert, Paderewski and Marteau were heard at Carnegie Hall.

With regard to music-schools, things were not so flourishing. As business enterprises, they had to entice students who could afford to pay. Students were only required to complete courses; they were not obliged to undertake lengthy studies or systematic work; diplomas were unknown. Mrs. Thurber's "National Conservatory of Art", a private school, was distinguished from all the rest in that it was actually run as an educational institution. For this reason and because it only accepted payment from those who could afford it, Congress had passed a Resolution giving it its title.

When his first astonishment at such conditions had abated, Dvořák was much impressed by the sincerity of those about him and by their genuine willingness to learn. At all events, he felt that he could work here and accomplish things, too; that he could do something to improve the standards of musical taste and performance. He was welcomed with great honors. Even before his arrival, Mrs. Thurber had it announced, expressly in honor of the famous composer Dvořák who was to become the new Director of the Conservatory, that a prize would be given for the best opera by an American-born composer; Dvořák was to judge the scores.

Newspapers and magazines published his photograph with articles about him. The American public already knew his works; now they heard about the man and a great deal to the effect that he was a "self-made-man" which especially pleased them. He had no sooner arrived at the Hotel Clarendon, (formerly on 18th Street, now no longer standing), than he was besieged by journalists. His interviewers were interested in every trifling detail of his life. They discovered that he didn't look as "wild" as they had expected; on the contrary, he had a pleasant face (minutely described) and agreeable manners.

The more objective appraisals often tended to exaggerated and false statements. American dramatists were urged to write him a worthwhile opera-text. People with a lively imagination prophesied that Dvořák would call forth a new American music out of the soil, that he would surely discover and develop unknown American composers; at the very least, he would himself compose great "American" masterpieces. His Czechish compatriots welcomed him with hearty good will; on November 9th, they held a gala reception in his honor at which 3000 guests were present.

Four days after his arrival, on the First of October, Dvořák was introduced by Mrs. Thurber to the teaching-staff of the Conservatory, then situated at 128 East 17th Street. Much to their delight he greeted them in excellent English.

Among other teachers at the Conservatory were: James T. Huneker; Henry T. Finck, for the History of Music; Max Spicker, Theory; and Adele Margulies, with whom Ottilie Dvořák soon began studying piano. Dvořák's friend, Kovařík, taking up his quarters with Dvořák's family, likewise became a member of the Conservatory staff, remaining a faithful collaborator during Dvořák's entire American stay.

Although the management had placed a piano at his disposal, Madame Dvořák found the hotel too expensive; he himself preferred quieter lodgings. So they moved into a five-room apartment at 327 East 17th Street, not far from the School, so that Dvořák had only a few minutes to walk. Steinway furnished a piano gratis.

In a New York with no skyscrapers, very little traffic, and no motor vehicles, Dvořák was surprised to find himself extraordinarily "at home": the life of the times and the cleanliness of the city both pleased him; he felt perfectly at ease with the unexacting democratic ways of Americans. He considered it an exemplary institution which permitted the laboring man to hear at popular prices the same concert to which the middle-class had to pay higher admission.

"Why should not the ordinary citizen, hard at work all week, be able to make the acquaintance of Bach and Beethoven?" was the way he put it.

His daily life, habits and hobbies remained as much as possible the same. True, his hobbies required much more attention and consumed more time than at home, but they brought him fresh revelations. Chief among these was his passion for locomotives. A locomotive was to him the highest achievement of the human inventive faculty and he often said that he would give all his symphonies had he been able to invent the locomotive.

In the New York of those days, it was not so easy to get to the railway stations; they were inconveniently situated and only travelers were allowed on the platforms. There was slight sympathy for locomotive statisticians even when they were famous composers. He used to drive one whole hour to 155th Street in order to see the trains for Chicago go thundering by; Dvořák was tremendously impressed by their speed.

The Harbor, however, lay close at hand and on sailing-days anybody could go on board ship. Dvořák did not wait to hear this twice. He fell into the habit of visiting each great vessel that left New York, making a thorough inspection of every feature from bow to stern, interviewing Captain, officers and crew until it was sailing-time. He remained on the pier until the last minute in order to see the liners with their attendant tugs sheer off into mid-stream. When he had to be at the Conservatory, he at least made every effort to see them sail.

Twice a week he went down to the docks, twice a week he visited a railway station, and the other two days he went walking in Central Park. Evenings were spent in fascinating speculation as to where a certain ship would be about that time and how many knots she could make. He knew to the day and hour what ships were arriving and departing, and prided himself on being able to address his letters to Bohemia, stating exactly on which ship they would be carried.

For the rest, his love of Nature had to be satisfied with Central Park. There were pigeons, too, in this extraordinary town, though you did not get to know them so well as in Vysoká.

He was always an early riser and persisted in going to bed at an early hour. Social gatherings, theaters and concerts that interfered with bedtime he avoided as much as possible. The composer, Heinrich Zöllner, at that time conductor of the German "Liederkranz" choral society, relates that he once invited Dvořák to conduct his own Overture, "In Nature's Realm"; Dvořák declined because he did not like to go out in the evening. The single exception he made was for the Concerts of the Philharmonic Society. Otherwise, in three years, apart from the Philharmonic, he attended only two symphony concerts, two chamber-music recitals and two opera performances.

He and his family took all their meals at a nearby boarding-house. Nervous about crossing the street, Dvořák never went for a walk except with a companion, usually Kovařík. In the afternoon, he liked to read the papers in the Café

Boulevard on Second Avenue. There they had the "Na-rodní Listy" from Prague, and of course he knew on what days it arrived. Here in a foreign land, political news did not excite him so much as at home; whenever he read the Prague parliamentary debates, at most he would grumble a bit. He was not much concerned about American internal politics; nevertheless, he listened attentively and, when topics of the day were discussed, liked to have everything carefully explained.

At home in the evenings he loved to play cards; Kovařík had to learn the game. But when Dvořák had lost several times in succession, he would become very angry and toss the cards in the air. He soon got over it when Kovařík would propose to contribute his winnings towards the doll they were going to take home to his youngest daughter in Vysoká. Sometimes Dvořák would spend the evenings with Seidl in the Café Fleischmann on Broadway at 10th Street.

Dvořák was now quite happy in the peaceful way of life he had established in New York. Only occasionally he suffered acute pangs of homesickness for his children, and the friends and scenes of his native land. He wrote frequently, with loving greetings and admonitions to his children; and he used to beg his friends to make him happy by writing as often as possible.

Dvořák and American Folk-music

THREE TIMES A WEEK, Dvořák gave a two-hour lesson in composition, and twice a week he conducted the Conservatory Orchestra for two hours, a duty less to his liking.

The school instrumentalists were only moderately trained and they ran off as soon as they could, in order to make money. He proposed to Mrs. Thurber that the teaching plan be reorganized, but did not meet with ready comprehension on her part.

The composition periods were much more agreeable. Among the pupils were some real talents: there were Rubin Goldmark, a nephew of Carl Goldmark; Harry Rowe Shelley; Laura S. Collins, later a well-known song-composer; Harvey Worthington Loomis and Camille Zeckwer. Finally, there was William Arms Fisher, who later wrote a popular arrangement of The Largo from "The New World Symphony" for choir with baritone solo.

Dvořák himself remained, of course, the same sort of teacher he had been in Prague.

Several Negroes soon turned up among his classes. Dvořák encountered them with sympathy if for no other reason than because he knew they were excluded from so many walks of life. An announcement in the newspapers, in May, 1893, extended an especially cordial invitation to Negroes. How greatly Dvořák loved their music will be seen.

As a conductor, Dvořák enjoyed signal success. His first concert in Carnegie Hall, on October 21st, 1892, took the form of a gala reception in his honor. The "Star-Spangled Banner" was sung, the founder of the Boston Symphony Orchestra welcomed Dvořák to America and, at the conclusion of the program, consisting of the Te Deum and Three Overtures, the National Hymn was again sung. Another great success was the Philharmonic Concert on November 17th, on which occasion Busoni played the Beethovan Concerto in G major, conducted by Seidl, and thereafter Dvořák conducted his own D major Symphony. The audience was still applauding long after Dvořák had gone home. Eleven o'clock was too late for him.

In Boston, on November 29th and 30th, Dvořák conducted two performances of his Requiem, one of them at popular prices, for working men. This again was a triumph for Dvořák, who in his letters had much to say of the Orchestra's splendid reading under his baton. Another banquet in his honor followed.

On April 6th, 1893, he conducted in New York, this time the Philharmonic Society, his program including the Hussite Overture and the Spectre's Bride. Besides in his own concerts, his works were being frequently performed elsewhere.

Several critics, dyed-in-the-wool Wagnerians, railed at Dvořák as a reactionary. He wrote home that he would like to have more enemies; he could stand it. Incidentally, about this time, Dvořák was elected a member of the Berlin Academy of Arts.

Naturally there were those who were "disappointed", those to whom Dvořák's coming did not seem to "pay for itself" quickly enough. Now and then there were rumors that he admitted as much, that he had had enough, that he wanted to return to Europe.

Perhaps the Conservatory had disseminated such rumors in order to be able to ward them off with all the more effect.

Mrs. Thurber published a declaration that, in the short time he had been here, Dvořák had accomplished much more than had been expected. He was, she said, an extraordinary worker and an exemplary director who, in contrast to most creative spirits, was concerned about every smallest detail. She announced a further prize competition.

Newspaper interviewers were ordered to get stories from Dvořák; how he liked America, what he thought of American music, and whether or not he was satisfied with his work. There was a sensational feature article in the New York Herald of May 21st, 1893. In it Dvořák stressed the importance of Negro music for America, challenging American composers to make use of the wealth of material in this treasury of genuine folk-music. His attention had been called to Negro music by one of the instructors on the staff of the Conservatory, the music-critic, James Huneker, and by his pupil, H. T. Burleigh, whom he often asked to sing the Spirituals for him.

This article aroused a great deal of comment, exactly as Mrs. Thurber and the newspaper writers had intended. Following up this story, the Herald "interviewed" various great European musicians and music-scholars, asking what they thought of Dvořák's views and opinions. Among those allegedly approached were Bruckner, Brahms, Rubinstein, Mandyczewsky and Hanslick. Some of them were said to have replied that they were waiting with intense interest to see results.

Another article in the New York Herald, likewise supposed to have been written on the basis of utterances by

Dvořák, emphasized still more plainly that America, indeed, possessed a folk-music—the Negro Spirituals and their derivatives—and that therefore this country in the long run was bound to develop its own great music. It was already possible to study music in America without having to go abroad.

By this time, however, Dvořák felt that enough had been written: he had perhaps said too much, or he had kept silence too long with regard to the things that were said in his name.

It was not until 1895 that another article appeared, this time in Harper's Magazine, expressly written by Dvořák in collaboration with Edwin Emerson. In this article, Dvořák made excuses for his temerity as a foreigner speaking about American problems. He felt himself impelled, however, as a teacher of music, to demand why, in a land of so much opportunity, enthusiasm and patriotism, so little was being done on behalf of music?

In Europe, he declared, music was everywhere a matter of national interest, the state supplying the money with which to further and develop musicians of talent. He himself had for many years received a stipendium from the Austrian Government. On the other hand, in New York conditions were such that he had lost a very gifted pupil because his employer had told the young man that he would not even permit music in his workers' free time.

There were as yet, he continued, scarcely any American publishers of serious music. Just as little were there any operas in English; and this despite the fact that this country had plenty of good voices and its own folk-music, that of the colored people, as beautiful and distinctive as perhaps only the folk-music of the Scotch and Irish.

The composers of this country should make the most of their music; he suggested that we even ought to collect the words and music of our street-cries. Dvořák felt it his task to guide and encourage young American composers in the development of their own native sources. In this way America would certainly soon become a land of music just as it was already the land of technical achievement, a land that had a great literature and, most priceless of all, had established its own freedom.

Whatever our opinions on this subject, Dvořák was certainly one of the first musicians who, even before Americans themselves, recognized the individual character, wealth and variety of stimulus to be derived from our Negro and Amerindian music. Many students hold the view, hinted at by Dvořák in his article, that America's so-called Negro Music is in reality a mixture of the musics of the white, black and Amerindian races: something indigenous and typical of America alone.

Our American Negro Spirituals and plantation-songs, as we know them today, arose at least in part at camp-meetings and revivals where the slaves made use of and simulated the traditional hymns they had been taught. But they did so in their own fashion, adorning them with their own melodic peculiarities and that unerring sense of rhythm they had brought with them from Africa. Amerindian influences doubtless played some role.

The result is pentatonic melody—a musical scale without the fourth and seventh step, common to many primitive peoples and periods—having a minor key with a lowered seventh and a style of syncopation revealing traces of a Scottish element (likewise characteristic of Slavic and Hungarian music). To Dvořák, such syncopation was perfectly familiar as innate in Czechish songs and dances.

The unspoilt, primal sources of American Negro music were also recognized by Delius who, in his preface to a book of Spirituals, several decades later, concurs with Dvořák, even maintaining that, when the time comes for America to give to the world a truly great composer, he will surely have Negro blood in his veins.

"From the New World" Symphony

AT ALL EVENTS, this music it was that inspired Dvořák to write his American Symphony and to compose several chamber-music works while in this country. He also undoubtedly received stimulus from Amerindian music: the frequent repetition of tonic and dominant, the plagal cadence and peculiar drum-rhythms. Would it be correct to say that, in so doing, Dvořák incorporated American folk-melodies in his works? A great deal has been written and said on this subject. A careless word let fall by Seidl, calling the New World Symphony "a lot of Indian music", an appellation utterly unjustified, probably moved Kretzschmar, in his "Guide to Concert Music" ("Führer durch den Konzertsaal") to talk about "original American melodies" as embodied in this Symphony.

After Dvořák's death, William Ritter asked the surviving members of his family what they had to say about this. He was told the same thing Dvořák had already said: The New World Symphony contains no "original American melodies", but it is composed out of a spiritual affinity with American folk-music. If we compare certain Spirituals like "Swing low sweet chariot", "Somebody is knockin' ", "I am seekin' for a city", "Roll Jordan Roll", "Didn't my Lord deliver Daniel", etc., with The New World Symphony or with the Quartet Op. 96, we may perhaps be inclined to feel that the latter betray a hint of reminiscence here and there.

Even supposing they did, Dvořák was such a master that he could without any pangs of conscience have allowed himself such liberties. If he had deliberately borrowed, that would not have detracted in the least from his fame. He would simply have been using "citations". Consciously, however, he had always disdained direct citation, even from his native Bohemian and Moravian folk-music.

In 1900, when Nedbal was about to conduct the New World Symphony in Berlin, Dvořák sent him Kretzschmar's analysis, with the remark: "But leave out that nonsense about my having made use of original American melodies; I have only composed in the spirit of such American national melodies." And on another occasion, Dvořák calls the works he composed during his American period "genuine Bohemian music".

The dispute about all this is tedious and simply shows a wanton lack of perception. Such an artist as Dvořák could hardly have reacted in happier fashion to the tremendous impressions of the New World and, at the same time, to its folk-music to which he felt himself closely akin. He certainly was not obsessed by any racial muddiness of thinking and so could give himself up to the enjoyment of that magic exercised by American folk-music.

In his American compositions, he was moved not only by the spirit of these folk-songs but also, to a certain extent, by the unexacting standards and freedom from prejudice of the 'New World.' For in these works composed in America, theme follows theme without going into prolonged development such as is otherwise characteristic of Dvořák (and Schubert). On the other hand, in the sovereign right of his artistic license, yet bound by the ties of his native land (and how gladly bound!), he would often transpose and employ the very same motives in Bohemian idiom. Syncopes, of course, were no novelty to him. One of the main attractions of the New World Symphony is that both elements, American and Czechish, are so effectively used and, beneath the sway of such an expansive spirit as Dvořák's, reveal a definite kinship.

Similarly, the answer is patent to the simple-minded question whether or not in these works Dvořák was trying to call into being a genuine American music. Anybody who knew him would never attribute to him any such intention. It cannot be too often reiterated that Dvořák could only write *his own* music. Indeed, he could not even have shown one of his students, or any other American composer, how they ought to create "American music". He remained himself and his work had its own individual significance.

Apart from all this, we should mention another influence on the Dvořák of those years and on his works of that period: this was Henry Wadsworth Longfellow in whose poem, "The Song of Hiawatha", the old American Indian legends are interwoven. In Longfellow's saga, Hiawatha is depicted as a sort of national hero and savior of the Indians, liberating his people from the sorcery of dark demons, teaching his kinsmen the arts of agriculture and picture-writing, and decreeing the laws of goodness and love. He foresees the coming of the White people and seeks to awaken understanding for them among his own. When he believes his mission accomplished, he disappears into the primeval forest whence he had come.

Dvořák, who made the acquaintance of this poem in a Czechish translation, was spell-bound by the dignity of the Indian legends and the descriptions of the American landscape. There was some talk of shaping this material into an opera libretto, or at least a cantata, for him. Perhaps Dvořák entertained the idea; but he realized that, for the purpose of an opera, Hiawatha, in spite of all its lyric beauty, did not provide much dramatic possibility.

During the last few weeks of 1892, while he was still working on "The American Flag" cantata, out of the sum of all these stimuli arose the germ of what was to be a great, new work. Five of Dvořák's note-books, evidently used alternately, bear witness to this. In them are to be found many motives, some for later works, and some dated.

The very first entry, in December 1892, contains the primal form of the slow introduction to the New World Symphony. On the same day he makes a note of the theme that he was later to use for the variations in the String Quintet in E flat major; incidentally, the same melody that he had thought of for a new American National Anthem:

He never got round to composing it, however. But these sketch-books contain many another theme of that period, one of which is to be found in the later "Rusalka", and one in the Eighth "Humoresque".

Dvořák came to an important decision shortly after New Year's, 1893. Hitherto he had definitely counted upon returning to Bohemia in the early summer. Now, however, it was proposed that he should take advantage of the opportunity to make the acquaintance of America farther West. And Hiawatha urged him on. A prominent newspaper publisher, Bohemian by birth, who owned "The Omaha Bee", invited Dvořák to come and visit him. The deciding vote was cast by Kovařík, who every evening would tell him how beautiful was his home-town of Spillville, Iowa; besides there were so many Czechs in the vicinity, a lot of fine people from Písek and Protivín, who would be thrilled. . . .

To cut a long story short, one day about mid-February, Dvořák came home from the Conservatory and told his wife that he had declined an invitation to the Carolinas because he wanted to go to Spillville: he was going to send for the other four children in Bohemia, have them come over, and they would all spend the summer together in Spillville; he and his whole family would therefore not return to Bohemia until the following year. Kovařík had to write home to his parents in Spillville, asking them to take a house for the Dvořáks.

Dvořák cabled the children in Bohemia at once: his widowed sister-in-law was to bring them over. To his friends at home, Dvořák wrote saying with how much joy he anticipated visiting his own countrymen in this foreign land. It seemed, he said, that they had their own Czechish school and a Church with a pastor from Wittingau. In Spillville, he was told, there were two pairs of horses waiting for him, pigeons as in Vysoká and even his favorite Czech cardgame. True, it was a far cry, farther than from Kremsier to London (the addressee lived in Kemsier), but by this time he had become completely American and did not even think of distance.

He was already working on the Symphony. It was to be his Ninth and, as with several other masters, this Ninth was to be his last. In the three weeks beginning January 10th, he had completed the sketches for the first three movements; the Fourth he did not begin to put into form until he had already written the score of the other three. On May 24th, the work was finished, composed in its entirety in

New York City. He made a few changes in the Second Movement after his return from Spillville. It was not christened *"From The New World"* until mid-November.

Perhaps slightly under the influence of their triumphal success, Dvořák in a later letter to Göbl characterizes The New World Symphony and his other two "American" chamber-music works as his greatest. The New World Symphony is one of the most often played in musical literature, and throughout America there is hardly an orchestra that is not prepared to perform it year after year.

Taken as a whole, its simplicity, lucidity and homogeneity are superb. Each succeeding movement takes over in prominent position the leading themes of the foregoing, nevertheless without programmatic "significance". The genius of a born musician here reacts to his experience of the New World, of New York and of the mighty forces of primeval Nature as yet apprehended only through poetic imagery. In addition, there is his nostalgia for his beloved native land, to which this Symphony in particular ("a homesick work") seems continually to be sending greetings.

At the very outset, the slow introduction to the First Movement reveals characteristic American syncopations. The New World offers the composer two themes in the Allegro:

This is an invention exactly in the style of American folk-music: a downward leading-tone, reiterated circlings about a central tone, the monotone D of the horns, the primitive fifths in the bass. Finally, the no less American

Compare this with the Spiritual, "Swing Low, Sweet Chariot".

The beautiful Largo is intended to remind us of the burial of Minnehaha, the companion of Hiawatha; the elegy of the middle section recalls Hiawatha's lament at her grave; the notebook entitles this "Legend". Seidl, the first to conduct this work, denoted the Largo: "Desolation of the Prairie in the Far West"!

In all this exotic coloring, however, Dvořák's longing for the homeland breaks through: the third theme of the Movement, reminiscent of "Rusalka" and of the "Wood-pigeon", is not without its effect. The pentatonic melody of the first theme, carried by the English horn, is unequivocally American:

In the further course of a crescendo, besides the first subject of the Largo, the first and third theme of the First Movement are superimposed one upon the other. The Scherzo, again inspired by Longfellow, purports to recall an Indian dance. It is soon transformed into a grotesque waltz—and suddenly, in the trio, we seem to find ourselves in a Bohemian village inn, where Schubert himself might be present:

The Scherzo returns; in the coda, the First Movement is again cited. In the Finale, there is another American-tinctured first subject and, in contrast, a Czech song, the whole culminating in a tower-upon-tower recurrence of themes from the Largo, Scherzo and Finale. In this, as in earlier works by Dvořák, we recognize that the themes are actually interrelated. The style is beautifully integrated.

Seidl, Wagner's friend and collaborator, "consecrated", as it were, in 1886, at Bayreuth, almost ten years younger than Dvořák (Seidl died at the early age of forty-eight), conducted the world première of the New World Symphony on December 16th, 1893, in Carnegie Hall. This was a phenomenal triumph even for Dvořák. The Symphony had to be repeated twice the same season, and was heard, soon after its New York première, in Boston. Published by Simrock in 1894 as Op. 95, it was performed that year in Prague and London, and in 1896 in Vienna. Its suc-

THE HOUSE IN WHICH HE LIVED AT SPILLVILLE, IOWA

THE ORGAN WHICH DVOŘÁK PLAYED

cess was everywhere unparalleled. There was talk of arranging the Largo for voices. This was done, and other arrangements soon followed.

On the last page of the score, next to his usual " Thank God!", Dvořák wrote: "The children have arrived in Southampton. We received a cable at 1:33 this afternoon." In his joy over this event, Dvořák forgot, while writing the last few bars, to write in the part for the trombones, as it turned out at rehearsals. Beside himself with excitement, he dashed hither and yon. One week later, on May 31st, the boat was in. An hour ahead of time, Dvořák was on the pier.

At last, Dvořák had his whole family together. He was almost out of his mind with joy. Three days later, on June 3rd, 1893, his entire party of eleven—Dvořák and his wife, the six children, Mme. Koutecká, who had brought them over, Kovařík and a housemaid—plentifully supplied with provisions, boarded the train for Spillville.

Spillville—Further American Works

THE STATE OF IOWA, in the northeast corner of which lies Spillville, is about half-way across the Continent. At that time, with a population of 2,500,000, Iowa had absorbed about 60,000 Czechs, mostly from southern Bohemia, especially peasants emigrated from the vast Schwarzenberg estates, who had come to America to satisfy their hunger for land. Today, the Czechish element still plays an important role in Iowa. There are Czechish schools and churches, shops, societies, even banks, and some of the villages bear the same Czechish names, such as Tábor, Písek, Protivín and others.

Naturally, it was no small matter to undertake a journey to Spillville, about 1200 miles. But Dvořák did not mind long railway journeys; he always found something to do, was full of curiosity and delighted with everything. The whole family was together, they had plenty to eat and still more to see. The only things that upset him were the many stops and the lack of beer. They arrived in Chicago on the forenoon of June 4th and spent ten long hours sight-seeing and resting.

The following morning, Dvořák beheld the Mississippi for the first time, and before noon their rail-journey came to an end at Calmar. Here they were heartily received by Kovařík's father, Johann J. Kovařík, by the pastor of Spillville, Thomas Bílý, and another clerical compatriot, Vrba. Dvořák could easily see with what joy and pride they were waiting for him. From Calmar they had to drive five miles to Spillville.

Founded by a Bavarian by the name of Spielmann, Spillville is actually the oldest Czechish settlement in America; about 1854, eleven families from Moldautein in Bohemia settled here, giving the place a markedly Czechish character, so much so that other settlers—German, Swiss, and Norwegian—of the second generation, were forced to speak Czechish. Spillville today has 329 inhabitants, and there are about the same number in the likewise purely Czechish village of Protivín, Iowa.

Dvořák was enchanted with everything he saw and heard. He felt altogether "at home" in the prosperous and tidy village with its comfortable houses and its Church of St. Wenceslas. The beautiful surroundings, too, reminded him of the homeland: here were fruitful fields, thick woods, and not far away, the Turky river. The spacious one-storey, eight-room house on Main Street (still standing) which they had found for him, was just the thing. It was owned by a German, Herr Schmidt. Kovařík, of course, was staying with his parents near-by.

Dvořák, the master, lived here precisely as he had in Vysoká. The first day he was up at four, exploring the countryside. At last, after eight months, he could again hear the birds sing! He arrived at Church on the dot for seven o'clock Mass, sat down at the organ and, much to the surprise and delight of the congregation, began to play the old Czechish hymns.

With that alone he had won their hearts. He received the Czechish appellation roughly corresponding to "Squire Dvořák", particularly since the local butcher was also called Dvořák. Returning from his morning walk, Dvořák always stopped for a few minutes' chat with the shoemaker, whose name was Benda, like the teacher in Dvořák's later opera, "Jacobin".

It was not easy to find a piano. Since there was no other solution, they had to cart over the one belonging to the Kovaříks, which was then thoroughly polished and tuned. When evening came, just as in Vysoká, Dvořák used to sit down to a game of cards. Then again, late at night, he would sometimes be heard playing old Bohemian folk-songs on his violin.

Dvořák was a very happy man.

As soon as his peace of mind was established, in the midst of his beloved Nature and this second "native land", something drove him to work. On June 8th, three days after his arrival, he had already begun a new composition, the *String Quartet in F major*, Op. 96. Three days later, the sketches were ready. "Thank God! I am content: it has gone very quickly" he wrote down after the last bar. On the 23rd, he had finished the score.

Attempting to interpret his many fresh impressions, this whole work exhales an air of delight in his new-found refuge. Departing from his usual custom, as he had done in the New World Symphony, here again he places his themes in short settings, one after another, instead of developing them through to their logical conclusion. Imbued with the spirit of his immediate environment, these themes are exotically tinted. This newly adopted manner of his corresponds to the American character as he saw it and attempted to portray it in his forms. The peculiarities of construction thus arising are among the chief reasons why Dvořák's American chamber-music works have become so popular.

The three main themes of the First Movement, depicting that idyllic Nature immediately about him, are interspersed with echoes of the Far West. Beauty and joy are the very breath of their being:

The slow Second Movement, pervaded with alien melancholy, is a nostalgic singing over ostinato syncopations. A frolicsome Scherzo replies: the two intervals of a single theme, related to the first motive of the beginning, alternate with each other. A counterpoint in the high register of the first violin

came to him from some "damned bird (red, only with black wings)" that kept singing:

(virtually, a rhythmically altered version of the preceding theme.)

The last movement is swift-paced and gay.

The Quartet in F major (Simrock, 1894), together with the *String Quintet in E flat* (a discussion of which follows), was played for the first time by the Kneisel Quartet in Boston on New Year's day, 1894. On January 12th, Kneisel played both works in New York; Carnegie Hall was crowded to the doors; the success was perhaps even greater than that of the New World Symphony.

Dvořák, however, to whom the Quartet had already brought so much happiness, was far too impatient to wait for a public performance. He insisted that it had to be tried out at once, in Spillville! He himself played the first violin, and assuredly had not played anything so difficult for the past twenty years. Papa Kovařík played second violin; his daughter, viola; and her brother, 'cello. They also played Dvořák's latest work, as usual a sister-composition, the Quintet in E flat.

Three days after finishing the Quartet he had begun the Quintet, and on July 27th it was finished. Just about this time, Dvořák had his first experience of hearing American Indian songs. Three roving Iroquois had come to Spillville as "medicine men". Every evening they sang and danced to their drums, and Dvořák never missed their performance. Hence, according to Kovařík, the drum-like rhythm and strange theme in the First Movement of the Quintet are derived.

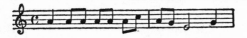

In the Scherzo, the Second Movement, accompanied by the drum-rhythm,

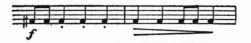

there is an exotic theme alternating with another of a Czechish national hue!

Another "outlandish" feature, for Dvořák, is the Minore in place of a trio. The slow Third Movement introduces the theme Dvořák had sketched in December, 1892, with the idea of using it for a new American national hymn; here it appears with some figurations. The American element in this theme is contrasted with another, essentially Bohemian, somehow reminiscent of Beethoven's Harp Quartet. The expansive gaiety of the Rondo Finale, again with alien intonation, is impressive. However closely related to the Quartet in F major, the Quintet is more definitely stated, more self-aware and conscious of the outside world than the former, which is an exceptionally introspective work, engendered by Dvořák's personal experience of Nature and of life. Quartet and Quintet have shared alike the widespread enthusiasm for Dvořák's "American" chamber-music.

The first stages of his reconciliation with Simrock were covered during that peaceful period in Spillville. About the beginning of 1893, Dvořák had decided to have all his new works published by Novello. But in mid-June, he received a letter from Simrock, begging for some new works and complaining that he now only had news of Dvořák by way of Hanslick. Dvořák replied: "From now on, thank God, I compose only for my own pleasure; I am practically independent. . . . I can therefore wait for publication"—especially when, he goes on to say, there are certain considerations affecting their business relations, as Simrock, his old Berlin friend, can confirm by referring to his files.

None the less, Dvořák listed his latest works: The Three Overtures, Rondo for 'Cello, the 'cello arrangement of "Woodland Peace", The New World Symphony, The Quartet and Quintet. Simrock could have all these for 7,500 marks. The latter accepted and, because of the great distance and necessity for haste in publishing, asked Brahms to undertake the proof-reading.

Brahms not only agreed, but wrote Simrock: "Please tell Dvořák how much I rejoice to hear of his joy in composing!" Dvořák, deeply moved, wrote to Simrock, in February, 1894: "I can scarcely believe there is another composer in the world who would do as much!" At the same time, Dvořák cautioned Simrock about the necessity of registering American copyright, then something new for a European publishing firm.

In spite of everything, the peace and quiet of Spillville was unexpectedly disturbed. July had no sooner come than there appeared a Czech deputation from Chicago, requesting Dvořák to conduct a concert at the Chicago World's Fair on "Czechish Day". He finally agreed, especially as

Mrs. Thurber supported their plea with a telegram. But there was one condition: the leader of the deputation, Josef Vilím, formerly a pupil at the Prague Conservatory, had to sit down at once and play in Dvořák's house-quartet.

On August 6th, Dvořák left for Chicago with his wife, his daughters, Ottilie and Anna, and, of course, accompanied by Kovařík. On the seventh, they were met in Chicago by the deputation. An old admirer of Dvořák's, Theodore Thomas, Founder and Conductor of the Chicago Symphony Orchestra, welcomed him. Since 1880, Thomas had conducted at least one of Dvořák's works every year. Theodor Spiering (who later befriended Gustav Mahler in this country) was also on hand to greet Dvořák. There was, moreover, a delegation from Prague which had come to Chicago especially to take part in the "Czechish Day" festivities. And, among them, Dvořák met again his good friends, the writer, Herites, and the stage-director, Šmaha.

Dvořák went sightseeing in the city and then to the Exposition. Arrived at the Austrian Pavilion, he was welcomed by the Ziehrer Orchestra's playing one of his own Slavonic Dances. On Czechish Day, August 12th, there was a parade of 30,000 Czechs from all over the United States; at noon, in the Exposition, Dvořák conducted his G major Symphony, three of the Slavonic Dances, Op. 72, and his Overture to "Josef Kajetan Tyl" which concludes with the Czech National Hymn. There was no end to the ovations he received.

From Spillville, there was yet another journey he had to make, and no small matter at that. He had promised to visit

Mr. Rosewater, a friend of Mrs. Thurber's and a Czechish compatriot, publisher of the "Omaha Bee"; and he had likewise promised to visit Pastor Rynda in St. Paul, Minnesota. The combined distance was a journey of more than 750 miles. However, he wanted to keep his word.

Accompanied only by his wife and Kovařík, he left Calmar on September 1st, arriving at 2 A. M. in Omaha. There he was met by Rosewater, of whom Dvořák wrote home: "He is a Jew and has, they say, changed his name. But he is a well-educated man, much loved throughout America, especially in the West. He is wealthy, a Republican, exercising great political influence. Ex-President Harrison, President Cleveland and many other prominent people are among his friends."

Dvořák had no sooner descended from the train than Rosewater warned him he would have to prolong his stay because so many festivities had been arranged in his honor. Outside the station, a great crowd of Czechs was waiting to welcome him. Rosewater was an amiable host, and that morning conducted Dvořák on a tour of inspection, first to see the great printing-press of the "Omaha Bee", and then to admire the beautiful scenery. In the evening, his Czechish countrymen serenaded Dvořák.

Hearing that there were two neighbors from Vysoká living in Omaha, Dvořák much to their delight visited them the very next day. The third day, there was a gala banquet at which Kovařík played, accompanied by Dvořák. With a send-off of still further ovations Dvořák left that night for St. Paul.

In St. Paul, all three were the guests of Pastor Rynda, who came from Moravia. Here again there was a great deputation of Czechs, and nothing would do but that their famous countryman should be guest of honor at a festive banquet for 3,000! Dvořák also found time to visit the Minnehaha Falls, the beauty of which absolutely carried him away. Then and there, he wrote down on his starched cuff a theme later used in the Slow Movement of his Violin Sonatina.

On September 5th, he was back again in Spillville, declaring that nothing could get him to budge from there; it was bad enough that he had to return to New York on September 16th. When that time came, there were heartfelt adieus all round, his new-found friends well aware that he would probably never return; and, of course, he had to promise to take their greetings back to the old country. In Spillville today, they are still proud to recall that memorable visit. In a spot Dvořák especially loved, they have erected a simple monument. In 1929, twenty-five years after his death, an Iowa State Commission decided to christen the sixty-mile road from Calmar, via Spillville and Protivín, to Preston, Minnesota, the "Dvořák Highway".

On the return journey, they stopped off in Chicago for two days for the sake of the children, went on to Buffalo to see Niagara Falls, and then to Albany where they took the boat down the Hudson to New York. Unable to forget the tremendous impression left by Niagara, Dvořák said to Kovařík: "That is going to be a symphony in B minor". In Dvořák's sketch-books, there are actually motives for such a symphony, though undated; and, with the exception of a scherzo-theme that reappears in the Eighth Humoresque for Piano, they were never used.

The Second Year in America

THE HOMESICKNESS that attacked Dvořák the first few days after his return to New York was soon forgotten in his work. The family kept to themselves more than ever and no longer took their meals away from home. Dvořák finished his arrangement of the "Dumky Trio" for four hands, supervised the entrance examinations at the Conservatory, altered the Second Movement of the New World Symphony and wrote the instrumentation for his "Woodland Peace".

About this time he began to think of his Op. 100. This was to be a sort of jubilee work, something very special. It was natural therefore, in harmony with Dvořák's native modesty and love of family, that he should decide upon a jubilee composition that his children, Ottilie and Antonín, might be able to play. This was to be a short sonata for violin and piano. Begun the second half of November, it turned out to be, after all, as Dvořák wrote to Simrock, a work that adults, as well, would love to play.

This was perfectly true. The *"Sonatina" in G major* contains some of the most remarkable refinements of his melodic and harmonic ideas. In the First Movement, we note the length of the first subject and, in the development of the three themes, the unusual modulation. The "clou" of the whole is the Second Movement, conceived, like all his slow movements in America, as a Larghetto, with a pentatonic run as follows:

This is the theme that Dvořák had hastily written down when he saw the Minnehaha Falls.

Presumably without consulting Dvořák, Simrock later published various arrangements with fantastic names, such as "Indian Lullabye" or "Indian Lament" (Kreisler). It is possible, however, that Simrock may have heard from Kovařík that Dvořák really had in mind Hiawatha's brooding on the waters at play. A Scherzo with all the gaiety of a Mozart is followed by a very joyful Finale for which, in the third theme, Dvořák had saved up a special melodic surprise. This Sonatina with exquisite taste transmutes Dvořák's American impressions into a music eloquent of human-kindness. Altogether worthy to rank as his jubilee composition, it was especially dear to him: his children now had something to play for him in the evening. Their first rendition of it was, he said, his favorite première.

At all events, such a composition was a real relief to Dvořák from the urgent problems with which he was confronted. His contract with the New York Conservatory would expire in the summer of 1894, and Mrs. Thurber already wanted to know if he was thinking of extending it.

But he could not make up his mind. The advantages to him in America were great and becoming ever greater. On the other hand, his native land was calling him. What should he do?

He had also to think about the performance of the three "American" works, the Symphony, Quartet and Quintet, for which he was being besieged. These works were a bond between the New World and him, part of their common destiny. Seidl, whom he frequently met at the Café Fleischmann, was anxious to conduct the Symphony. Dvořák and Seidl got on better and better.

Seidl had to tell him all about Wagner, and Dvořák found lively rejoinders to much that he said; but they never quarreled. Dvořák later used to say that without Seidl he would have been bored to death in New York. An artist must be able to talk to artists on his own level about art and craftsmanship. It will be remembered that Dvořák finally chose Seidl to conduct the New World Symphony.

In spite of the tremendous expectations which the newspapers had done their best to arouse, there was certainly no disappointment: on the contrary, the memorable 16th of December, 1893, was a day of jubilant triumph surpassing all anticipation. Dvořák wrote to Simrock: "The papers say that no composer ever celebrated such a triumph. Carnegie Hall was crowded with the best people of New York, and the audience applauded so that, like visiting royalty, I had to take my bows repeatedly from the box in which I sat. It made me think of Mascagni in Vienna".

Immediately after the General Rehearsal, the newspapers

again launched a "questionnaire". Those musicians who were interviewed expressed their unanimous enthusiasm, although all very rightly (with the exception of Seidl) declared that the New World Symphony was not an "American" work of art. There were insistent demands for repeated hearings and also for the first performance of the two chamber-music works.

In January, the New York Conservatory gave a concert in which, with the exception of one white girl who appeared as piano virtuoso, the student musicians were all Negroes. Dvořák conducted Mendelssohn's Overture to "Midsummer Night's Dream," the first work other than his own he had conducted in America, and, thereafter, his own, very restrained arrangement of Foster's Plantation-song, "*Old Folks at Home*", for solo voices, choir and orchestra. It met with such instant appreciation that they had to play it through again. Deluged with applause, Dvořák was presented with a conductor's ivory baton. The newspapers sang a chorus of praise.

Mrs. Thurber, who evidently wanted to bind Dvořák still closer to America by having him compose another great "American work", did her best to have Longfellow's Hiawatha turned into an opera libretto for him. A special jury was to pick the best version. Nothing came of this, so the energetic Mrs. Thurber ordered a libretto from Vienna. Outside of thematic sketches, Dvořák never got any further with this plan.

Instead, he composed a new work for piano, a "*Suite in A major*", published by Simrock as Op. 98 in the same year,

1894. In the third year of his American stay, Dvořák orchestrated this Suite, known since then as Op. 98-b.

In five parts, like the Suite in D of 1879, it too, combines a personal, intimate style with marked American intonation. The first theme of the opening movement seems to begin where the Finale of the Violin Sonatina left off. It is followed by a fast Second Movement, a Third which begins like a Polonaise, and a Fourth, a slow movement with a colorful Indian lullabye. The Finale introduces a lively Gavotte and, in the end, returns to the first subject of the First Movement. This Suite, however, certainly has not the immediacy of appeal nor the significance of his other "American" works.

In March, Dvořák began to think of composing a new symphony. What he actually wrote was something quite different: *"Ten Biblical Songs"*, published by Simrock as Op. 99. The deep seriousness of these songs was probably motivated by the death of both Gounod and Tchaikowsky, whose obituaries Dvořák had read. Moreover, he had just heard that his father, who had gone to live in Welwarn, was rapidly weakening. It was, indeed, not long before his father died. Easter, too, turned his thoughts to spiritual matters.

The Ten Biblical Songs have nothing whatever to do with Negro Spirituals. This work offers fresh testimony, perhaps in a stronger sense than any other so-called "sacred" composition, of Dvořák's deep religious fervor. He himself chose the texts from the Czech translation of the Bible, a Sixteenth Century achievement of the Bohemian Friars, obviously imbued with a Czechish national quality. Dvořák's personal choice was from the Psalms, and the beauty and power of his music is admirably suited to them. Melody and style are here happily combined with profound spirituality. The personal connotation is further carried out in the closing song, "Sing unto the Lord a new song". This is the last lyric dispensation of a mature master who, all his life long, had endeavored to "sing a new song".

This composition was so closely welded to the Czechish text that Dvořák had to exercise the greatest care in handling the problem of translation. He insisted that Simrock print the songs, as originally composed to the Czechish text, between the same covers with the German translation in the identical musical setting. Simrock consented, and so the work was published in 1895. Shortly after, Dvořák orchestrated the first five Biblical Songs for small orchestra and himself conducted them in Prague in 1896. Apparently he later mislaid the score of this orchestral version; not found until after his death it was then published by Simrock in 1914. The late Dr. Zemánek, former Conductor of the Czechish Philharmonic Orchestra, orchestrated the remaining five Biblical Songs and, in 1914, himself conducted the whole cycle.

Dvořák's continued companionship with Seidl brought it about that the latter used to send him tickets to the Metropolitan Opera. Apparently he wanted to convert Dvořák to a different point of view regarding Wagner, whose best work, Dvořák maintained, was "Tannhäuser". Seidl wanted him to hear Siegfried. It seems, however, that Dvořák did not care for the oft-repeated rhythm of the Forging of Nothung in the first act; several other things displeased him, too, so that, after the first curtain, he left. Perhaps he was also disgruntled because he was not in evening-dress and therefore had taken a seat in the rear of the box placed at his disposal. He was much more disturbed, however, by the inattentiveness and loud talking of his neighbors in the other boxes.

Nevertheless, when he again received tickets, this time to hear Rossini's "Semiramis", he gladly went, especially as he had been violist in the Prague National Theater Orchestra when this opera was performed. This time he came in evening-dress and stayed throughout the performance. These were the only occasions on which he ever went to the Metropolitan. But, the outcome of his reawakened interest in the theater, stimulated by Seidl, was the revision of "Dimitrij" in 1894.

Homeward Bound

AFTER MUCH DELIBERATION concerning his contract with the New York Conservatory, Dvořák had at last found a solution: he would return home to Bohemia for the summer but be back in New York again that autumn for another year. With his wife and six children he sailed on May 19th, 1894, on board the S. S. "Aller" for Europe—a fatiguing trip, but otherwise without untoward incident. After having been away for almost two years, he arrived again in Prague on May 30th.

He was met at the Station by countless welcoming

friends, every one of whom wanted to be first to shake his hand. A great crowd was gathered in the streets to welcome him with cries of "Long live Dvořák!" On the eve of these celebrations the Czechish National Theater had given his "Jacobin". But Dvořák was in haste to get to Vysoká. He wrote, declining Simrock's invitation to Karlsbad, and left Prague on June 4th.

It was one of the happiest days in his life when, at last, in Vysoká he saw the familiar Church tower, inspected his garden, chatted with the pigeons and then sat down at his piano. He found his desk and everything in perfect order. That evening the villagers paraded with lanterns and music before his house. Surrounded by this homely guard of honor, he had to repair to the inn where they were all, individually, determined to tell him how much they loved him and how glad they were to see him again.

June and July he spent in Vysoká. Life went on as usual: he got up not later than five in the morning, immediately went for his morning walk, at six played the organ for early mass in the neighboring village of Třebsko, returned home for breakfast at seven and then worked for two or three hours. He would then spend a quiet hour in the garden or the woods, and occasionally pay a visit to his ailing brother-in-law, Count Kaunitz, whom he held in high esteem. Before and after luncheon, he would do some more work, and, towards evening, he would sit on his favorite bench in front of the house and listen to the birds. At other times, he would spend the evening at the little inn run by Mayor Fencl, smoking his pipe (something frowned upon at home), playing cards or telling the peasants and miners all about America.

Notwithstanding this uneventful period of external and internal calm, he composed nothing new. The revision of Dimitrij took him until the end of July. About the beginning of August he turned to his American sketch-books and composed, in rapid succession, from the 10th to the 27th, a cycle of eight pieces for piano, later called *"Humoresques"*, Op. 101. Originally he had intended to call them "New Scottish Dances" as they were somewhat similar to those earlier Scottish Dances of 1877, of which he had composed quite a few. The repeated eight-bar sections of the first Humoresque are in much the same manner.

The remaining Humoresques are written in two-quarter time, with regular eight-bar periods. The thematic ideas he took from the plentiful stores in his sketch-books. The theme of the First Humoresque he had already noted down in 1893, intending it for the Funeral March in an orchestra suite. The Fourth contains the leitmotif, descriptive of the childhood of Hiawatha, for the projected opera. The model for the Eighth is to be found in his sketchbook, and in the middle of the Sixth is a New Year's Eve song he had heard in the streets of New York. It is therefore not at all extraordinary that most of these themes are typical of his "American Period": pentatonic melody, a diminished seventh in the minor, and syncopated rhythm.

These Humoresques are unaffected, amiable, refreshing, carefree and often really humorous pieces, mostly in the three-part song-form, with the exception of the First and

Fifth, which are in the rondo form. The best known is the Seventh; played everywhere, it alone soon became a gold-mine for the publisher who, of course, brought it out in all sorts of arrangements. One is with a gay little text, another with a melancholy English text, and in this country we have a version for choral singing, an arrangement by Dvořák's pupil, William Arms Fisher.

Dvořák asked and received 4,000 marks from Simrock for these Eight Humoresques. As frequently happens, he wanted to follow them up with a second series, and actually sketched out two more: a Lullabye, and a Scherzo with a lilting tune like an Italian folk-song. However, he did not write any more; preparations for his return journey to America swept them out of his mind. Those last two pieces, found among his effects, were published posthumously by Simrock, with slight retouches by Josef Suk, as *"Two Piano Pieces"*, a "Berceuse" and "Capriccio".

On Dvořák's birthday, September 8th, there was a great celebration in the village Church. For Dvořák had donated 800 gulden to buy them a new organ which, consecrated that same day, was presented with appropriate ceremonies. This event was recorded in the Golden Book of the village school, and Dvořák wrote on the margin: "and I played this organ".

In order to conduct several concerts, he had to return to Prague sooner than usual. On October 13th, as the crowning work of a Dvořák Program in the National Theater, he conducted for the first time in Prague (and the first time in the Old World) his New World Symphony. Needless to say, it enjoyed the same tremendous success that it had in America.

Second Journey to America

He had only been waiting to conduct this concert. Three days later, October 16th, 1894, he left for Hamburg, boarded the S. S. "Bismark" and arrived in New York Harbor on the 25th; the ship was freed from Quarantine the following day, and Dvořák went ashore. By this time an expert traveler, he boasted of the quick crossing: "3,100 miles in six days and a few minutes!". They had had two bad days of storm, but as usual that had not inconvenienced him.

This time, since he had decided to stay in this country but one year, he had brought only his wife and son, Otakar. They leased the very same flat. The faithful helper, Kovařík, was on hand as usual. Dvořák went to work at the Conservatory and, in November, became the object of further ovations and honors when Theodore Thomas in Chicago, and immediately thereafter, Seidl in New York, both conducted the New World Symphony. On the latter occasion, the New York Philharmonic Society elected Dvořák an Honorary Member. It was, however, no longer the same thing and somehow or other, he did not feel as well as usual. He was tortured by homesickness, his recent impressions of Vysoká were still too strong, he did not have the children with him, and there were no new American experiences to throw everything else in the shade. If he had been able to settle down to the composition of an American opera, he would certainly have found a fresh bond of inner relationship to this land of so much hospitality. But there was no plausible opera text and, when the one arrived from Vienna, the jury declared it unsuitable.

The only work he composed during his last year in America was not at all "American", but imbued with all his unabated longing to return home. This was the very well known 'Cello Concerto in B minor, written from November, 1894 to February, 1895. Only the final sixty bars were altered in Bohemia, in June, 1896.

The immediate stimulus to the inception of this work is presumed to have been Dvořák's hearing of a 'cello concerto by Victor Herbert, at that time solo 'cellist of the New York Philharmonic; according to others, his friend Wihan had begged Dvořák for a concerto. What he produced was a music completely romantic, with all the glamor, opulence and pathos of the romantic age. For the orchestration, Dvořák chose not the classic orchestra of his earlier concertos, but the multicolored romantic orchestra in which the wind instruments were accorded an especial role.

Dovetailed with its role in the symphonic whole, the solo 'cello part is beautifully written, demanding a brilliant technique. This is entirely due to Dvořák's artistry and not, as was believed, to any collaboration on the part of Wihan, who was only permitted to make five slight alterations in the First Movement.

Dvořák would not tolerate any further changes and went so far as to make it a condition, with Simrock, that the solo voice in the Concerto must appear in print as he had written it, without Wihan's cadenzas. Wihan was at first rather huffed about this. And so it happened that he did not play the solo part on the occasion of the Concerto's world première in London, March 19th, 1896. Instead, it was played by Leo Stern, who made a special journey to Prague and spent two whole weeks going over it with Dvořák. That same year, Stern likewise played it in Prague.

It was only later that Wihan took it up; by that time, however, he did interpret it in a spirit of especial sympathy. Since then, it has become a particularly favored work with all great 'cellists and is, for instance, a regular feature of Casals' repertoire. In this connection, it is amusing to record that Dvořák, paradoxically, often declared that he did not consider the 'cello a solo instrument and that he had actually written this Concerto only because Wihan asked for it.

The second measure of the first subject in the First Movement again betrays the "American" tone-scale without the leading seventh. But then, immediately, the old Bohemian "Musikant" is heard singing and romancing to his heart's desire. Dvořák's third theme later returns in his opera, "Rusalka"; in the repeat, he even throws in a fourth theme. The Adagio has the joyful sonority and sensitiveness of the latest American works, but returns in short order to the earlier Dvořák of the broad-and-blissful Czechish cantilena. In the middle section there is an almost verbatim quotation of one of the Lieder, Op. 82, presumably in farewell to his recently deceased sister-in-law, Countess Kaunitz, with whom he had once been unhappily in love. The Adagio closes with an intimate dialogue between 'cello and orchestra. The Finale, in the minor key, definitely expresses his jubilation over the approaching return to Bohemia; one theme after the other, in colors of the homeland, denotes his joyful expectation; in particular:

The 'Cello Concerto in B minor, acquired by Simrock for 6,000 marks, was published in 1896 as Op. 104.

In America, Dvořák's works were still being frequently performed, especially those he had written over here. Kneisel alone played the F major Quartet fifty times in one season. But Dvořák only listened with one ear, as it were, to all this enthusiastic re-echoing; his mind was quite elsewhere, his heart in only one place. He wrote eleven pages of "Hiawatha" themes in one notebook, but he did not use them either then or later. It was impossible for a man of his temperament to write anything "American" when, in spirit, he was already in Bohemia.

Furthermore, in February, 1895, he heard from Vienna that the venerable Society of the Friends of Music had elected him an Honorary Member. Ambroise Thomas, Grieg, Gevaert and Reinecke, all of them highly esteemed, were elected at the same time. Thus Dvořák, while still alive, joined the ranks of the Immortals, in the society of such masters as Beethoven and Schubert who in their day had been singled out for similar honors. He was especially pleased because it was in that same Vienna that, on "nationalistic" grounds, his works had frequently aroused such enmity.

It may be of interest to insert at this point a brief résumé of an article, one of several that appeared under Dvořák's name during his stay in this country. This one, devoted to Schubert, was published in the Century Magazine, 1894, as one of a series: "Portraits of Great Musicians". Written on assignment, this contribution was prepared in collaboration with Henry T. Finck, and no doubt owes its literary form to him. It is safe to assume, however, that Dvořák inspired his treatment of the subject, and, at all events, it contains nothing opposed to Dvořák's views. Grove, the Editor of the well-known Dictionary of Music, in his own exhaustive article on Schubert mentions Dvořák's contribution to the Century as the best that he had read.

Dvořák asserts that, most composers having written too much, this prevents the public from becoming thoroughly acquainted with their individual works. On the other hand, this business of writing a great deal—and here he seems to be speaking in self-defense—is something that no composer can avoid if he has many ideas. The same is true, according to Dvořák, with regard to length. On another occasion, Dvořák is known to have said: "Schubert is too long, but not for me."

In this article, Dvořák has more to say in admiration of Schubert's instrumental works than of his songs. It had taken a long time for general opinion, and even the science of music, to catch up with Schubert's qualities as a writer for the orchestra. Dvořák calls attention to Schubert's early symphonies, of which he had made a thorough analysis when conducting the Fifth and the Sixth Symphonies with the Conservatory Orchestra. He points out the "Tristan" harmonies in the slow movement of the Fourth Symphony. Dvořák esteems the "Unfinished Symphony" even more than the Great Symphony in C.

He has especial praise for Schubert's piano-music in which he finds a Slavic trait. (As a Schubert biographer, the author of this book may be permitted to observe that, in perfect agreement with Dvořák, he feels this Slavic trait is to be found not only in Schubert's piano-pieces but in some of his other works.)

What Dvořák most admired in Schubert's songs was the way the mood of a given poem, as for instance the "Leiermann" (The Organ-grinder), was so thoroughly expressed in music. There had been nothing like it before Schubert.... The whole article, imbued with the most beautiful reverence, testifies anew to the spiritual kinship of Dvořák and Schubert.

In March, 1895, Dvořák began a new work, his *String Quartet in A Flat,* but only wrote a few pages. The greater portion of it therefore seems to have been written in Bohemia.

On April 16th, Dvořák, his wife and son sailed on board the S. S. "Saale", the same ship that had brought him to America the first time. This time he was leaving America for good. True, he did not leave Mrs. Thurber without the

hope that he might return. But inwardly he knew otherwise. His roots had by now taken hold too firmly in the
soil of his native land.

Not that he had forgotten or would ever forget what he
owed to America. There he had found many fresh stimuli,
the far-seeing perspective of early middle-age, true and devoted friends and, last but not least, material security for the
rest of his life.

He, on his part, had given this country, which delighted
to honor him with especial distinction for those three years,
many fresh impulses. To young American composers, he
had emphasized the necessity of turning to the sources of
their own rich treasury of folk-song. He and America remained proud and grateful friends. The New World Symphony alone had proved epoch-making in the history of
American music. Very likely there is some justification for
the assertion that it has had the same significance for this
country that the production of "Figaro" had for Prague.

In view of these facts, it is not at all surprising that another attempt was made to bring Dvořák back to the United
States for the third time. What little biographical material
there is tells nothing of this. But, when Miss Margulies was
living in Vienna, she showed the author of this book the
correspondence that, on behalf of her friend, Mrs. Thurber,
she had conducted with Dvořák relative to his eventual
return.

It seems that two years after Dvořák had left America,
Miss Margulies was again in Vienna, intending to visit
Dvořák either in Prague or Vysoká. These letters, covering

the period from June 29th to August 20th, were later, through the intervention of Dr. Löwenbach, placed in the Prague Dvořák Museum. It was my privilege to edit and publish them in a Czechish review and later, just before the German annexation of Austria, to have them translated and published in "Musical America", New York.

From these letters, as well as from what Miss Margulies had to tell me, it appears that, although he did not refuse to consider the plan, Dvořák continually offered fresh objections. On July 18th, things were so far that he was ready to accept an engagement for two months' duration. But then he said that if this concession of his were published, he would withdraw his acceptance. There are no further letters on the subject and at all events, Dvořák remained at home, in Bohemia.

At the time of Dvořák's death in 1904, the chief organs of public opinion and leading figures in the world of music throughout the United States paid tribute to the great master, reverently evaluating his memorable three-years' stay in this country. He was honored and mourned as would have been any great American. The newspapers carried long obituaries and appreciations of his work, once again stressing the interplay upon one another of that genius of the old world and this spirit of the New.

DVOŘÁK ON HIS SIXTIETH BIRTHDAY

CHAPTER IV

"THE GRAND OLD MAN"
The Last Quartets—Final Voyage to England

WHEN DVOŘÁK ARRIVED in Prague on April 27th, 1895, only his most intimate friends had been advised of his coming. Without having formulated any particular plans, he went home to Vysoká. Occasionally he would manage to tear himself away from the one place he loved best, but only in order to visit friends, such as Judge Rus in Písek. In mid-August, he met Simrock and Hanslick in Karlsbad. By now people in America were convinced that, for the time being at any rate, he was not going to return. At first, it was the general impression that he had only gone home in order to finish some important compositions. But the decision once taken, he remained firm.

On the other hand, he did no work in Vysoká. Never in his life before had there been an interval of seven months' leisure. This, however, was a fallow period before he collected his forces and began fresh undertakings. It was just as natural for him to rest and wait as it was for him to create. When the time came, the works would pour forth, copiously and without restraint, from his fertile brain and imagination. Meanwhile, Dvořák was neither worried nor concerned.

That autumn he returned to Prague and resumed teaching. This time, in expectation of his return, so many students had registered for the composition class that it had to be held in two periods. His methods of teaching remained the same; only he had now gained greater insight.

He kept to his old ways of life, retaining the same small apartment, and began the day with an early morning walk in the Karlsplatz Park, in the course of which he would step into the St. Ignatius Church. Or he would pay a visit of inspection to the locomotives in the Franz-Josef Railway Station. In the afternoon he would drop in at a café.

A few evenings a week he liked to spend at Mahulik's Restaurant, in Myslikgasse, where he ran into theatrical people, academicians and, above all, the young musicians, such as Novák, Tregler and the others. They all foregathered in a special room, nicknamed "The Trunk". With all due ceremony, Dvořák was elected Chairman of "The Trunk", but nothing could prevent him from going home at nine in the evening, no matter how lively the entertainment. He also liked to be present at the musical soirées in the home of Professor Hlávka, President of the Academy, where he would be sure to find the poets, Zeyer and Vrchlický; the sculptor Myslbek; the statesman, Rieger, and other interesting people. The Bohemian Quartet often played there, particularly Dvořák's works. And, too, they usually liked to hear some of his compositions arranged for four hands, most often with Dvořák and Mme. Hlávka at the piano.

Finally, in November, he began to work again, his composition entering upon a new period that was to be his last. Strangely enough, these last nine years of his life carried him, as it were, straight back to his own beginnings, to those days when, under the influence of Wagner and Liszt, he had begun to seek new forms. It was a definite reversion to romanticism, characterized by the predominance of the symphonic poem and opera, those typical romantic forms.

For, romanticism is, after all, an obliteration of all boundaries, a declaration of faith in the oneness of the arts. Music receives its stimuli from poetry precisely as do opera and the symphonic poem. Notwithstanding, with Dvořák both symphonic poem and opera are evoked from the deepest well-springs of his own people, their poetry, legend and literature. And Dvořák's works owe their individual stamp to this fact and this alone.

First, however, there were two further transitional works from his American period: the *String Quartets in A flat major*, Op. 105, and in *G*, Op. 106. Actually, the latter, that in G, was composed first, whereas that in A flat had been begun in New York, but left unfinished. By the end of December, that is in less than eight weeks, both were finished. All his old freshness and delight in his work are here once more to be found. In between the two Quartets, he paid a visit to Vienna, of which more presently.

The G major Quartet reminds us of his American stay because of the birds' chirping in the main theme of the First Movement and the minor-seventh, not in the ruling key, of the episode that immediately follows. In the development, however, the style betrays a new and fully-matured mastery, introducing a work that tells of the pure joy of insight and understanding. In the following Adagio, we recognize the composer of the "Dumky". He builds his form with great freedom upon a single theme, only now and then imbued with darker nuances. The Scherzo is an idyllic mixture of gaiety and contemplation. In the Finale, as in an intermezzo in the First Movement, some reminiscences of American Indian music are heard again.

Of the A flat major Quartet, nothing of that which he wrote in America remains except the exposition. As far as their character is concerned, the main and subordinate themes practically exchange roles. The Scherzo begins as a Furiant and winds up in a contemplative mood. (Here, as in the G major Quartet, the Scherzo is the Second Movement, the same impulse being twice allowed full play in Dvořák's unmistakable manner of "pairing" two works.) Into the same Scherzo there slips a reminiscence of the Lullabye from "Jacobin". A dialogue between violin and 'cello then leads to a second reminiscence from the climax of the same opera when, to the general satisfaction, everything turns out happily.

Satisfaction, contentment—this is the mood out of which Dvořák now creates. For the first time in three years, he writes to Göbl, he will be able to celebrate Christmas in Bohemia. This complete happiness sings its praise and adoration in that slow Third Movement; and in the Finale there is another declaration of national loyalty expressed by a typically Bohemian theme.

Both works were awaited with great impatience. Simrock published them in the summer of 1896, but, even before that, they were being requested by chamber-music societies all over the world. That is why the Quartet in G alone had its world première in Prague, in October, 1896. Dvořák arranged a private performance of the A flat major Quartet, played by pupils of the Prague Conservatory. The first public performance was that given by the Bohemian String Quartet on January 15th, 1897, in Vienna. In New York, it was heard shortly prior to this. In Vienna, the applause was so insistent that the Scherzo, one of the most beautiful Dvořák ever composed, had to be played through again.

In December, 1895, he had visited Brahms, whom he wished to thank for having corrected his proofs the whole time Dvořák was in America. He also wanted to see Richter. Dvořák and his wife stayed at the Hotel "Goldenes Lamm" on the Wiedener Hauptstrasse, not far from Brahms, who lived in the Karlsgasse. The joy of their reunion still further contributed to the great respect and friendship he felt for Brahms, who reciprocated precisely those sentiments for Dvořák.

Richter, who had become First Conductor of the Vienna Imperial Opera, was delighted to see Dvořák, the more so as Richter was about to conduct the New World Symphony and wanted to discuss it with him. When the Vienna première took place, on February 16th, 1896, it was for Dvořák—just arrived from Prague—an almost unprecedented triumph.

The recipient of every honor that went with a Philharmonic première, Dvořák sat with Brahms in the box reserved for the Board of Directors of the Friends of Music Society. And, together with Brahms and Richter, he was afterwards invited to Miller-Aichholz, a prominent Viennese patron of the arts. Brahms extended the invitation on his own, thereafter notifying Miller-Aichholz by letter, assuring his host that he would give Dvořák something to eat and drink from his own plate and glass. But one thing was certain: Dvořák would make no speeches. As a social lion, Dvořák was notoriously a silent specimen.

Soon after, for the ninth and last time, Dvořák went to England as guest of the London Philharmonic Society. His wife and his daughter, Ottilie, went with him. The Concert took place on March 19th, 1896, in Queen's Hall, with Dvořák conducting his 'Cello Concerto, the Symphony in G major and the Biblical Songs. He also conducted the Overture to Bartered Bride, and Emil Sauer played the Beethoven Piano Concerto in E flat major.

Externally, this time he did not care at all for London. The food and the fog bothered him. He made up for this by dining as often as possible in the home of Littleton, with whom, however, he was not staying. The tremendous success of his concert naturally exorcized every depression and irritation. Nevertheless, he was glad of the excuse to leave at once because he had to return to Vienna for another concert.

On March 25th, he was to conduct the "Glasbena Matice"

Choral Society from Laibach (Ljubljana). In return for Vienna's charitable aid at the time of the Laibach earthquake, the Glasbena Matice Society was giving two concerts for the benefit of Vienna's public welfare institutions. One of them was to be a performance of The Spectre's Bride. Although Dvořák's conducting obviously contributed to the financial success, he would accept no payment nor anything for his expenses. The Laibach Choral Society elected him an Honorary Member.

While in Vienna, Dvořák sat for his portrait bust by the sculptor, Hedley. Dvořák also met Grieg, who was giving a concert recital in Vienna. For March 27th, there was scheduled a concert by the Bohemian String Quartet, who were to play Dvořák's Sextet in A, Brahms' Piano Quartet in C minor and Bruckner's String Quintet. All three great contemporaries were thus to be heard on one program, and the impresario, Albert Gutmann, wanted to invite them all to be present. It was decided, however, that Brahms and Bruckner, because of the enmity between their followers, should not be given to understand that they were each being invited. The members of the Quartet, in company with Dvořák, agreed to deliver the invitations personally. Dvořák was glad of the opportunity of meeting Bruckner, whose works he esteemed.

Their visit to Brahms unexpectedly turned out to be most agitated. Brahms did everything in his power to persuade Dvořák to come and teach composition at the Vienna Conservatory (obviously to counterbalance Bruckner).

And when Dvořák again averred that the cost of living in Vienna was too high for him and his numerous family, Brahms offered him (not for the first time) his entire fortune, for which, he declared, he had otherwise no use. Dvořák was deeply moved and thanked him, but declined.

He was, however, profoundly shocked when Brahms, turning to religious subjects, quoted some of Schopenhauer's skeptical sayings. As they left, according to Suk (memoirs published in the "Merker"), Dvořák exclaimed, despairingly: "Such a great man! Such a great soul! And he believes in nothing!"

Brahms, after all, did not appear at the Concert, but came to the general rehearsal. Hanslick, too, was there, but displeased Dvořák by declaring that he was going to leave before they played Bruckner's Quintet. (Hanslick had a habit of ostentatiously leaving whenever any of Bruckner's works were played.)

There is pathos in the story of Dvořák's calling on Bruckner with the Bohemians. Suk tells how they found Bruckner in his shirtsleeves, obviously ill and preoccupied, deep in his work. He at first appeared not to understand what they wanted of him, but finally declared he was in the midst of writing the Adagio for his Ninth Symphony and could not leave the house. As they were about to go, Bruckner was suddenly moved to tears. He accompanied them to the door of his lodging (he was then an Imperial Pensioner) and kept waving to them until they were out of sight.

This was six months before his death, and Dvořák never saw Bruckner again.

Dvořák's Symphonic Poems

AT THIS PERIOD, Dvořák had committed to paper the sketches for three new symphonic works. The scores of two were already finished. And they were all three of an entirely new genre for him. The first news about them hinted that they were "orchestra ballads". Actually, they were Symphonic Poems. Dvořák had begun their composition on January 6th, 1896, and, a bare three weeks later, they were all on paper.

Entitled the "Water Goblin" (*Wassermann*), "Noonday Witch" (*Mittagshexe*), and "Golden Spinning-wheel" (*Goldene Spinnrad*), all three were suggested by poems in a collection of folk-ballads known as "Nosegay" by K. J. Erben. The same poet had furnished the text of The Spectre's Bride and several of Dvořák's Lieder.

The pathway to program music—music requiring an extraneous, non-musical, or literary impulse—had once upon a time led Dvořák to the composition of his "Alfred". Even in his periods of "absolute" music, he had produced piano-pieces that were more and more distinctly programmatic. Finally, he had composed the three "Program Overtures", of which Dvořák himself had written to Simrock: "Of course they are program music." And, in New York, Seidl had unquestionably again recommended to Dvořák, the master, that trail blazed by Wagner and Liszt. Dvořák, the musician, was only ostensibly tranquillized about the formal problems of his art; apparently a naive creator, in reality he was a thinker in music. Brahms, from his point of view, had been quite right to warn Dvořák of the "danger" of America.

Once confronted with the necessity of thrashing out this problem, Dvořák was not troubled by any scruples; he was not to be restrained out of considerations for Brahms or for Hanslick. The latter, of course, wrote him that this was the path of declivity that must finally lead to Richard Strauss. On the other hand, he declared, Dvořák was a real musician who would not find it necessary to ask what Zarathustra might have said. Perhaps he did not even know who Zarathustra was!

K. J. Erben's Ballads take us into a world of fantasy rather than that of folk-tale. Nevertheless, their folk-idiom and mood were bound to allure Dvořák: terror, or dread, is the chief motive of these Ballads; as to content, they have nothing much in common unless it be the motive of guilt. What with all the ethical components of his being, Dvořák was quite equal to dealing with the problems of guilt and atonement, crime and punishment.

Musically, these Symphonic Poems do not actually constitute a cycle. It would be unjust to consider them as the by-products or, shall we say, aberrations of a great musician. They are worthy continuations of that which Berlioz had planned, Liszt and Smetana, each in his own way, had carried out. In contrast to Richard Strauss, Dvořák's simplicity of means is striking. He writes music with motives of a penetrating intensity and dramatic logic. He has rarely if ever revealed a greater artistry of instrumentation. Janáček has said of Dvořák that he used each instrument only when he could give it "something to sing".

Most admirable of all is the economy of instrumental means which suffices Dvořák; there are often very few systems in his scores. One difficult task was presented to him by this new form: he, the master of the sonata, was now confronted by the primary demands of the poem and, at the same time, he must discover that form best suited to the musician. In view of the variety of these three poems, this was especially difficult for him; nevertheless, he was, each time after a different fashion, almost invariably successful.

The first of these Symphonic Poems was the "*Water Goblin*" ("Vodník"), Op. 107, composed in January and February, 1896, and published the same year by Simrock. Together with the two which followed, "Noonday Witch" and "Golden Spinning-Wheel", it was first performed on June 3rd by the Prague Conservatory Orchestra, conducted by Anton Bennewitz. The actual world première was that conducted by Hans Richter, with the Vienna Philharmonic, on November 22nd, 1896.

This particular Ballad by Erben is motivated by horror as well, and apology for this is made in the program notes, pointing out that such horror is often to be found in Slav fairy-tales, not merely in this one.

This Water Goblin sits on the shore of the Lake, sewing his wedding garb. His victim is to be a Maiden from the neighboring village. Though warned by her Mother not to venture outside the garden, it being "Unlucky Friday", the Maiden is impelled by some mysterious force to go down to the Lake. The pier beneath her breaks and she sinks, held fast in the Water Goblin's arms. As his wife, she bears him a child to whom she croons a mournful lullabye. At last, she succeeds in persuading the Water Goblin to let her visit her Mother for one day only, but he keeps her baby as hostage. To her Mother, she laments her unhappy lot, and both determine that she shall not return to the Lake. At night, the Water Goblin raps impatiently on the door, demanding his wife, but is mocked by the Mother. A terrible storm breaks out, and something is hurled upon the doorsill. It is the headless corpse of the Water Goblin's child. . . .

Inasmuch as everything centers about the Water Goblin, beginning with and returning to him, Dvořák has here employed the rondo form: A-B-A-C-A-B-A. A denotes the Water Goblin and the Lake; B, the two women; A, the Water Goblin drags the maiden down into his watery kingdom; C, Water Goblin and Maiden in the depths; A, the Water Goblin grants the Maiden's plea; B, the two women again; A, the Water Goblin's revenge. There is a poignant contrast between the almost maliciously indifferent Water Goblin motive and the tenderly moving motive ascribed to the Maiden; then there is the Maiden's tragic lullabye. In conclusion, Dvořák seems to continue the poem by composing for the two women an epilogue of mourning.

One remarkable feature of this Symphonic Poem is that several of the motives precisely imitate the scansion of Erben's Czechish verse. This innovation is almost analogous to Janáček's opera-motives, in which the attempt is made to hold fast the melody of Czechish folk-idiom.

Immediately after the "Water Goblin", Dvořák composed the *"Noon-day Witch"* ("Polednice"), Op. 108, likewise in January and February, 1896, published the same year. Its première, conducted by Richter in Vienna, took place on December 20th, that is, scarcely one month later than that of "Water Goblin".

The story is as follows: The Child's crying annoys its Mother, who threatens to call for the Noon-day Witch; (This is a peculiar figure of Slav mythology, analogous to the "Pan-ic" noonday terror. It is not good to walk in the forest at midday lest one should meet the Witch.) Thereupon the Witch appears, a shriveled hag, who demands: "Give me the child!" The Witch's shadowy figure approaches, growing larger and larger, until the Mother falls unconscious. The returning Father finds her lying on the floor; the Child is dead.

Here again, the Witch's demand is reproduced by a motive scanning exactly like the words. Her coming is accompanied by a twilight-motive: muted violins and violas above a sustained note in the bass-clarinet (according to Janáček, a masterly description of a ghostly world). Sheer genius is implicit in Dvořák's handling of the form which, unlike the poem, does not begin with the child's crying, but first portrays a homely idyll contrasted with a demonic witches' dance.

In spite of Dvořák's various concert tournées, *"The Golden Spinning-Wheel"* ("Zlatý Kolovrat"), Op. 109, was finished in April. It was first performed by the Prague

Conservatory Orchestra, and the first public performance was that on November 3rd, 1901, conducted by Hellmesberger with the Vienna Philharmonic Orchestra.

The story: The King, on his splendid horse, is returning from the hunt. Thirsty, he stops before a lowly hut in the forest; a beautiful Maiden hands him a cup of water and goes back to her Spinning-Wheel. The King determines to marry her, but he must ask her Stepmother, who is expected the following day. The King asks her hand, but the Stepmother tries to persuade him to marry her own, no less beautiful Daughter. The King insists on the Stepdaughter, ordering her to appear at his Castle the next day.

In the forest at night, the Stepmother and her Daughter murder the Maiden of his choice, carrying off her eyes, hands and feet to the Castle. The King does not notice the deception when the Stepmother presents her own Daughter, disguised, as his choice. Their nuptials celebrated, the King rides off to war. In his absence, a strange Old Man comes to the Castle, offering the Queen a beautiful Golden Spinning-Wheel in exchange "for two feet." He is given the feet of the murdered girl and, in exchange for the distaff and spindle, her eyes and hands. These members he restores to the corpse in the forest and, by a magic spell, calls the Maiden back to life. The victorious King returns, to be welcomed by the impostor "wife" sitting at her Golden Spinning-Wheel. As she begins to spin, however, the Spinning-Wheel recites the tale of the murder. The King hastens to the forest, finds his real betrothed and, with pomp and circumstance, they are married. The Stepmother and Daughter are appropriately punished.

With exquisite charm, Dvořák unites the theme of the King (exactly following the word-accent of the poem's first verse), with the ravishing motives of the Spinning-Wheel and the Beautiful Maiden. But here the musician in Dvořák overcomes his scrupulous adherence to the story: by enlarging upon his motives and formal constructions he does not always do justice to the poem. Then, again, as if to make good this negligence, he writes descriptive music, faithfully, word for word. He is therefore not so successful in mastering the formal problem here presented as he was in the two foregoing Symphonic Poems. For this reason, particularly in concerts of the Prague Philharmonic Orchestra, Suk's condensed version of the Golden Spinning-Wheel has been preferred. At all events, whoever simply listens for pure, musical beauty, in all this wealth of melody and harmony, is sure to find his reward.

In the same year, 1896, in Vysoká, Dvořák composed a Fourth Symphonic Poem, also based on one of Erben's poems, "*Woodpigeon*", ("Die Waldtaube"; Czechish, "Holoubek"). Simrock wanted to print the full text of the poems along with the music, but Dvořák insisted on a brief synopsis, and thus they were published. Chancing to find a German translation of "Woodpigeon", by Julius Zeyer, in the program of one of Nedbal's concerts in Berlin, 1900, Simrock wrote to Nedbal that, if he had known of this translation, he would have printed it with the score. But

Dvořák would not provide him with the translation, preferring to leave the interpretation to the listener, and thus, Simrock alleged, misunderstandings had arisen.

Hans Richter had written several urgent letters to Dvořák in Vysoká: he wanted the Three Symphonic Poems as soon as possible, to conduct on his tour of eight cities in England. Dvořák replied:

"My Most Honored Friend!

"I was away for three days, so that only yesterday I received your telegram and your kind letter. I at once wrote an urgent letter to Simrock in Berlin, and await his reply. Apparently you misunderstood me: the Three Symphonic Poems are independent works and each one can be performed alone. The Water Goblin takes 18 minutes, the Noonday Witch, 13; the Golden Spinning-Wheel is the longest, requiring about half-an-hour. I should prefer to have only one at a time performed because the effect of one may detract from that of the others. In Prague, this June, it is true, all three were given at one time, but that was a private performance; I wanted to give my friends in Prague a complete picture of my recent works. I beg you, please conduct only one of them at a time.

"These pieces are rather more in the folk-tone, with the dramatic element sometimes strongly emphasized. They are Ballads, and in each piece there are three or four persons I have attempted to characterize. Each piece is accompanied by a prose synopsis so that it will be more easily understood by the audience.

"As soon as I hear from Simrock, tomorrow or the day after, I shall at once communicate all further details to you. I am thinking of coming to Vienna in order to discuss everything else. In the meanwhile, with best greetings,

"Your grateful,

"Antonín Dvořák."

In spite of all admonitions, the proofs were not ready on time, so that Richter could not conduct the Symphonic Poems until he gave a concert in Vienna. In England, he had to be satisfied with the Scherzo Capriccioso. Shortly after this, Dvořák recommended his pupil, Suk (by now secretly engaged to Ottilie), to his publisher, Simrock, just as, nineteen years previously, Brahms had recommended Dvořák to Simrock. About this time, too, he was overjoyed to receive a visit from his young friend and faithful helper in America, Kovařík, revisiting Bohemia.

Dvořák completed *"The Woodpigeon"* towards the close of 1896 in Vysoká. Published by Simrock three years later as Op. 110, it was first conducted by Janáček in Brünn, and later by Gustav Mahler with the Vienna Philharmonic Orchestra on December 3rd, 1899.

The synopsis is as follows: With lamentation, all the time knowing that she has poisoned her husband, the young Widow follows his coffin to the grave. A slow funeral march contains a motive that is then transformed into the theme of guilt, the actual leading motive. Here again, we find, before its entry, that "masking" of the first subject which is a favorite device with Dvořák. There is a transition to the Allegro. A gay and smartly dressed young man encounters the beautiful Widow; comforting her, he persuades her to forget her sorrow and marry him. Here there is a diminution of the main motive, gaily scanned to the exact words of the Czechish text. There is a fresh, coquettish diminution to the words: "But one week, and she has forgotten the dead; but one month, and she is sewing a new wedding-dress." Here the music is gay, almost in dance-rhythm, followed by tender confidences: two forms of the same motive are here combined in masterly fashion.

The Widow is tormented by pangs of conscience and driven to visit her murdered husband's grave. New variation of the motive, in apprehension of coming evil. The Woodpigeon coos from the branches of the oak above the grave. Dvořák, an ardent breeder of pigeons, imitates the language of his favorites, tame and wild, with the virtuosity of a connoisseur: flutes, oboes, harp-tremolos in the high register, sometimes accompanied by the bass-clarinet—all mixed with the artistry of genius on his instrumental palette.

The Widow throws herself into the water. The poem ends, but Dvořák poetizes further: he portrays a sort of reconciliation and forgiveness, thereby returning musically in a cycle to the beginning. His composing in cyclic forms is, indeed, a return to the same manner of solution he applied to such problems in the works of his youthful period; in the Symphonic Poems, he is altogether closer to the manner of his earliest works. In view of the scant motivation and brief events in the tale of the Woodpigeon, he has been particularly successful in mastering the problems of form. Here, the music and poem are in beautiful harmony; and here he has been richly rewarded in his struggle with the limitations of the symphonic poem.

He continued to receive gratifying news of the many performances of his works in other countries. The names of his pupils, Suk, Novák and Nedbal, were everywhere making themselves heard. Basking in the reflected glory of his fame overseas, he was fast becoming, at home and abroad, "The Grand Old Man" of Czechish music.

"The Devil and Kate"

THE FLOWER of Czech music was now in full bloom. Besides the influence of Dvořák, Fibich was still to be reckoned with, and the mighty shadow of Smetana, his influence ever more powerful, lengthened down into the present. Of living contemporaries, Dvořák's friend, Karel Bendl, suffering from mental derangement, had come to the close of his career.

Of the younger generation, J. B. Foerster, the intimate friend of Mahler, was at that time living and working in Hamburg. Janáček, although living in obscurity, was doing good work. And such a conductor as Kovařovic, likewise successful as a composer, was propagating the great works of his compatriots as well as those of foreign composers. A vigorous musical life was guaranteed by the Prague Philharmonic Orchestra, the Czechish Society for Chamber-Music and a German chamber-music organization. There were several attempts to constitute a secession, or revolutionary group. In illustration of this, an "outsider" by the name of Lošták—incidentally a great admirer and imitator of Dvořák—published a manifesto decrying the rigidity of established musical canons. Dvořák's pupils were likewise very much alive, and many a fresh impetus and many a new work arose out of their sessions in "The Trunk" at Mahulík's Restaurant.

In October, 1896, Dvořák heard that Brahms was very ill and that in all likelihood his end was near. Writing to Simrock for news, Dvořák meanwhile thoroughly studied Brahms' latest works, especially the "Four Serious Songs"; but, for a time, shyness prevented him from visiting his friend in Vienna. Busy with the revision of his earlier works, Dvořák did not even interrupt his composition and teaching when Richter invited him to Vienna for the première of his 'Cello Concerto, to be interpreted by Hugo Becker, on March 7th, 1897.

He did not go to Vienna because he knew Brahms' Fourth Symphony was to be heard for the first time (on the same program with Dvořák's 'Cello Concerto) and the opportunity would be given for the master to be present— and acclaimed—probably for the last time. Actually, Brahms was present—the shadow of the former Brahms— and, on this occasion, the crowning triumph of his lifetime, there was a touching reunion with his audience.

One week later, Dvořák visited his friend for the last time. It was a tragic meeting; only Dvořák's native optimism could have dictated his words to Simrock: "Let us pray that it is not too late to hope." A few days later, on

April 6th, 1897, standing beside Brahms' grave, he was moved to tears when Richard von Perger delivered the funeral oration. The death of this friend, so close to him and so important for his whole career, had for some time a paralyzing effect on Dvořák.

Once again, he could not decide what to do, what work to undertake. Sketches that he had begun for a choral version of "The Song of Songs" were laid aside because the text seemed to him "too sensual". When Simrock asked him to orchestrate a few of Brahms' last piano-pieces, reminding him of his promise to Brahms, Dvořák did not react. He did nothing but orchestrate his revised version of "Jacobin", the third act of which he had completely re-written.

This, at last, gave him fresh impetus. He sketched another Symphonic Poem, his Fifth and last: *"The Hero's Song"*. It was likewise to be his final orchestral work and, together with "Woodpigeon", the last that Simrock would publish during his lifetime. Composed in October, 1897, as Op. 111, Dvořák's own four-hand piano-score was brought out in 1899. The world première took place on December 4th, 1898, in Vienna, conducted by Gustav Mahler, with Dvořák present. Another triumph! Although not so much appreciated at home, this "The Hero's Song" ("Píseň bohatýrskà") was often played: in London, 1899; in Berlin, November, 1899, at a Philharmonic Concert with Nikisch conducting and Dvořák present; and frequently since then.

"The Hero's Song" is not in praise of a warrior but is the credo of a champion of great ideas. Musically, it depicts

Power, Decision, Disappointment and Lamentation, New Hope, Battle and, finally, the Triumph of the Idea. The reproach was made to Dvořák, especially in his own country, that the argument is in contradiction to his simple nature. There were comparisons with the "Hero's Life" of Richard Strauss, and there were other false evaluations.

The truth was that Dvořák had actually composed, in part, his own autobiography. In this there could not fail to be some colloquial turns of phrase which, of course, were held against him as trivialities. It is characteristic that the clarinet, which plays such a great role in Czechish music, decidedly has a great deal to say in "The Hero's Song". "Formlessness" was another reproach, notwithstanding the fact that the form is here definite and easily perceptible. The four movements of the classic symphony are united in one: an Introduction, a Slow Movement, a Scherzo and, returning cyclically to the beginning, the Finale.

All four movements constitute, if you will, a single great exposition. Three themes are introduced: that of Decision, with eight variants, each virtually an independent theme; that of Disappointment, in several diminutions; and that of Consolation and Hope, first appearing in the middle of the Adagio. Riemann was among the first to recognize that in this work the classic symphonic form is successfully combined with the new tendencies of the symphonic poem.

Dvořák was perfectly justified in drawing upon his own life and achievements to illustrate the triumph of his Hero. Peace of mind, comfort, recognition, prosperity and rejoicing in his loved ones—these had been granted to him. The

Vienna Ministry of Education had raised the annual subvention to the Prague Conservatory from 8500 to 10,000 gulden on condition that Dvořák must receive 1000 gulden of that amount. Thus he was placed on equal footing with professors "of the sixth rank", according to the remuneration they received from the State.

As successor to Brahms, Dvořák was named a member of the Austrian State Commission which recommended to the Ministry of Education those composers to receive the annually awarded Austrian State Stipendium. The other members were Ignaz Brüll and Mandyczewski, with whom Dvořák became fast friends. This election delighted him because he could now assist talented young composers just as Brahms had once helped him. On the other hand, he could not bring himself to compose a Festival March for the Emperor's Jubilee in 1898, the fiftieth year of his reign. Instead, Dvořák wrote to the Ministry of Education, which had made the request, that he would like permission to dedicate a beautiful March, if one occurred to him, to the Emperor. But nothing ever came of this.

Regarded superficially, Dvořák's life had, perhaps, not been so heroic. But those who took the trouble to trace its course would find that, in order to live such a life, one would indeed have to have something of the heroic. They would be forced to the conclusion that Dvořák was a true warrior in the spirit and that his "Hero's Song" is the imaging-forth of his own struggles and triumphs.

Dvořák's external way of life did not alter and his joy in teaching certainly did not diminish. His personality and genius attracted more and more students from near and far. Nobody noticed the somber, plainly furnished class-room when he could see before him that famous and yet unassuming man. This was the man who could teach with such fervor and who, notwithstanding, now and again could be childishly enthusiastic or, if occasion demanded, fly into a rage.

He had, too, his share of fame, and there was always good news of performances of his works here and there. "Ludmila" was heard in Vienna and Prague, 1897; his Violin Concerto was played by Hoffmann, the First Violinist of the "Bohemians". At the rehearsals, Dvořák and Hoffmann had a rather violent difference of opinion as to the tempo in which it should be played. Dvořák wound up by saying: "If you cannot play it in my tempo, you shall not play it at all." Hoffmann was very much hurt. But as they were walking home together, Dvořák suddenly came to a standstill before a house that particularly pleased him and that he contemplated buying, and declared: "I am going to buy this house and you are going to play my Concerto". When it was finally performed, and Hoffmann had beautifully interpreted his part, Dvořák came out onto the platform and shared the applause with him, something he had never done before.

Suk, the Second Violinist of the Bohemian String Quartet, reported the sensational success Willem Mengelberg had had in Holland, conducting the New World Symphony, the Violin Concerto and the Program Overtures, "In Nature's Realm". Suk was at that time living in the same house as Dvořák and hence saw a good deal of Ottilie. But Dvořák pretended not to notice anything and only once asked his daughter if it were true that one of the Quartet-members was paying court to her.

Dvořák found himself once again in the atmosphere of the opera, close to the world of the theater. With the simple directness of his nature, he strove so vigorously and creatively to produce something adequate to the demands of the stage that it was inevitable that he should make his mark. Possibly he overlooked some of the theater's most exacting and peculiar requirements. At any rate, he devoted to it his whole being, with its almost mythical sources and traditions, and the whole of his music, ever and again seeking to express his affinities with the people, his suffering and his triumph. Perhaps he could succeed by means of the fairy-tale. Fairy-tales were taking possession of the stage about this time: there were "Hänsel and Gretel", "The Sunken Bell", and the operas of Rimsky-Korsakoff. Almost a legendary figure himself, Dvořák was closer than many another to the fairy realm.

Therefore he set about composing a new opera, "The Devil and Kate" ("Čert a Káča"), the text of which had been brought to him by a young Prague schoolmaster and writer, Adolf Wenig. He began the sketches of this, his Op. 112, in Vysoká, May, 1898; but it took him, contrary to his habit, until February, 1899 to complete it. Preparations for the forthcoming marriage of Ottilie and Suk had turned his household upside down, and he was the last who could remain indifferent in the midst of festivities.

Among all peoples, there are tales of the stupid Devil. According to Wenig and Dvořák, the story runs: There are high jinks in the village inn at the time of the country fair. Only Jirka (George), the shepherd for the gentry, has to work on this otherwise general holiday; the stern Administrator has sent for him to come to the Castle. He obeys, but the Musikants accompany him. Kate, a vigorous girl, not very pretty and hampered by her mother, comes to the inn. She is all on fire to dance, but nobody wants to dance with her. All make fun of her and she, for her part, declares that she would be content to dance with the Devil.

At once there appears an uncanny-looking Stranger, of savage appearance, in hunting costume, dragging one leg as he walks. Exceptionally gallant, he pays for Kate's beer and invites her to dance. What with Kate's substantial figure and powers of endurance, however, he has no easy time of it. She assures him—just as the polka is turning into a galop—that she could dance on like this for the rest of her life.

The Stranger has made inquiries about the Administrator and the Princess who owns the estate, and the villagers have nothing good to say. In the attempt to be freed from dancing, he invites Kate to come with him: he has a beautiful red castle in which it is nice and warm in winter-time. Kate is wondering what to do about her mother when Jirka, crestfallen, reappears. The Administrator has taken offence because of the Musikants who were with him and, discharging him, has told him to go to the devil. The Stranger laughs queerly.

Kate makes up her mind to go with him. There is a thunder-clap, and, amidst smoke and flame, the Stranger and Kate disappear through a hole in the floor. (This Stranger is none other than Marbuel, who, as emissary of Lucifer, the ruler of Hell, was sent to find out if the Princess and her Administrator really merit damnation for their mistreatment of the people.) Kate's mother is in despair. But never fear, Jirka will fetch her daughter back again! Having lost his job, he is going to the Devil anyhow.

The second act is staged in Hell. The Devils are playing cards, making such a racket that Lucifer has to demand silence. Marbuel carrying Kate, arrives, limping badly, having got hold of a captive who won't let go of him. Furious that she finds herself in Hell instead of in a Castle, Kate cruelly torments poor Marbuel. How to get rid of her? Jirka arrives, and Marbuel promises him anything if he will take Kate away. Jirka knows how to handle Kate: first show her gold, then she runs after it and Marbuel will be free. This is done, Jirka dances with her to the gates of Hell and, at the right instant, pushes her outside. The Devils are all delighted. As a reward, when Marbuel comes to fetch the Administrator and sees Jirka, he will pretend to run away from him in fright. The Administrator will be sure to recompense Jirka, letting him return to work. There is one condition: Jirka must not on any account attempt to rescue the Princess, for whom Hell knows no pardon.

In the Third Act, at the Castle, the Princess is downcast. The Devil has just dragged off her Administrator, and threatened to come back for her. She sends for Jirka, but he declares that it is out of his power to help. The Princess thereupon calls together her retainers, promising them to make an end of forced labor and to give them all their freedom. Overjoyed, Jirka hides Kate in the Princess' chamber, and when Marbuel appears, advises him to get away as quickly as possibly before Kate can lay hands on him. In a flash, the Devil disappears through the chimney, minus his prey. The Princess appoints Jirka her Privy Councillor and gives Kate a fine house. Kate at last has found what she had always wished. A husband, too, should not be far to seek. There is great rejoicing among the liberated people, and Jirka promises never to mistreat the citizens of his own village.

This book has the advantages of a lively, popular story, with sharp contrasts and well-defined leading roles. It has, of course, its dramatic weaknesses, but, what is more important and decisive, it is completely in Dvořák's line. These are the themes he loves, that do not change with him: gaiety in the village and countryside, rewards to benevolent masters and resistance to wicked ones ("The Peasant Rogue, "Jacobin", etc.). Given a strong character like Kate, he well knows how to reproduce musically the best qualities of his own people, sound and happy, with their feet on the ground and fearful of no-one, not even the Devil. If the people are able to get along with the gentry, then nothing can upset their wholesome gaiety.

The music makes the most of all this spirit of joyful solidarity among the country-folk. Dvořák's concentration of dramatic motive is especially effective in this comic opera, and his exact and sure musical diction is in fine harmony with it. Whenever this music sparkles effervescently out of the life-giving sources of folk-idiom, as in Kate's passion for dancing, it clings to the folk-dance. Fashionable even in Hell, the folk-dance gives Dvořák every opportunity to let his rhythms hold high revel.

"The Devil and Kate" is important for another reason: the renewed trend toward Wagner, probably the outcome of his discussions with Seidl in New York. Not only is there something Wagnerian about this whole conception, but also the technique of instrumentation and the thematic texture point to Wagner. We have previously remarked how the revived Wagnerian impulse corresponded to Dvořák's recrudescent youthful urge.

Nevertheless, this thematic texture has now been most remarkably thought out. There are, so to speak, collective leitmotifs in this opera, though not so distinctly and not so consistently carried out as in the two later operas. There is a leitmotif for each group of people and characters: whoever belongs to that group is designated by the group-motive in some variant or other. The antagonist to the group also has his variant. Furthermore, the individual of the group sometimes has his own peculiar motive; the antagonist occasionally receives an affiliated motive that is melodically an inversion. In this opera, the people constitute one group; hence, Kate and the Shepherd are each allotted a variant of the people's motive. Another group is the Hell with its Devils; and a third is the world of those living in the Castle. This new leitmotif technique is certainly not uncomplicated, but its general effect is uncommonly simple, natural and logical. It need hardly be added that Dvořák, the musical inventor, does not maltreat Dvořák, the lyrical singer.

In "The Devil and Kate" Dvořák has produced an altogether effective comic opera, especially considered in the light of its own background, such as was provided by the Czechish Theater. There are still further innovations in this opera-music: in the Overture to the Second Act, there are, for instance, whole-tone progressions. A motive such as this,

to designate the people, cannot fail to have its decisive effect. Seldom with Dvořák has the primitive appeal of the homeland and its people spoken so distinctly as here.

On its first performance in the Prague National Theater, on November 23rd, 1899, "The Devil and Kate", enjoyed an extraordinary success, and it soon became a fixture in the repertoire of that institution. It was first published, with text in German and Czechish, by M. Urbánek, in Prague, 1908. In 1909, there were several performances in Bremen. In 1924, the Olmütz Opera Company revived it in Vienna with great success. There were German performances in Brünn and at the Vienna Volksoper (1932); in the same year, an English production at Oxford, staged by Director

Strohbach of the Darmstadt Theater, brought the plot up to date.

In the summer of 1898, Dvořák wrote to Richter that at last he hoped to be able to visit Bayreuth, thus indicating his renewed veneration for Wagner. He was, however, unable to carry out this plan because of work on the opera and, too, he did not like to leave his family in the midst of feverish preparations for the wedding. Dvořák participated wholeheartedly in such festivities. He was fond of saying: "You have to expect that every spree will cost something." On November 17th, 1898, the wedding took place in the Church of St. Stephen where twenty-five years before, on that very day, Dvořák himself had married Anna; they were celebrating their Silver Wedding.

In November, on the occasion of Francis Joseph's Jubilee, Dvořák received a very rare and much coveted "Medal of Honor for the Arts and Sciences," otherwise awarded to only one musician, Johannes Brahms. It was worn about the neck and Dvořák, delighted to have it, called it his "big golden platter".

In the autumn of 1898, Hans Richter gave up conducting the Vienna Philharmonic Orchestra, recommending Gustav Mahler in his place. Richter had intended to conduct "Woodpigeon" and "The Hero's Song". On October 3rd, Mahler wrote that he would like to conduct "your new work". Dvořák answered that he had two new works, and sent them both. Mahler, deciding on "The Hero's Song", conducted it with great success on December 4th, 1898, with Dvořák present. Word came that Wihan had played

Dvořák's 'Cello Concerto in the Hague and in Amsterdam, both concerts conducted by Mengelberg, to the delight of Dutch audiences. Thus the New Year began auspiciously.

World-Wide Success—"Rusalka"

IN HIS FIFTY-EIGHTH YEAR, there came another pause in his creative activity. Ordinarily, his proclivity towards producing two similar works within a short time would have required that he compose a second opera. If he had only had a libretto, he would certainly have done so at once. Having none, he found it annoying to be forced to seek one.

Simrock impatiently urged him to write a new chamber-music work. But Dvořák, aware that the material circumstances of his family were now thoroughly assured, was deaf to all enticements. Completely under the spell of the theater and convinced that opera was of most importance to his people, all his strivings were consecrated to one end: to produce more operas. Symphonies and chamber-music works are performed perhaps once a year. An opera with national coloring, of national importance, may be performed once a month and even more often. Two months before his death, on March 1st, 1904, the Vienna "Reichswehr" published an interview in which Dvořák unreservedly admitted that he had but one more goal in life: the opera.

About mid-June, 1899, Dvořák went to Vienna to express his gratitude to the Emperor for his new decoration. Mandyczewski, at his request, had arranged for the audience. On arriving, however, Dvořák was informed that Francis Joseph was not feeling well and therefore all audiences had to be postponed. Not wishing to wait indefinitely, Dvořák returned to Vysoká.

That fall, rehearsals for "The Devil and Kate" took up most of his time. His intense passion for opera now led him to participate more fully in the production: he took a hand in everything, decided the tempi, worked with the singers and was even concerned about the acting. Once he said to a tenor: "You sang that very beautifully, indeed—but what I wrote is something quite different!" He took particular delight in the beautiful mezzo-soprano of his daughter, Magda, inherited from her mother. While still at the Conservatory, she promised to become an excellent concert-singer, but she married soon after and gave up singing in public.

In order to be on hand for the fourth performance of "The Devil and Kate", Dvořák had to decline Mahler's invitation to the Viennese première of his "Woodpigeon", on December 3rd, 1899. About the same time, the "Woodpigeon" met with great success in London. In the month of November alone, his "Hero's Song" was heard in London, Berlin, Hamburg, Leipzig and Boston. In Dvořák's honor, two concerts were given in Budapest, where, with the exception of Hesch, Kubelík and Wihan, all the assisting artists were Hungarian.

On December 20th, 1899, in Budapest, Dvořák himself conducted his "Hero's Song", the 'Cello Concerto and the "Carnival" Overture, the rest of the program being devoted to Haydn and Mendelssohn. The applause was frenetic and the Hungarian papers welcomed the "Czechish Schumann".

Of course, he went sightseeing in the lovely Hungarian capital, and of course he heard the Gypsy orchestras play. On his return to Prague, he declared: "It's extraordinary how much Gypsy music is like modern counterpoint: everyone plays what he likes, but it all comes out together and it sounds all right!"

In Prague, on April 4th, 1900, he was to conduct for the last time; it was, however, the first time that, with the Czechish Philharmonic Orchestra, he conducted other works besides his own. The program comprised: "Woodpigeon", Brahms' "Tragic Overture", Schubert's B minor Symphony and Beethoven's Eighth.

Rarely did Dvořák of his own volition appear as conductor; almost always it was a concert-manager who wanted him to conduct. Whenever he did conduct, however, he gave himself up to the task with all the ardor of his nature. The Budapest papers reported that, when he conducted, he appeared to be twenty years younger and that, at such moments, his face was really beautiful. At all events, wherever he conducted, in Germany, Russia, England and the United States, he assuredly did honor to his own works and to the whole of Czechish music, gaining new friends for both.

Perhaps he had decided that now, about the turn of the century, he no longer needed to campaign on behalf of his own works. He had found, in the person of Oskar Nedbal, a real apostle whose great gifts as a conductor were definitely demonstrated by his interpretations of the work of his teacher. Simrock invited Nedbal to conduct a Dvořák Concert in the Berlin Beethoven-Saal, on March 2nd, 1900.

The program contained The "New World" Symphony, "Woodpigeon", Three "Gypsy Melodies" and other Songs, the "Carnival" Overture and the Violin Concerto, played by Hoffmann. The souvenir program contained an essay on Dvořák by Nedbal, analyses of his Works by Peter Raabe, and Zeyer's translation of "Woodpigeon" (that had so pleased Simrock). The critics were all present at the General Rehearsal, and the reviews were all enthusiastic. Both for Nedbal and the assisting artists, it was an outstanding success; financially, it was less so.

With this concert, Nedbal began his career in foreign lands: the same year he conducted two concerts at the Paris World's Fair. Wherever he conducted, The "New World" Symphony was featured on his programs. Like one of the characters in Dvořák's operas, a man of the people, of the soil, witty, primitive and unspoilt, Nedbal well knew how to interpret and bring closer to his audiences every nuance of this masterpiece. It was his personal triumph and Dvořák's, too. That triumph was re-echoed when the young Toscanini conducted this work, victorious throughout the world, at the Scala in Milan.

About this time, early in 1900, Dvořák was requested to write a festival cantata for the seventieth birthday of the Conservatory's President, Dr. Josef Tragy. Dr. Tragy had, indeed, merited high honors for his work on behalf of the Conservatory and on behalf of music education in general in Bohemia; it was he who had been responsible for uniting the Organ School with the Conservatory.

The text provided was by Vrchlický, and Dvořák ac-

tually revered Dr. Tragy. But he flew into a temper when
the proposal was first made: no ideas had occurred to him
in the past fortnight! Two days later, discussing the matter
in his class-room, he was much calmer, saying: "The good
director is waiting for that composition, and I haven't even
begun it. Three times I've tried, and three times I've thrown
it into the stove."

At his next lesson-period, he was in the best of spirits,
declaring the Cantata was almost ready. In despair, he had
gone to Church and there he had heard an hymn that corresponded exactly in rhythm to the meter of Vrchlický's
verses. This had given him fresh courage. . . . In two days'
time, he had completed the entire cantata.

This *"Festival Cantata" for Mixed Choir and Orchestra*,
Op. 113, finished on April 17th, 1900, was a tour de force,
written to fit the occasion, and yet its music is of the most
noble and distinguished kind. Dvořák himself conducted
the chorus and orchestra, all members of the Conservatory,
on May 20th, as an internal affair in honor of their President. Strictly speaking, this was Dvořák's last appearance
as conductor.

He was by this time working steadily on his next (and,
next but last) opera, *"Rusalka"*. His finding of the story was
pure chance. The author was Jaroslav Kvapil, a young poet
better known later on as a dramatist, stage-director and
high official in the Art Department of the Ministry of Education. Probably influenced by the latest trend in poetry,
that of writing fairy-tales for the stage, and more especially
impressed by Gerhart Hauptmann's "The Sunken Bell",

Kvapil had taken the age-old "Undine" motive, to be found among the legends of so many peoples, and shaped it into an opera libretto. He had offered it successively to Nedbal, Foerster and Suk, but without arousing their interest. When this came to the knowledge of Dvořák, whom Kvapil had not had the temerity to approach, he literally pounced on the book. Begun at the end of April, he had finished composing this opera, his Op. 114, before December, 1900.

Kvapil had taken the features now of Undine, now of Melusine, combining them with a creation all his own, and, despite all affinities with Andersen and Hauptmann, he had produced an original work with a Czechish national flavor. Dvořák was especially intrigued by such devices as Kvapil's letting the people speak through the game-keeper and cook in a sort of chorus commenting upon the course of events.

There was more to it than this: Dvořák was enthralled by the fairytale element in the story, by that something intangible. It appealed to him because of the harshness of destiny, inexorably holding sway in spite of all the gentler emotions, and he was especially attuned to the concept of Nature as a protective and consoling Power. This Nature was the Nature he knew: a mighty Being whose kingdom no-one could defile, whose barriers no man could destroy and whose laws not even dwellers in the supernatural world could defy. In "Rusalka" humankind recedes into the background: this is a drama of the Elementals, of conflicts between irreconcilable spheres, a drama which therefore can have only one solution—tragedy.

On the other hand, as far as opera-goers are concerned,

some of the novelty of the story has been diminished by an acquaintance with Lortzing's "Undine". E. T. A. Hoffmann's "Undine" has none the less effectively demonstrated that there are other possible operatic solutions of the problems here posed.

This is the Dvořák-Kvapil version: In the clearing between Forest and Lake, the Elementals reign: The Water Goblin; the Nixie, Rusalka, and her sisters. And here, too, stands the hut of the powerful Witch, Ježibaba. Elves and Nixies dance and sing in the Moonlight, enticing the Water Goblin out of his Lake and teasing him. Rusalka sings to him her plaintive song: she loves a man, the Prince who often comes to bathe in the Lake, and she longs to find his love and to experience earthly passion. The Water Goblin warns her of danger, but hints that there is only one who can help her, the Witch, Ježibaba, who is capable of altering Nature herself!

Appealed to by Rusalka, the Witch agrees to transform her into a fleshly woman, but she will be speechless in the realm of humankind. Should her lover deceive her, she will become a Nixie again and he will succumb to a terrible curse. Rusalka is willing to take every risk. Once again, during her magic metamorphosis, the Nixies and the Water Goblin warn her of dangers to come. But by now Rusalka is a woman of unearthly beauty. The coming of the Prince is announced by hunting-fanfares, with a weird and sorrowful undertone. For the third and last time warned by the Elementals, Rusalka heedlessly follows the Prince.

Act II: In the garden about the Castle, there are great

preparations for the wedding of Rusalka to the Prince. There is something uncanny about the beautiful Stranger: why is Rusalka so mute, why so strangely cool? The game-keeper and cook comment in the vernacular upon these proceedings, especially on the fact that the Prince no longer evinces the same passion for Rusalka. Instead, he pays court to a Duchess among the wedding-guests.

Rusalka is being attired for the evening's festivities. The Prince and the Duchess are alone in the garden. There is dancing in the illuminated park, and wedding-songs are heard. In the Lake, the Water Goblin laments the fate of his playmate, Rusalka, who now seeks him out, pouring forth the tale of her woes. Water Goblin and Rusalka witness a love-scene between the Prince and Duchess, whereupon the Water Goblin, in his most terrifying guise, appears to the Prince, prophesying his doom. The Duchess mockingly deserts the Prince. Rusalka sinks with the Water Goblin to the bottom of the Lake.

The Third Act takes place in the clearing between Lake and Forest. Rusalka is pining away, pale, enfeebled, scarce more than a flickering chimera. Ježibaba tells her the only remedy: in order to be restored to her former Nixie-nature, she must kill her beloved. This Rusalka cannot do, for she still loves the Prince. The gamekeeper and the cook beg the Witch to rescue the Prince, who is under a spell. With objurgations on the race of humankind, the Water Goblin drives them away. The Elves resume their dancing, but when they learn of Rusalka's unhappy fate, sorrowfully disappear into the Forest. The Prince, his mind distraught, comes to the Lake, seeking Rusalka. She appears and he sinks in her arms, lifeless. Having atoned for her folly, the saddened Rusalka plunges into the Lake.

Dvořák, himself an elemental spirit, in his Rusalka introduces the romantic opera into the realm of Wagner. Employing Wagner's chromatic scales, his alterations, his chords of ninths, his admixtures of D minor, Dvořák transcends the musical idiom of "Tristan", arriving at the borderland of impressionism and even going beyond it. He intermingles the old opera of closed scenes with the music-drama style of continuous melody; he even goes back to the couplets of his earliest works. He still further intensifies his use of the leitmotif. And here again he introduces the group-leitmotif: there is one for the natural kingdom, one for the love of everything human, one for the common sorrowing of all creatures. In addition, there are individual leitmotifs for the Water Goblin (a reiterated phantom knocking), for the Prince and for the Duchess. Yet all of this is far removed from any schematic system.

Here is the especially characteristic "Nixie-yearning" motive, that of Rusalka, above the lulling accompaniment of the waves and the rigid organ-point bass in B, with the Undine-like crash to the diminished seventh chord:

Dvořák's homogeneity of mood most beautifully pervades every detail of the extremely delicate, lyric scenes precisely as it does the scenes of dramatic force. He achieves the greatest operatic effects in this work, and his lyric power remains irresistible. Such soaring flights of genius as his are based upon the sheer artistry of the composer of songs as well as upon the sound technique of the composer of symphonies.

The brief Overture, in which the entire opera is contained as if in embryo, is a veritable masterpiece. There is in it that same unity of mood, that tender mourning, that elemental force which are attributes of Dvořák's art. With artistic mastery, precise technique and an uncanny sureness, he expresses yearning, love and the certainty of tragic doom in all his arias, particularly in those of Rusalka. With great felicity he contrasts the world of the Elementals with the affairs of men in the Castle, particularly with the folk-being and folk-idiom of retainers and servants. In a grandiose repeat-crescendo, in the Third Act, the world of the supernatural regains possession of the stage, drenching the soul of the listener with poignant and magnificent emotional intensity.

The success of "Rusalka" was the greatest Dvořák ever experienced. True, it was so only in Bohemia, but there it became the closest favorite to "The Bartered Bride". The première, on March 31st, 1901, however, was not entirely auspicious since the tenor, Burian, who should have sung the Prince, had begun to "celebrate" too soon. Fortunately, Dvořák had provided for a competent understudy.

On hearing the news of its bombshell success, Gustav Mahler expressed the wish to produce "Rusalka" at the Vienna Opera. Rehearsals were carried on so zealously that the Vienna première was expected in December. Mahler even secured better terms for Dvořák than the Vienna Imperial Opera usually granted. Dvořák, making frequent trips to Vienna, declared himself wholly satisfied with the cast: Rusalka, Berta Foerster-Lauterer; Water Goblin, Hesch; the Prince, Slezak; the Duchess, Marie Gutheil-Schoder. (Hesch and Foerster-Lauterer had repeatedly sung in Dvořák's operas at the Prague National Theater.) Everything was finally set for the première in March, 1902. But Dvořák, for some reason mistrustful of the whole affair, had not signed the contract. At all events, Hesch fell ill, and "Rusalka" was postponed until the following season. And that was the last that was heard of a Vienna production.

Was the Vienna Opera Management annoyed because Dvořák had not accepted such a favorable contract? One thing is certain: Mahler had the best intentions, and there were positively no prejudices to wreck this production, the success of which would have given Dvořák especially great joy and the failure of which severely affected him.

"Rusalka" was not heard in Vienna until 1910 when it was performed by the Brünn Opera Company on tour, and again in 1924 when the Olmütz Czechish Theater brought it to the Austrian Capital. On both occasions it made a profound impression and, in 1924 especially, a number of Viennese critics declared it was incomprehensible that such great music had been so long neglected.

In 1924, a Czechish road company produced "Rusalka" in Barcelona and Madrid. In 1929, it was produced in German at Stuttgart and, soon after, by the German Theater in Brünn.

Official Duties and Distinctions—"Armida"

ON THE MORNING after the première, Dvořák came into the office of the Czechish National Theater, where Kvapil was engaged as assistant stage director, and, obviously in high spirits, demanded (according to Kvapil's memoirs):

"Quick! A new libretto!"

"I haven't any!"

"Then write me one at once, one that will stimulate me to compose, and be sure to put into it a good role for Maturová!" (the Rusalka of the première).

About this time Dvořák simply could not compose enough operas, and he was not even thinking of retiring. But he did not get his text: Kvapil was too busy with his work at the Theater; and nothing else turned up. Again there was a pause in Dvořák's work, this time enforced, and the longest in his life. On the other hand, there was no lack of concerts, and the coming event of his 60th birthday cast its shadow before. Hamburg and Budapest extended invitations. In Vienna, Mahler conducted his "Serenade for Wind Instruments", Op. 44; Ferdinand Löwe conducted the "Requiem", in March, 1901; and Hellmesberger, relieving Mahler, who was ill, conducted the Overture, "In Nature's Realm", with the Vienna Philharmonic Orchestra. In Berlin, Nikisch conducted "Woodpigeon", and when Dvořák stood to take his bows in the Management's box, the entire Orchestra rose to its feet in spontaneous ovation.

Once again, the Austrian Government gave Dvořák a great distinction. In mid-April, 1901, the Emperor named Dvořák and Vrchlický life-members of the Austrian House of Lords. Dvořák's compatriot, the Minister, Dr. Rezek, had proposed them for this honor, all the greater inasmuch as Dvořák was the first musician ever elected to the House of Lords. Of course, it was merely a gesture of Imperial favor. For Dvořák had not the slightest interest in politics and he could not bear to listen to debates.

He went to Vienna, to be present at only one session, on May 14th, when he was sworn in by Prince Windischgrätz, President of the House. Dvořák and Vrchlický traveled together, Dvořák as usual saying virtually nothing. When the train passed the Wittingau marshes, Vrchlický expressed his astonishment at the clouds of midges. Dvořák did not reply until, arrived in Vienna, they were walking on the Ringstrasse, when he opined: "That's probably because there's so much water."

In the House of Lords, many politicians of the day came to the last bench on the right-hand side of the House, where Dvořák was sitting. All wanted to congratulate him and each spoke with enthusiasm of his music. Rieger did all his answering for him. Dvořák only growled something, sat with his gaze glued to the door and was highly pleased when at last he could make his escape. That was the end of his political career, and he never again entered the House of Lords. As souvenirs, he carried off some magnificently sharpened pencils that lay upon his desk. Proudly beaming, he told his wife that these pencils would be of great help in his composing.

On July 6th, 1901, Dvořák became *Director of the Prague Conservatory*. It happened in this way: Bennewitz, now seventy, wanted to retire. A brilliant organizer, apart from everything else, he had headed the Conservatory for the past twenty years. The Board of Directors was confronted with a dilemma: in view of his musical eminence, Dvořák was the only one who came into consideration as Bennewitz' successor, but they were well aware Dvořák was no organizer.

Finally, they hit upon the solution. Bennewitz was elected Honorary Member of the Board (he died in 1926, at the age of 93, in Hirschberg); Dvořák was made Director, but all business affairs were entrusted to Professor Knittl. It was typical of Dvořák that, whenever he wanted to go to Vysoká, he would ask Knittl, his deputy representative, for leave. A young musician who came to the Conservatory once asked to see the Director and was told by the beadle: "He's not here. What would he be doing here?"

In Vysoká, Dvořák went on just as usual with his morning constitutional, his organ-playing, visits to the local inn, work in the garden and pigeon-breeding. But he was made restless by a fresh desire to compose. A poem with a social message by Svatopluk Čech, entitled "The Smith of Lešetín" came into his hands, and he set it for tenor and piano.

The folk-idiom and the general feeling of solidarity among the people, together with the national note it expressed, all impelled him to undertake this work, as the music bears witness. Harmonically it is not uninteresting. The arrangement by Josef Suk, entitled "Fresh from the Forge", together with various other posthumous works previously unpublished, was brought out by Simrock in 1911.

On August 20th, 1901, at sixty years of age, Fritz Simrock died in Lausanne, the last of the immediate descendants of Nikolaus Simrock. The famous House had for three generations published works by Beethoven, Mendelssohn, Schumann, Brahms and Dvořák, and the proprietors had always been on close personal terms with their composers. They had constantly entertained the most eminent people. To Dvořák, Fritz Simrock had been more than a mere publisher. They had sincerely esteemed each other and, in spite of their totally different characters, remained friends even during that short period when their business relations were interrupted.

Dvořák was very deeply moved by this sad news; it was all the more difficult for him to turn to other thoughts: his own 60th birthday was not far off. If only they would have forgotten him! As soon as some new honor was conferred upon him, he would ask: "Do they have to do that?" His distrust of the sincerity of public opinion was great and he often sighed, saying that a Czechish musician in his position certainly did not have an easy time of it. They had only allowed Smetana to live after he had been dead a long time. But there was nothing for it: just at that time Chvála, Krejčí,

Knittl, Boleška, Hostinský, Hoffmeister and several other musicians published a booklet in honor of Dvořák, containing their several uncommonly valuable contributions on Dvořák's life and works.

On Dvořák's birthday, Nelahozeves staged a gala celebration, but Dvořák could not be there. On that September 8th, 1901, he had urgent business in Vienna. On the same day, the Czechish National Theater in Prague began the production of the full cycle of Dvořák's operas, from "The Obstinate Children" to "Rusalka", and followed this with the Oratorio, "Ludmila". And when the cycle had ended, on November 6th, then the celebrations really began. While he was being detained at home through a ruse, a festive parade marched up to his house, a corps of singers entered the courtyard and serenaded him. He was compelled—at the cost of considerable effort—to appear at the window and thank them. In a towering rage, although affected to tears, when they would not stop crying "Long live Dvořák!", he roared: "Tell them to stop shouting!"

On the following day, the National Theater gave a special gala performance of "Rusalka". In the Rudolfinum there were three gala concerts of his chamber-music works, symphonic works and the Requiem. On November 10th, the Prague National Museum gave a gala reception: Professor Knittl delivered the ceremonial address, all the artists of Prague were present, and there was only one missing—Dvořák! On the other hand, he found it impossible to disappear when the "Umělecká beseda" (Art Society) gave a banquet in his honor. He even made a short speech:

"When I first heard about what you were planning to do, I was very much upset. But then I thought to myself that I would probably survive this, too." There were countless congratulations: from Minister President Koerber down, nobody had forgotten Dvořák's birthday.

He still was not allowed to enjoy his peace of mind. His daughter, Ottilie, was expecting a child, and he was much worried because she had heart-trouble. Nevertheless, she was happily delivered and, on December 19th, 1901, Dvořák was a grandfather. His grandson was christened Josef.

There were fresh performances of his works all over the world. From England, in January 1902, Hans Richter wrote a warm letter, begging Dvořák not to miss Bayreuth that year. This was his last letter from Richter, and Dvořák's reply, likewise his last, dated February 11th, was almost premonitory: "You have all my thanks for everything you have done for my works. It was my dearest wish to visit Bayreuth, but it is so difficult to get there!"

All this time, Dvořák continued in expectation of a long life. His own father had lived to be eighty, and he himself felt energetic and in the best of health. He was not even disturbed by the fact that a whole year, the first since the beginning of his career, had gone by, without his having conceived a single big work.

He had many plans, and any number of opera librettos passed through his hands. It is said that he renounced the idea of composing a "Death of Vlasta" in favor of the young composer, Ostrčil, later opera director of the National Theater. He also considered a "Cinderella" libretto by Hostinský. Vrclický proposed to him a new Oratorio, a complementary piece to "Ludmila", this time about another Czechish historical figure, St. Adalbert. Dvořák is said to have replied that he could not do anything with a text providing so few roles for women. There was also some talk of a "Nazareth" Oratorio, to be followed by a "Golgotha". But Dvořák declared that anybody attempting to compose a "Golgotha" must "have such a head", and he spread his hands wide.

Very likely, he only wanted to compose an opera. He was certainly not averse to a Biblical text. He loved reading the Bible, copies of which he possessed in English, modern and ancient Czechish. He would have preferred to compose to his own text: if he had been a poet, he said, he would have heard the music while writing down his verses. (This again was Wagner!) But since he was compelled to look for poets, when he could not find one, he became so disgruntled that, toward the end, he did not want to meet anybody. If only he could find another great work!

Finally, at long last, he decided upon a libretto by Vrchlický. Strangely enough, he, the composer in the national folk-idiom, turned to a story of universal implications, one of those great sagas of world literature: a translation, entitled "Armida", based on Tasso's "Jerusalem Delivered". There have been not a few "Armida"-operas: those of Lully, Händel, Vivaldi, Salieri, Gluck, Cimarosa, Haydn, Cherubini, Rossini and Dvořák's countryman, Mysliveček-Venatorini. Among all these, the only one that is heard nowadays, rarely enough, is that by Gluck. Incidentally,

Gluck composed his Armida at the same age as Dvořák did.

What attracted them all to this work was the quasi-mythical illumination of Tasso's characters and the contrast between two worlds, that of Christian Europe and that of the 'pagan' Orient. There was also the purely human conflict between love and duty, as in "Parsifal" and "Tannhäuser" —which Dvořák still considered Wagner's best work. He hoped to compose a Czechish "Armida" that should be worthy to rank with those masterpieces, and, perhaps, be heard on foreign stages.

Vrchlický had translated into Czechish the entire epic of "Jerusalem Delivered". But in his opera libretto he has not used a single verse of that translation. Instead, he has altered the plot motivation and created an entirely new poem.

The army of the Crusaders led by Godfrey of Bouillon appears before Damascus, and the pagan ruler, King Hydraot, is terrified by the tremendous strength of Godfrey's forces. Hydraot's ally is Ismen, King of Syria, who is also a magician.

Ismen advises Hydraot to send his beautiful daughter, Armida, into the camp of the Crusaders, where her beauty will be sure to stir up such confusion that the Islamites will be able to destroy them. Ismen has in vain been making love to Armida and, being spurned, now hopes to bring down calamity upon her. Armida refuses to enter the Christian camp. But Ismen conjures up the image of Rinaldo, one of the Crusaders, whom she had chanced to meet in the forest and with whom she had fallen in love at first sight. Thus Armida is persuaded.

In the Second Act, she begs the guards to lead her before Godfrey of Bouillon. Peter the Hermit will not permit this because he senses that she is in the service of the unbelievers. But Rinaldo takes her part and conducts her to Godfrey, to whom she spins a story intended to lure the Crusaders into Damascus. Having accomplished her mission, forgetting everything but her love for Rinaldo, she flees with him. They take refuge in a magic garden that Ismen has conjured up in the desert.

In the Third Act, Ismen reveals to two Knights of the Crusade how they may release Rinaldo from under the spell of Armida's love: this can only be done by means of the Magic Shield of the Archangel Michael, concealed in a magic castle. The Knights get possession of the Shield.

In the Fourth Act, Rinaldo repents having fallen into love's toils and returns to the Crusade. In the battle with the pagan host, Rinaldo kills Ismen and wounds to the death Armida, clad as a knight. Recognizing her, his love flares up again and he baptizes the dying Armida.

Ismen's love for Armida and her tragic death are both extraneous to Tasso's poem. The libretto, at any rate, affords the composer enough material and certainly enough contrasts: the poetry of the Orient, the Crusaders' life in camp, a magic garden, war, love and death. But the characters are obscured in fable, fairy-tale and myth. Whenever motivations fail, some sort of magic must be brought into play—not always effectively.

Dvořák began composing on April 11th, 1902. After the First Act, he wrote on the score: "Completed in Vysoká,

on June 30th, after the Fair, in very hot weather." The
whole work was not finished until a year later, on August
23rd, 1903. Dvořák had a difficult time with this libretto.
What he composed was a music of exalted ceremony, of
intoxicating sonority and often ravishing lyrical beauty.
The story demanded an alien coloring; the content of ideas
required a still closer approach to Wagner, particularly to
"Parsifal". Dvořák had never before turned more unresist-
ingly toward this genius who, all his life, had allured him.
This does not mean that he was dependent upon Wagner.
The motive of the Cross, reminiscent of Parsifal, in three
minor chords

is contrasted with the motive of the Crusader, solely characteristic of Dvořák:

Magnificent arias, especially that of Armida, lead up to
the climax of Armida's love-duet with Rinaldo. There are
many alterations and D major elements in the harmony.
Dvořák achieves especial refinement in the instrumentation:
with the simplest means, often by sparing use of a color, he
secures effects that actually seem to reproduce in tone the
magical power of the poetic Middle Ages. There are fewer
closed forms; the goal that he most strives for is the music-

drama. He attempts the same thing with the leitmotif technique that he had in the two foregoing operas: characterization of each group by its own particular theme, with variant themes for leading individuals belonging to the several groups. Dvořák, though he is evidently fascinated by the erotic magic of Armida, does not neglect Rinaldo or even Ismen.

It is a touching spectacle! Here is this master of the art of reproducing the genuine folk-idiom, folk-being and folk-character who, even in pathetic moments, always knew how to find some sort of solution or diversion such as a polka. And now we find him, in the last opera that he was to write, in fact the very last music of his career, succumbing to the mystic ardor of his own inner being. And the final chapter that he writes is a paean of praise to the world of great heroic pathos, to that world of which he supposedly knew nothing, to which apparently he was a stranger! He seeks protection in that faith of his in a Higher Power, which, after all the battles of his life, can still raise him to his feet undaunted, strengthened, with courage ever new. Of Dvořák it may well be said: He lived, he created, he conquered!

Although we feel the exaltation of this alien world, and it is certain that Dvořák experienced it, nevertheless the operatic fate of "Armida" was not immediately gratifying. It was no topical work for the day, it was certainly not likely to be popular with numbers of people. Not yet, at any rate. It was produced for the first time on March 25th, 1904, in the Czechish National Theater, and presumably there was not very much conviction behind that production. In that year it was performed only six times, and in the thirty years after his death, only twenty-one times. Very few theaters in Czechoslovakia ventured to produce it. No piano score has been published, and only eight excerpts from "Armida" were brought out in 1921 by Hudebni Matice.

Even with his head full of plans and his hands full of work, Dvořák took the liveliest interest in every artistic event, particularly in what went on at the opera. He spent more and more time at the National Theater, not so much at performances—for he always left early to go home to bed—as at rehearsals. He was especially fascinated by the revivals of "Wilhelm Tell" and "Les Huguenots," and he was careful not to miss the première of "Tosca" in November, 1903. It was, however, his passion for the opera that drove him, and not a predilection for the singers. "Their high C is nothing but a circus!" he used to say. One taste of Puccini was enough for him. As a man he was offended by the libretto, which he found "brutal", and as a musician by the constant outpouring of fifths.

"When I die," he once told a soprano, "if they should sing a lot of fifths at me that way, I'd jump out of my grave!"

The artist replied: "Yet you tell me that fifths are not worth-while when they can restore our beloved Master to life!"

He growled in despair: "This is what happens when you get drawn into conversation with a woman!"

He did not particularly care to hear the productions of

Berlioz' "Carmen" or Charpentier's "Louise", the latter of which was new at that time. But their music could not leave him unaffected. After having heartily scolded "Louise", two months later, following the première, he bought the piano-score and made himself thoroughly acquainted with it. He made crosses and question-marks on the margin, with remarks such as "These fifths are very beautiful, but I can't stand it."

Contrariwise, he was immensely proud when the Czech-ish National Theater produced "Under the Apple-tree", a music-"melodrama" by his son-in-law, Suk, with book by Zeyer. This was sound work with no fifths, and he found it good.

From abroad, he heard more and more news of success-ful performances. And whenever foreign artists of rank visited Prague, they always made it a point to pay their re-spects to Dvořák. Safonoff, who gave a recital in January, 1903, was an old acquaintance. He took pleasure in again meeting Edvard Grieg, who gave a recital of his own com-positions in Prague. Dvořák felt a great sympathy for Grieg and knew it to be reciprocated.

Grieg, who was not feeling very well, gave orders that he wished to see no-one but Dr. Dvořák; thereafter, he re-turned the visit. According to his habit of recording impor-tant events, Dvořák wrote on one page of his "Armida" sketches: "The day of Grieg's concert, March 25th, 1903". After Dvořák's death, Grieg wrote a long, warm-hearted obituary and tribute for one of the Norwegian newspapers. In his letter of condolence to Dvořák's daughter, Magda,

Grieg begged her to believe that he had loved and esteemed not only Dvořák the artist, but Dvořák, the fine and upright man.

With great diligence and affection, Dvořák continued his teaching until the end. He was always surrounded and besieged by pupils. About this time, he noticed the unusual talent of Rudolf Karel. If, however, it occurred to any unfortunate pupil to try out some of the latest fashionable innovations, he was met with a scornful outburst. For a while, after the success of "Louise", everybody was writing for "stopped trombones". Dvořák insisted it was not permissible for the trombones to "blow their noses" too often in one work!

The early months of 1904 were none too auspicious for the rehearsals and première of "Armida". There was not the same zeal at rehearsing this difficult work in a new style. The singers for the most part grew slack in their roles, and "the Old Man" grumbled, which did not mend matters. Scenically and musically, as far as the orchestra was concerned, the production was not on the same high level. The final rehearsals and General Rehearsal were stormy, indeed. Dvořák came, of course, to the première, but had to leave before it was over. He was suffering from "an indisposition". No-one dreamt that this was the first intimation of the end.

The End

HE WAS SUFFERING from uremia and progressive arteriosclerosis. For the first time in his life, he was seriously ill, more seriously than the members of his family or even the physicians supposed. Later on, it was maintained that the excitement attendant upon operatic production had accelerated his trouble. A false assumption. His was an organic disease, although the wear and tear of the theater was anything but beneficial. He had complained about pains in his side; to quiet him, the family physician, Professor Hnátek, assured him they were nothing but rheumatic pains, and Dvořák accepted that diagnosis.

About this time, preparations were under way for the First Czechish Music Festival in Prague, when several of his works were to be produced. He had also agreed to be present at the revival of "Dimitrij" in Pilsen; and in Kremsier, on May 7th and 8th, he was to conduct "The Spectre's Bride", with his daughter Magda singing the soprano solo. It was a severe disappointment to him not to be able to take part in the Music Festival, for which an excellent program with the best artists was planned. And there was to be a choir of 3000.

In April, 1904, the week before Easter, Dvořák's "Ludmila" opened the Festival, followed by his Violin Concerto and The New World Symphony. His condition was very much worse. He had gone for his regular morning constitutional to the Railway Station and spent some time chatting about his beloved locomotives. Apparently, he had stood too long in the chill air. He caught cold and was laid up when the various participants in the Festival came to see him.

In the early days of April, his health grew rapidly worse.

Professor Janovský was called into consultation and upheld Professor Hnátek's diagnosis: uremia and arteriosclerosis. Dvořák was reassured, and his family felt confident that his strong constitution would help him to overcome any danger. He was in a passably good mood, sometimes quite cheerful, and kept on asking if he would be well soon enough to conduct the concerts in Kremsier. He was promised that he would.

He was not very happy, however, about the plans of his household for moving. His family had finally persuaded him to take a new and larger apartment on May 1st. He himself was quite satisfied to remain in the old, very small flat, and he particularly prized the quiet, old house because in the entire neighborhood no-one played the piano. But that move, at any event, was not to be for him. Towards the end of April, he suffered a decline. On the 27th, they telegraphed Kremsier that, in view of the unfavorable weather, it was unthinkable that he should travel and he could not conduct.

The first of May was a day of brilliant sunshine, everybody was in good spirits, and Dvořák was so much better that the Doctor allowed him to have luncheon at the table with his family. He was feeling rather weak from lying still for so long, and in order to restore his sense of balance, made a tour of the dining-room. He sat at the head of the table and ate his soup with appetite. Suddenly turning pale, he muttered that he did not feel at all well, and was helped back to bed. Almost immediately he lost consciousness. Dr. Hnátek, who lived across the way, hurried over, but could only establish that the end had come swiftly with a brain-stroke. It was early afternoon.

Thus a great and noble life came to its end.

On May-day half of Prague was out-of-doors on excursions in the countryside; only his immediate family and friends could be notified. The first visitors to bring condolences were the Conductor of the National Theater, Šubert; Mme. Maturová, the singer; Anger, the friend of Dvořák's youth and his faithful companion; Professor Knittl, and the publisher, Urbánek.

The family were stunned. They had been in no sense prepared for his sudden demise. Dvořák's abrupt end had a dire effect on his daughter, Ottilie, whose heart-trouble became so accentuated that she died a year later, on July 6th, 1905.

The sculptor, Maratka, who lived in the same house as Dvořák, made the death-mask and an impression of the right hand.

That evening, when the ticket-holders were coming to the Czechish National Theater to hear Smetana's "Brandenburger in Bohemia", they were astounded to see black drapes on the building. On the following day, the whole world heard the tragic news. Long, heartfelt and sympathetic obituaries were published everywhere, not only in Bohemia, but in Austria, Germany and England. Whole pages in the American papers were devoted to Dvořák. Memories were rife of all that Dvořák had meant to the "New World" and of the joyful expectations awakened when he was in this country. The family received countless declarations of sympathy, particularly from official quarters and musical organizations all over the world.

On May 3rd, the Municipal Corporations in charge of the funeral met in the Prague City Hall; the ceremonies were to be conducted by the City of Prague and the "Umělecká Beseda" (Art Society). On May 5th, the funeral was attended by a vast and touching demonstration. Thousands had come from near and far to line the way or to follow the cortège. The Governor of Prague headed the official dignitaries, and all the artists and art societies were represented.

The body was laid out in state in the Church of the Savior. After the Blessing, the procession wound its way past the Czechish National Theater, whence the tones of Dvořák's "Requiem" resounded. Dvořák was laid to rest in the Vyšehrad Cemetery, the Funeral Oration being delivered by Professor Knittl. Two years later, the sarcophagus was transferred to a place of honor in the arcades of the Cemetery. Dvořák's daughter, Anna, who died in 1923, and his wife, who died on July 14th, 1931, at the age of 77, were buried by his side.

CHAPTER V

THE MAN AND HIS WORK

THE FOREGOING CHAPTER was, of course, only the biographical conclusion of Dvořák's life. It is now high time to look upon Dvořák in his full stature, the man and the artist, apart from all biographical detail, and to consider his work as distinct from everything temporal and contemporary; as distinct, that is, from mortality. What is there about Anton Dvořák destined to remain indelible in our memories and engraved upon our hearts? Let us examine his spiritual heritage, transmuted and transfigured out of the mere incidents of life, the accidents of birth and of this earthly pilgrimage.

To all external appearances, what happened was this: there was a boy, born in the blessed, fertile valleys of Bohemia, before the Revolution of 1848, destined for a practical life and spiritually bound up with his people through their common love of music. But was that all?

When, at an early age, he left home and familiar surroundings to become identified with the City and when, later, he left the City to enter the great outside world of which he had long since become a spiritual citizen, he remained a plain and simple human being, of great goodness of heart although, his life long, he liked to bluster in order to conceal it. His deep religiousness led him at all times and in all places to recognize and revere the guidance of a Higher Power. Ethical purity and the love of Nature in all her creations, were a matter of course. His believing soul nevertheless on occasion liked to indulge in philosophical speculation.

By preference he spoke the language of the people and was in every sense a lover of the colloquial idiom and of folk customs. The vernacular and folk-poetry invariably touched the depths of his musician's heart. The roots of his creation are the melody and rhythm of folk-song and folk-dance. He did not imitate them, he did not simply borrow them, but he created completely in their spirit, delving into the same sources that were those of his inmost being.

Furthermore, he went outside the charmed circle of his Czechish environment to the music of other Slavs, to the Southern Slavs, Slovaks, Ukrainians, to the Poles, and to the Russians themselves. But however often he struck the Slav note, he never did so simply in order to localize or diminish the circumference of his art. On the contrary, through the medium of his own great gifts, but without any pretentions, he conducted the stream of Slav folk-music out of its mountain-glens and rivulets into the great ocean of the world's music.

He grew ever greater in stature in the region of art and the spirit, still retaining both feet on the ground, on the soil of his native land. His growth was not sudden, in fits and starts, but came by degrees, slowly, steadily, organically. The first years in Prague were devoted to the acquiring of craftsmanship, the later years to a modest citizenship in local music.

His genius burst the bounds of these limitations.

His pilgrimage to Vienna opened up to him the realm of music in Austria and, later, in Germany. His encounter with Brahms alone, at first a meeting in the spirit, was the "Open, Sesame!" Even before that, such a man as Ehlert in Wiesbaden had detected in the national being of Dvořák that which was natively and universally valid.

Dvořák, the inventor and musician in the grand manner, first conquered England and then America. It was a hazardous enterprise for the simple man that Dvořák was, although he bore the titles of Doctor and Professor, to make the transition to an entirely different world. On the other hand, the Americans made it easy for him, meeting him in human, friendly fashion, respecting that which was quaintly old-world about him because they distinctly felt his dignity and his undeniable genius.

The fruits of his three years in the United States are, indeed, a horn of plenty. Who knows what more he might have sown and harvested? But he had to return home—his heart commanded him; with the matter-of-fact certainty that governed his external life, he must go back to his native land. If there had been no other reason, the need of the Czechish Theater was sufficient.

The portrait of Dvořák is made up of individual features each of which has been discussed in this book. The total impression is that of an instinctively good, noble, tender-hearted and none the less determined man, capable of making definite decisions, who lived only for those he loved. But those he loved were also his pupils and his countrymen, and, furthermore, he had a profound understanding of human beings in general. He could also fly into a rage, but his rages were of short duration and without malice.

Possessing complete confidence in Providence and an All-Wise Guidance, he permitted the demands of external life to present their claims. Prosperity, honors, and fame were all his portion. Nevertheless, there is a slight trait of melancholy in his portrait, a melancholy not merely derived from his Slavic heritage. Perhaps he dreamt—with that yearning of ripe years that knows most wishes never can be fulfilled—of more things and of other things than were granted to him.

In this life there was, perhaps, something of tragedy. Be that as it may, Dvořák bore every trial manfully, faithfully, in his inmost being and in the depths of his soul a figure of destiny, almost a legendary incarnation. His faith in God, anchored deep within, was not only the firm foundation of his faith in life but also the actual driving-force of his creative activity.

It is, however, incumbent upon us to linger for a while in contemplation of his works. With an instinct we can only admire, Dvořák began his composing with works of chamber-music. He may have reaped fame from other sources, but the significance of his chamber-music was not to be surpassed. Whether composing for four or five stringed instruments alone, or for strings with piano, he left his stamp on a world of chamber-music closely akin to that of Brahms, although entirely independent of him. Dvořák's goal was the classic form, derived from Beethoven in its spiritual import and from Schubert in its sensibility and sonority, but adapted to a new content of ideas and a new manner of expression.

With Dvořák, the form alone is rarely victorious. More often than not, the very essence of South-Slav late romanticism molds the form to his will. Harmonically neither in advance of nor behind his times, betraying great but not startling craftsmanship, Dvořák, in his contrapuntal voice-leading, gives of his highest and best with full and yet delicate sonority. This is true both of his chamber-music and his symphonies, the instrumentation of which aims at a singing tone and at the euphony of each individual voice.

A master of instrumentation, he knew how to give an orchestral texture of great beauty to his own compositions and to some of Brahms' piano-pieces. Into that texture he wove his own, unique colors, but he never strained after gaudy effects.

In his treatment of form, he soon brought the sonata (in the first and last movements) to its full development, often cunningly disguising his first subject until it appeared in its own right, together with frequent modulations, especially in the mediants (as with Schubert), with a poignant song-theme and powerful climaxes. His developments are exhaustive, but almost never hair-splitting. Only in his "American" works is he not as thoroughgoing as usual. As long as he remains in the European sphere, he never relaxes that thoroughness with which at home in Bohemia every piece of work had to be executed.

His first and last movements are often imbued with gaiety but just as often with brooding seriousness, seldom with resignation or defiance. He is practically always sparing in that form of introspection peculiar to the symphony because, by nature a believing spirit, he is not often given to abstruse problems. Yet he does not evade such elucidation when unavoidable, as in his D minor Symphony, and, there, too, he is equal to the task.

It cannot be asserted that his chamber-music works and symphonies are especially overburdened at any one point: his first and last movements and the combined weight of the intermediate movements are carefully balanced against each other. Not one of his works promises more in some particular part than it fulfills throughout. Nowhere is there a doubtful over-accentuation of a single movement; and, throughout a given work, he practically always retains the same corps of instruments with which he began, without later augmentation of orchestra or of voices.

We are impressed by the beauty of melody in his slow movements, expressive of yearning or of Slav melancholy, in which his innate sensibility often attains Beethoven's heights. In the Scherzo, however, it is his affinity with the primal rhythm of his people that stands him in good stead. Sometimes he seems to fight shy of this affinity as if he feared to be composing an altogether too-popular dance. But then again he affirms precisely this derivation: we have already seen how in several suites and symphonies and in his chamber-music, Dvořák introduced the folk-dance in his art. There is no mistaking the national idiosyncracy of these works which were to become not only the pride of his own people but the delight and enchantment of the whole world.

Dvořák bequeathed symphonies and chamber-music with their distinctive Czechish melos, just as Smetana bequeathed the Czechish opera of the same genre—and, in the concert of the musics of the world, that melos is no longer to be missed. Quite cheerfully a lyric composer, Dvořák nevertheless rises to heights of dramatic majesty and tragic greatness, carrying away his hearers with daring constructions and crescendos. Our attention is caught and held by his peculiar periods, departing from the octave, and his drastic manner of crescendo-writing by the repetition of a section on the next-higher chromatic step.

In several of Dvořák's symphonies and chamber-music works, a certain relationship or identity of themes is found. This straightforward composer, although he disliked brooding speculation, certainly did not lack inventive power. Towards the close of his life, he returned again to consider the artistic and musical problems of his youth, and was thus stimulated afresh to discover new forms and new ideas. Many of his works somehow seem to be seeking again their own point of departure, thus inevitably falling into the cyclic form. Such a pioneer is never content to have achieved the next pinnacle, but is ceaselessly in search of new paths and fresh peaks to explore.

When we think of the outspoken character of his

Czechish national awareness, there was something almost miraculous, like the hand of Destiny, about the sequence of events leading up to his departure for the New World.

There is something of divination, too, about his modest yet well-defined attitude that was not particularly impressed by New York City or by the much-boasted civilization of the Eastern States, but, with a sure instinct, turned to the folk-music of the West and South, since become so very popular. American folk-melodies and rhythms gave Dvořák fresh stimuli even before we in America knew what to do with them ourselves. More than this, the spirit of America's natural wonders, the grandeur of the American landscape, took possession of Dvořák. It is remarkable that such an artist as he, who was not at all "literary", should become acquainted with this country first through books (Longfellow) and then find everything he had read confirmed by reality.

In spite of the love of order displayed in his work and in his life, Dvořák was ultimately not to be contented with the spacious, well-joined structure of traditional form. At the outset and close of his life, he was striving to transcend it; at the beginning, in his chamber-music (and in the opera) and, toward the end, in the symphonic poem. Both at the beginning, when the trail was still unblazed, and afterwards, when he had surveyed its possibilities, he sensed that there can be no ultimate satisfaction, and that he must ever discover fresh trails into the unknown Infinite. This is the eternal mission of the artist.

The romantic age before and after Wagner early

awakened this yearning in him. Close on Beethoven's achievement, Berlioz had already consciously aimed at and revealed the possibilities in new fields. Actually, Beethoven himself had previously done so. Liszt and Wagner are the completion, the realization of that dream of two generations. It follows that Dvořák, in his way, was not only a revolutionary in the opera-form and even in the content of opera, but he also burst the bounds of chamber-music and the symphony; he composed symphonic poems.

Still, he remained the unliterary artist: overwhelmed by the beauty of poetry, he must try to emulate it. If he should succeed—and he did succeed more often than not—so much the better. He was not so much concerned about the extent to which he did not succeed because, for him, the emphasis was on the music and the forms pertaining to music.

The soul of this apparently so simple man became involved in the historical, and for him contemporary, conflict concerning music. How often is the artist aware that a certain highway leads to a dead end! His people, together with whom he fought for a place in the sun, and of whom he wanted to be the champion, were in every phase of life to help him find the necessary solution. His people, too, were to help him mold fresh forms that would lead to a new synthesis of music and poetry. Not only was such the premise for his symphonic writing, but it was also the articulate urge of the day in which he lived.

In the Wagnerian epoch, there was certainly no more pre-Wagnerian opera. It was only after the close of that epoch that, here and there, outside the German realm, a reawakened national consciousness explored other trails—that led, however, to an utterly different goal. Dvořák, too, was tempted by the music-drama, and would have himself rejoiced to write a poetic libretto equal to that form. Wagner's imperative appeal was heard both at the beginning and towards the close of Dvořák's period of creative activity. His life was a culmination of cycles within cycles.

Even the comic opera, which, in the name of his people and of his great predecessor, Smetana, Dvořák was driven to compose, assumed the mantle of that Wagner of the Meistersinger. It was only later that Smetana showed him the way to Mozart and, therewith, finally and irrevocably, to the primacy of music over poetry. He had always found it difficult to abandon melody, to push back the singer behind the orchestra; now, he no longer attempted to do so. The orchestra became more than ever important to the expression of his ideas, but the singing voice was restored to its rights.

Dvořák's concern for spiritual unity led to the growth of his leitmotif, later becoming the collective-leitmotif: the leitmotif for an entire group, with variants for friend and foe. At first he derived his texts from mythical sources: "Alfred", "Wanda". But later it was the people that gave him the greatest inspiration: "The Peasant Rogue", "Jacobin", "The Devil and Kate", "Rusalka". Finally, in his search for the opera-stage that was to be the whole world, Dvořák made another foray into the world's treasury of myth and legend and, undismayed by the many who had tried and failed before him, composed his "Armida".

In his Lieder, the battle between music and poetry was soon fought out, decidedly in favor of the musician. With Dvořák, the melody and the mood are perfectly synthesized. His voice is heard most clearly in the delicate, folk-song-like airs of the "Moravian Duets". This is pure folk-music conceived by a great artist; and in his piano-works the dance and rhythm, or song and mood, of the people, transfigure the whole. In all vocal literature there is nothing like the strength of religious feeling that exalts his "Biblical Songs". They belong to the sphere of his great works in sacred music. In these songs, both composer and listener are overcome by the adoration of his spirit.

In larger forms, the liturgical exaltation of the "Mass in D" and "Requiem" reveal him to be, in his unique fashion, truly worthy of the task. At one moment he is "God's Musikant" (particularly, a Bohemian Musikant, as in the Oratorio, "St. Ludmila") and at another, he is the pupil of the great Masters of classic music. His "Stabat mater" proclaims in no hollow tones the teaching and sublimity of pain; here speaks his wounded, sorrowing heart. Here, too, he reveals that his soul comprised both heights and depths: his sacred music is the antithesis of that joyous unconcern evident in so many of his instrumental compositions. Yet everything that Dvořák writes, whatever for instruments or voices, has the spiritual sonority of a clarified soul.

The only thing "average" about Dvořák was the regulated life of the middle class, to him a predisposing condition for good work: order in outward circumstances was fundamental. Nevertheless, his intellectual, spiritual and emotional life remained unaffected by middle-class conventions. Whoever was as closely bound to the folk and the earth as he was, lives and creates out of all the urges, from elemental necessity to demonic obsession: a spirit tireless, thirsting to create, and God-imbued.

The only formula we can write for Dvořák is this: the elemental artist.

Whereas Smetana was a great thinker and, through the arts, the interpreter of his age to his own people, Dvořák is a veritable child of the good, sound, Czechish earth. In contrast to the fighting musician, spiritualized by suffering, who was Smetana, Dvořák is a discoverer, motivated by natural forces, who is at one and the same time the favored child of life and fortune. With humility and gratitude he enjoyed the blessings that came to him. Tragic tensions are alien to him, yet intuition revealed to him the meaning of Destiny, intensive contemplation ripening to wisdom. He was not naive, as people sometimes thought, but he was entirely free from artifice. One thing he was above all, and that was elemental.

On the great National Memorial in Weimar, there was found room for two great poets: Goethe and Schiller. It would be perfectly appropriate for Czechish music to erect twin monuments to Smetana and Dvořák, and not far away there should stand another pair, Fibich and Janáček.

The fact that Dvořák, the neo-classic artist of the late romantic period, the standard-bearer and preserver of melody and form, should be so well understood by Janáček, the "impressionist" (or, if preferred, "expressionist"), is a recommendation for both. It is also a testimonial to the enduring beneficent virtue of a Dvořák, whose teaching, master-craftsmanship and spiritual strength still hold sway in his people. If there were surviving no others than Novák, Suk, and Nedbal to go on creating in the spirit of their master, Dvořák's heritage would be assured. To the younger generation, however, Dvořák is no mere adjunct to be placed on an already enduring national monument, but a force still at work, a portion of their essential art life.

These final words are written while remembering a long and delightful conversation about Dvořák, in which Alois Hába led the talk. When he had finished speaking, we were gazing across the square at the reflected lights from many peaceful windows. It was on the Market Place of that beautiful old city, Litomysl, where Smetana was born. Meditating on what had been said, our hearts were stirred by a great faith in all that is enduring and good; the sound earth held us in fast embrace; we could not help feeling Dvořák's unity of being with the universal spirit of the world, and out of that feeling veneration deepened. Our thoughts and emotions were altogether consecrated to Dvořák and to the glowing wonder of living Czechish music—an art steeled in the fires of our time, an art of infinite creative possibilities.

That art and the people to whom it belongs need have nothing to fear from tyrants.

[THE END]

Dvořák's Works

Compiled by Otakar Šourek, 1934

Dvořák's works were originally numbered chronologically but, following upon various revisions, he listed them anew, discarding many and using their opus numbers for other works. Thus, several opus numbers appear twice. Simrock also arbitrarily changed various opus numbers to give the impression that he was publishing new works. Dvořák disapproved, but perforce had to agree.

PUBLISHED WORKS

Op. 2: Four Songs with Piano (Poems by G. Pfleger-Moravský, also in German), composed as "Cypresses," July, 1865; revised, 1882; Starý, Prague, 1882.

Op. 3: Four Songs with Piano (Vitězslav Hálek, also in German), June, 1876; Hofmeister, Leipzig, 1881.

Op. 5: "The Orphan," Ballad for Voice with Piano (K. J. Erben, also German), 1871; Urbánek, Prague, 1883.

Op. 6: Four Songs, (Serb folk-poems) with Piano, also in English and German, 1872; Simrock, Berlin, 1879.

Op. 7: Six Songs from the Koeniginhof Manuscript (also English and German), 1872; Starý, Prague, 1878; Nos. 1-4, Simrock, 1879.

Op. 8: "Silhouettes," 12 Piano Pieces, 1879; Hofmeister, 1880.

Op. 9: Four Songs with Piano (words by E. Krasnohorská and V. Hálek (also in German), 1871, and 1876; Schlesinger, Berlin, 1880.

Op. 11: "Romance" for Violin and Orchestra (Piano), 1873; Simrock, 1879.

Op. 12: Dumka and Furiant for Piano, 1884; Urbánek, 1885.

Op. 14: "King and Charcoal-burner," (Král a uhlíř), Comic Opera in Three Acts, book by B. Guldener; completely rewritten, 1874; revised, 1887; Hudební Matice, Prague, 1915.

Op. 15: Ballad for Violin and Piano, 1885; Urbánek, 1885.

Op. 16: Quartet in A minor, 1874; Starý, 1875; Bote & Bock, 1893.

Op. 17: "Obstinate Children" ("Tvrdé palice"; "Die Dickschädel"), Comic Opera in One Act, book by Štolba, 1874; Simrock, 1882.

Op. 19: "O Sanctissima, Ave Maria and Ave Maris Stella," Duets for Contralto and Baritone with Organ, 1879; Starý, 1883.

Op. 20: Four Duets for Two Voices and Piano (Moravian folk-poems; also in English and German), 1875; Simrock, 1879.

Op. 21: Trio in B flat major for Piano, Violin and 'Cello, 1875; Schlesinger, 1880.

Op. 22: Serenade in E major for Strings, 1875; Bote & Bock, 1879.

Op. 23: Piano Quartet in D major, 1875; Schlesinger, 1880.

Op. 25: "Overture to Wanda," Opera in Five Acts, by Beneš-Šumavsky, 1875; Cranz, Leipzig, 1885.

Op. 26: Trio in G minor for Piano, Violin and 'Cello, 1876; Bote & Bock, 1880.

Op. 27: Five Chorals for Male Voices (Lithuanian folk-poems), 1878; Urbánek, 1890.

Op. 28: Two Minuets for Piano, 1876; Starý, 1879; Bote & Bock, 1893.

Op. 28: Choral in Praise of Czech Peasant Life, for Mixed Choir and Orchestra (words by Pippich), 1885; Urbánek, 1885.

Op. 29: Four Songs for Mixed Choir (words by Heyduk and folk-poems), 1876; Starý, 1879.

Op. 30: "Hymnus" for Mixed Choir with Orchestra; poem "The Heirs of the White Mountain" by Hálek; English and German, 1872; revised 1880; Novello, London, 1885.

Op. 31: Five "Evening Songs" with Piano, words by Hálek; 1876; Urbánek, 1883.

Op. 32: "Airs from Moravia" ("Klänge aus Mähren"), Thirteen Duets for Soprano and Contralto with Piano; English and German: 1876; Starý, 1876; Simrock, 1878.

Op. 33: Concerto in G minor for Piano and Orchestra, 1876; Hainauer, Breslau, 1883.

Op. 34: Quartet in D minor, 1877; Schlesinger, 1880.

Op. 35: "Dumka" (Elégie), for Piano, 1876; Bote & Bock, 1879.

Op. 36: "Theme with Variations" for Piano, 1876; Bote & Bock, 1879.

Op. 37: "The Peasant Rogue" (Šelma sedlák), Comic Opera in Two Acts, book by Veselý; also in German, 1877; Simrock, 1882.

Op. 38: Four Duets with Piano, (Moravian folk-poems); English and German, 1877; Simrock, 1879.

Op. 39: Suite in D major ("Czechish Suite") for Orchestra, 1879; Schlesinger, 1881.

Op. 40: "Nocturne" in B major for Strings, 1870; Bote & Bock, 1883.

Op. 41: "Scotch Dances" for Piano, 1877; Starý, 1879; Bote & Bock, 1893.

Op. 42: Two Furiants for Piano, 1877; Bote & Bock, 1879.

Op. 43: Three Slovak Folksongs for Male Choir and Four Hand Piano, 1877; Starý, 1879.

Op. 44: "Serenade" in D minor (2 oboes, 2 clarinets, 2 bassoons, contra-bassoon, 3 horns, 'cello and double-bass) 1878; Simrock, 1879.

Op. 45: Three "Slavonic Rhapsodies" for Orchestra, 1878; Simrock, 1879.

Op. 46: Eight "Slavonic Dances," First Series for Four Hand Piano, also for Orchestra, 1878; Simrock, 1878.

Op. 47: "Bagatelles" for 2 Violins, 'Cello and Harmonium or Piano, 1878; Simrock, 1879.

Op. 48: Sextet in A major (2 Violins, 2 Violas, 2 'Cellos) 1878; Simrock, 1879.

Op. 49: "Mazurek" (Mazurka) for Violin and Orchestra (Piano) 1879; Simrock, 1879.

Op. 50: Three Modern Greek Songs for Voice and Piano, words by Nebeský; also German 1878; Hainauer, 1883.

Op. 51: Quartet in E flat major, 1878-79; Simrock, 1879.

Op. 52: Four Piano Pieces, 1880; Hofmeister, 1881.

Op. 53: Concerto in A minor for Violin and Orchestra, 1879-80; Simrock, 1883.

Op. 53: Polka with Galop, for Piano, 1861-62; Starý, 1882; Bote & Bock, 1893.

Op. 54: Eight Piano Waltzes, 1879-80; Simrock, 1880; Nos. 1 and 4 also for String Quartet.

Op. 54: "Festival March" for Orchestra, 1879; Starý, 1879; Bote & Bock.

Op. 55: Seven "Gypsy Melodies" for Voice and Piano, words by Heyduk; also English and German, 1880; Simrock, 1880. ("Songs My Mother Taught Me" is the Fourth Gypsy Song.)

Op. 56: Six Mazurkas for Piano, 1880; Bote & Bock, 1880.

Op. 57: Sonata in F major for Violin and Piano, 1880; Simrock, 1880.

Op. 58: "Stabat mater" for Solos, Choir and Orchestra, 1876-77, (originally Op. 28); Simrock, 1881; also Novello, Latin and English.

Op. 59: Ten Legends for Four Hand Piano, 1881; Simrock, 1881; also for Orchestra.

Op. 60: Symphony in D major, 1880; Simrock, 1880. (Called "First Symphony.")

Op. 61: Quartet in C major, 1881; Simrock, 1882.

Op. 62: "My Home" ("Mein Heim"), Overture for Orchestra to "Josef Kajetán Tyl" by Šamberk, 1881; Simrock, 1882.

Op. 63: "In Nature's Realm" ("In der Natur") Five Chorals for Mixed Voices (words by Hálek), 1882; Cranz, 1882.

Op. 64: "Dimitrij" Opera in 4 Acts, book by Marie Červinková, 1881-82; Starý, 1886; Hudební Matice, 1911.

Op. 65: Trio in F minor for Piano, Violin and 'Cello, 1883; Simrock, 1883.

Op. 66: Scherzo Capriccioso for Orchestra, 1883; Bote & Bock, 1884.

Op. 67: "Hussite Overture" ("Husitská"), 1883; Simrock, 1884.

Op. 68: "From the Bohemian Forest" ("Aus dem Böhmerwald"), 6 Pieces for Four Hand Piano, 1883-84; Simrock, 1884; No. 5, "Woodland Peace", for 'Cello and Piano, 1891; 'Cello and Orchestra, 1893; both, Simrock, 1894.

Op. 69: "The Spectre's Bride" Ballad for Solos, Mixed Choir and Orchestra; words by K. J. Erben, also English and German, 1884; Novello, 1885.

Op. 70: Symphony in D minor, 1884-85; Simrock, 1885. (Called "Second Symphony.")

Op. 71: "Saint Ludmila," Oratorio for Solos, Choir and Orchestra; book by Vrchlický; also English, 1885-86; Novello, 1887.

Op. 72: "Slavonic Dances", Second Series (Nos. 9-16) for Four Hand Piano, also for Orchestra, 1886; Simrock, 1886.

Op. 73: "Im Volkston" ("In Folk-Tone"), Four Songs with Piano, (Czech folk-poems) also English and German, 1886; Simrock, 1887.

Op. 74: Terzetto in C major for Two Violins and Viola, 1887; Simrock, 1887.

Op. 75: Four Romantic Pieces for Violin and Piano, 1887; Simrock, 1887.

Op. 76: Symphony in F major, 1875; revised, 1887. (Originally Op. 24); Simrock, 1888. (Called "Third Symphony.")

Op. 77: Quintet in G major for Two Violins, Viola, 'Cello and Double-bass, 1875, (originally Op. 18); Simrock, 1888.

Op. 78: Symphonic Variations for Orchestra, 1877, (originally Op. 40); Simrock, 1887.

Op. 79: "The 149th Psalm" for Mixed Choir and Orchestra (for Male Choir, 1879), 1887; (originally Op. 52); Simrock, 1888.

Op. 80: Quartet in E major, 1876; (originally Op. 27); Simrock, 1888.

Op. 81: Piano Quintet in A major, 1887; Simrock, 1887.

Op. 82: Four Songs for Voice and Piano, poems by Malybrok-Stieler, also English and German, 1887-88; Simrock, 1889.

Op. 83: Eight Love-Songs ("Liebeslieder") for Voice and Piano, English and German; Poems by Pfleger-Moravský; originally entitled "Cypresses", 1865; revised, 1888; Simrock, 1889.

Op. 84: "Jacobin" Opera in 3 Acts, book by Marie Červinková, 1887-88; revised, 1897; Hudební Matice, 1911.

Op. 85: "Poetic Mood-pictures" ("Poetische Stimmungsbilder"), 13 Piano Pieces, 1889; Simrock, 1889.

Op. 86: "Mass" in D major for Solos, Choir and Orchestra, 1887; Novello, 1893 (Latin and English).

Op. 87: Piano Quartet in E flat major, 1889; Simrock, 1889.

Op. 88: Symphony in G major, 1889; Novello, 1892. (Called "Fourth Symphony.")

Op. 89: Requiem for Solos, Choir and Orchestra, 1890; Novello, 1891.

Op. 90: "Dumky" Trio for Piano, Violin and 'Cello, 1890-91; Simrock, 1894.

Op. 91: "In Nature's Realm" ("In der Natur"), Overture, 1891; Simrock, 1894.

Op. 92: "Carnival" Overture, 1891; Simrock, 1894.

Op. 93: "Othello" Overture, 1892; Simrock, 1894.

Op. 94: Rondo for 'Cello and Piano, 1891; 'Cello and Orchestra, 1893; Simrock, 1894.

Op. 95: "From the New World" Symphony in E minor, 1893; Simrock, 1894. (Called Fifth Symphony.)

Op. 96: Quartet in F major, 1893; Simrock, 1894.

Op. 97: Quintet in E flat major, 1893; Simrock, 1894.

Op. 98: Suite for Piano ("American"), 1894; Simrock, 1894; for Orchestra, 1895; Simrock, 1912.

Op. 99: Ten "Biblical Songs" for Voice and Piano, 1894; Simrock, 1895; Nos. 1-5 for Voice and Orchestra, 1895; Simrock, 1914.

Op. 100: Sonatina in G major for Violin and Piano, 1893; Simrock, 1894.

Op. 101: Eight "Humoresques" for Piano, 1894; Simrock, 1894.

Op. 102: "The American Flag", Cantata for Tenor and Bass solos, Choir and Orchestra; Text by J. R. Drake, 1892; G. Schirmer, New York, 1895.

Op. 103: "Te Deum" for Soprano and Bass solos, Choir and Orchestra, 1892; Simrock, 1896.

Op. 104: Concerto in B minor for 'Cello and Orchestra, 1894-95; Simrock, 1896.

Op. 105: Quartet in A flat major, 1895; Simrock, 1896.

Op. 106: Quartet in G major, 1895; Simrock, 1896.

Op. 107: "The Water Goblin" ("Vodnik", "Der Wassermann"), Symphonic Poem, 1896; Simrock, 1896.

Op. 108: The Noonday Witch, ("Polednice", "Die Mittagshexe"), Symphonic Poem, 1896; Simrock, 1896.

Op. 109: The Golden Spinning Wheel, ("Zlaty Kolovrat", "Das goldene Spinnrad"), Symphonic Poem, 1896; Simrock, 1896.

Op. 110: "The Wood-pigeon" ("Holoubek", "Die Waldtaube"), Symphonic Poem, 1896; Simrock, 1899.

Op. 111: "The Hero's Song" ("Pisen bohatýrská", "Heldenlied"), Symphonic Poem, 1897; Simrock, 1899.

Op. 112: "The Devil and Kate" ("Čert a Káča", "Die Teufelskäthe", Opera in 3 Acts, book by Adolf Wenig, 1898-99; Urbánek, 1908; Hudební Matice, 1910.

Op. 113: "Festival Cantata" ("Festgesang") for Choir and Orchestra, words by Vrchlický, 1900; Urbánek, 1910.

Op. 114: "Rusalka" Opera in 3 Acts, book by Jaroslav Kvapil, 1900; Urbánek, 1907; Hudební Matice, 1910.

Op. 115: "Armida" Opera in 4 Acts, by Vrchlický, 1902-03, 8 Scenes published by Hudební Matice, 1921.

Published Works Without Opus Numbers

"Cypresses" Ten Love Songs for String Quartet, 1856, revised 1887; Hudební Matice, 1921.

Concerto in A major for 'Cello and Piano, 1865; revised for 'Cello and Orchestra by Günther Raphael, Breitkopf & Härtel, Leipzig, 1929.

"Dramatic (Tragic) Overture" (originally Overture to "Alfred"), 1870; Simrock, 1912.

"King and Charcoal-burner" (Král a Uhlíř). Comic Opera in 3 Acts, first version, 1871. Potpourri, Starý, 1873.

Symphony in E flat major (originally Op. 10), 1873; Simrock, 1912.

Quartet in F minor (originally Op. 9), 1873; Breitkopf & Härtel, 1929. (Completed and edited by Günther Raphael.)

Symphony in D minor (originally Op. 13), 1874; Simrock, 1912.

Rhapsody in A minor for Orchestra (originally Op. 15), 1874; Simrock, 1912.

"The Soldier's Farewell" Duet for Soprano and Contralto with Piano. (From the Duets, Op. 32, Moravian folk-poems) 1876; Hudební Matice, 1913.

Chorals for Male Voices; words by Heyduk, 1877; Hudební Matice, 1921.

"Song of the Czechs" for Male Voices, 1877; words by Kamenický. Hudební Matice, 1921.

"Capriccio" ("Concert Piece", originally Op. 49) for Violin and Piano, 1878. Arranged by Günther Raphael, Breitkopf & Härtel, 1929.

"Humnus ad Laudes in festo S. S. Trinitatis," for Voice and Organ, 1878; Sodalitas S. Cyrilli, Prague, 1911.

Polonaise in A minor for 'Cello and Piano, 1879; Universal Edition, Vienna, 1925.

Polonaise in E flat major for Orchestra, 1879; Urbánek, 1883; Peters, Leipzig, 1892.

Waltz for Piano, 1880; Urbánek, 1880.

Four Eclogues for Piano, 1880; Hudební Matice, 1921.

Two Impromptus for Piano, 1880; Hudební Matice, 1921.

"On Our Roof" Duet for Soprano and Contralto. Words from a Moravian folk-poem, 1881; Starý, 1882.

Incidental music for the play, "Josef Kajetán Týl", 1880-81; Starý, 1882.

"Album Leaves" (3) for Piano, 1881; Hudební Matice, 1921.

Impromptu in D minor for Piano, 1882; J. R. Vilímek, Prague, 1883; Simrock, 1915.

Humoresques for Piano, 1884 (?); Urbánek, 1884.

Two Songs for Voice and Piano; words of Czech folk-poems ("Lullabye", "Disturbed Devotion") 1885; Hudební Matice, 1921.

"Two Pearls" for Piano, 1887; Urbánek, 1888.

Gavotte for 3 Violins, 1890; J. R. Vilímek, Prague; Simrock, 1914.

"Woodland Peace" for 'Cello and Orchestra (Op. 68, "From the Bohemian Forest").

Two Piano Pieces (Berceuse and Capriccio) 1894; Simrock, 1911.

Lullabye for Voice and Piano, words by F. L. Jelínek, 1895; Supplement to the Review, "Květy mládeže", Prague, 1896.

"The Smith of Lešetin", for Voice and Piano (Poem: "Lešetinský kovár" by Svatopluk Čech), 1901; "Fresh from the Forge," arrangement by Suk, Simrock, 1911.

UNPUBLISHED WORKS

Two Polkas.

Op. 1, Quintet in A minor with two Violas, 1861.

Op. 2, Quartet in A major, 1862.

Op. 3, Symphony in C minor ("The Bells of Zlonitz"), 1865.

"Cypresses" (18 songs), words by Gustav Pfleger-Moravský, 1865; revised as "songs", Op. 2, "Love Songs", Op. 83 and "Cypresses" for String Quartet.

Op. 4, Symphony in B flat major, 1865.

String Quartet in B flat major. (?)

"Alfred The Great" Heroic Opera in 3 Acts; book by Theodor Koerner, 1870. Only the "Tragic Overture" has been published.

"King and Charcoal-burner" ("Král a uhlíř). First version 1871; second version, 1874.

Op. 9, Quartet in D major, 1870.

Op. 10, Quartet in E minor, 1870.

Quintet in A major, 1872.

Op. 12, String Quartet in A minor, 1873.

"Wanda", Opera in 5 Acts, 1875.

Bibliography

Josef Zubatý: "Anton Dvořák," Hug Brothers, Leipzig, 1886.
Otakar Šourek: "Dvořák's Works Considered Chronologically, Thematically and Systematically," Simrock, Berlin, 1917. In German.
"Život a Vilo Ant. Dvořáka," Hudební Matice, Prague, 1916-1933. 4 Vol. In Czechish.
"Antonín Dvořák," Zlatoroh, Prague, 1929. In Czechish.
Josef Bartoš: "Antonín Dvořák," Pelcl, Prague, 1913. In Czechish.
Karel Hoffmeister: "Antonín Dvořák," J. R. Vilímek, Prague, 1924. In Czechish.
"Antonín Dvořák," English Version by Rosa Newmarch, John Lane, London, 1928.
Otakar Šourek and Paul Stefan: "Dvořák: Life and Works," Dr. R. Passer, Vienna, 1935. In German.
Hans Sirp: "Anton Dvořák," Berlin, 1939. In German.

OTHER WORKS

Libuše Bráfová: "Rieger-Smetana-Dvořák," F. A. Urbánek, Prague, 1913. In Czechish.
Otakar Šourek: "Dvořákové symphonie," Hudební Matice, Prague, 1922. In Czechish.
W. H. Hadow: "Studies in Modern Music," Seely Service & Co., London, 1926.
Daniel Gregory Mason: "From Grieg to Brahms," Macmillan, New York, 1927.
Otakar Šourek: "Anton Dvořák's Chamber-music," Simrock Year Book, Vol. I, Berlin, 1928. In German.

Wilhelm Altman: "Antonín Dvořák's Relations with Fritz Simrock," Simrock Year Book, Vol. II, Berlin, 1929. In German.
Article on Dvořák in Cobbett's "Cyclopedic Survey of Chamber Music," London, 1929.

REVIEWS AND MAGAZINES

Dr. Jan Löwenbach: "Dvořák in America," Hudební Review, Prague, 1911, one of two Dvořák Numbers of the Review issued in that year.
Henry E. Krehbiel: Article on Dvořák, Century Magazine, New York, 1892.
Anton Dvořák: "Schubert," in collaboration with Henry T. Finck, Century Magazine, New York, 1894.
"Music in America," in collaboration with Edwin Emerson, Harper's Magazine, New York, 1895.
Harry Patterson Hopkins: "Student Days with Dvořák," The Étude, Philadelphia, 1912.
Harry Rowe Shelley (and others): "Dvořák as I knew Him," The Etude, Philadelphia, 1913.
H. Pellegrini: "Personal Memories of Dvořák," Neue Musikzeitung, Stuttgart, 1914. In German.
Jeanette M. Thurber: "Dvořák as I knew Him," The Etude, Philadelphia, 1919.
Ramona Evans: "Dvořák at Spillville," The Palimpsest, State Historical Society of Iowa, 1930.
H. G. Kinscella: "Dvořák at Spillville," Musical America, New York, 1933.
Nejedly Zdeněk: "Smetana and Dvořák," Prague Rundschau, Prague, 1934. In German.
Paul Stefan: "Dvořák Once More in America?", Hitherto unpublished letters, Musical America, New York, 1938.
H. von Emde: "American Negro Music," Die Musik, Berlin, 1905. In German.

BIBLIOGRAPHY

Henry E. Krehbiel: "Afro-American Folk-songs," Schirmer, New York, 1914.

F. H. Burton, Editor: "American Primitive Music," Moffat Yard & Co., New York, 1909.

"Religious Folk-songs of the Negro," Hampton, Virginia, 1924.

Index of Names

Adalbert, St., 14, 51, 291
Adler, Guido, 18
D'Albert, Eugen, 193
Ambros, 18
Andersen, Hans, 279
Anger, Moriz, 35, 37, 38, 301
Arnim, 20

Bach, J. S., 175
Barnby, 127
Becker, Hugo, 262
   Jean, 102, 103, 106
Beethoven, 18, 31, 32, 33, 54, 55,
   67, 70, 88, 92, 119, 127, 135,
   136, 165, 200, 219, 237, 248,
   276, 288, 307, 308, 311
Benda, Franz, 17, 28
   George, 17, 28
Bendl, Karel, 29, 33, 47, 261
Beneš, Šumavsky, 68
Bennewitz, Anton, 52, 170, 181,
   253, 287
Berger, Otto, 181
Berlinger, Oskar, 127, 128
Berlioz, 18, 252, 297, 311
Biber, H. von, 16
Billroth, 126
Bílý, 214
Boleška, 289
Bondini, 17
Bote & Bock, 42, 59, 70, 101, 108,
   122
Botstiber, 136
Brahms, 48, 49, 61, 68, 76, 77, 78,
   80, 83, 84, 85, 86, 87, 88, 89, 95,
   96, 100, 109, 112, 124, 126, 134,
   136, 140, 154, 162, 167, 189,

   201, 220, 247, 248, 249, 250,
   251, 252, 259, 262, 263, 265,
   273, 276, 288, 305, 307
Brentano, 20
Bruckner, Anton, 18, 87, 175, 201,
   219, 250
Brüll, Ignaz, 126, 265
Buck, Dudley, 133, 185
Bülow, Hans von, 67, 68, 112, 118,
   124, 140
Bürger, G. A., 132
Burian, 283
Burleigh, H. T., 201
Burney, Chas., 16

Casals, Pablo, 231
Čech, Adolf, 39, 111, 122, 158, 159
   Karel, 159
   Svatopluk, 287
Čermak, Josefa, 35, 108
   Anna, 35, 51
Černohorský, B., 15
Červinková, Marie, 113, 120, 125,
   159
Charpentier, Gustave, 297
Cherubini, 291
Chvála, 288
Chopin, 70, 107, 169, 174
Cimarosa, 291
Cleveland, Grover, 222
Collins, L. S., 199
Columbus, 189
Cranz, 69

Damrosch, Walter, 193
Delius, Frederick, 204
Door, Anton, 186

331